The Traumatised Society

The Traumatised Society
How to Outlaw Cheating
and Save our Civilisation

FRED HARRISON

SHEPHEARD-WALWYN (PUBLISHERS) LTD

First published in 2012 by
Shepheard-Walwyn (Publishers) Ltd
107 Parkway House, Sheen Lane
London SW14 8LS
www.shepheard-walwyn.co.uk
www.ethicaleconomics.org.uk

British Library Cataloguing in Publication Data
A catalogue record of this book
is available from the British Library

ISBN-13: 978-0-85683-287-1

This book is printed on Forest Stewardship Council certified paper

Cover design by Tentacle
www.tentacledesign.co.uk
Typeset by Arthouse Publishing Solutions Ltd,
www.arthousepublishing.co.uk
Printed and bound in the United Kingdom
by Short Run Press Ltd, Exeter

Contents

Prologue: The Existential Crisis

FOLLOW the money. The trail is murky: the crooks have had centuries to cover their tracks. But we shall discover that it leads to the greatest crime ever committed in the history of mankind.

It is the crime that destroys civilisations. Is there time for us to intervene in the unfolding events that threaten our civilisation? I believe that there is, but not without a popular reawakening, a democratic revolution. That is unlikely unless enough people take control of the future of their communities. For one consequence of the crime is the comprehensive failure of leadership. I would go so far as to say that the West has been and is being betrayed by those who presume to govern, to philosophise and to moralise. They have access to the knowledge that would consign the great crises of our age to history, and they fail to use it.

Following the money will first require a re-examination of our forensic tools; tools that have been blunted by the cheats of old. Their mission was to ensure that we, as victims, would not know what was being done to us. They succeeded. One outcome is that what passes for democracy is not an authentic democratic process. Our world has been distorted by the culture of cheating. The story of one victim dramatizes the nature of the deprivation which we all now endure.

Raphael Lemkin (1900-1959) was a lawyer who nearly succeeded in outlawing behaviour at the heart of the privileges of the people who get rich by cheating the rest of us. He coined the word *genocide* and succeeded in piloting the concept through to the point where it became a crime against humanity. But he failed in his ultimate mission. We are all paying the price for that failure.

Lemkin was a Polish Jew who worked as a public prosecutor. He observed how the Nazis systematically dismantled his country. He was able to forensically assess the destruction of a nation because, by then, he had examined the way the people of Armenia had been massacred by Turkey, and Assyrians had been massacred in Iraq. He defined genocide in these terms:

Generally speaking, genocide does not necessarily mean the immediate destruction of a nation, except when accomplished by mass killings of all

members of a nation. It is intended rather to signify a co-ordinated plan
of different actions aiming at the destruction of essential foundations
of the life of national groups, with the aim of annihilating the groups
themselves. The objectives of such a plan would be disintegration of
the political and social institutions, of culture, language, national
feelings, religion, and the economic existence of national groups, and
the destruction of the personal security, liberty, health, dignity, and
even the lives of the individuals belonging to such groups.[1]

I have added the emphasis. Lemkin considered these words to represent the most important part of genocide. He fought for the inclusion of *cultural genocide* during the drafting of the UN Convention on Genocide. He argued that "Cultural Genocide is the most important part of the Convention".[2] Cultural genocide was deleted from what became a crime against humanity. In his autobiography, he recalled:

I defended it (cultural genocide) successfully through two drafts. It meant
the destruction of the cultural pattern of a group, such as the language,
the traditions, the monuments, archives, libraries, churches. In brief:
the shrines of the soul of a nation. *But there was not enough support*
for this idea in the Committee … So with a heavy heart I decided not to
press for it.[3]

Despite the atrocities of World War II, nations which had declared their commitment to human rights refused to recognise cultural genocide as a crime against humanity. Why?

Culture represents the collective consciousness of a population, its memory and all the intellectual and institutional supports that individuals need to live as members of the human species. Erase culture, and you erase what it means to be human. Lemkin came to see this with crystal clarity, and he fought to make the destruction of culture a crime. He wrote:

The world represents only so much culture and intellectual vigour as
are created by its component national groups. Essentially the idea of a
nation signifies constructive co-operation and original contributions,
based upon genuine traditions, genuine culture, and a well-developed

---

1 Lemkin (1944: 79).
2 Moses (2008: 12).
3 Quoted in Docker (2004).

national psychology. The destruction of a nation, therefore, results in the loss of its future contributions to the world.[4]

I have emphasised a part of this statement. I invite the reader to refer back to Lemkin's words while reading my account of *humanicide*. If Lemkin had succeeded in persuading the United Nations to accept his definition of genocide, the tumultuous second half of the 20th century would have evolved in an entirely different direction. *For the policy changes that would have been necessary to avoid committing Lemkin's definition of genocide would have guided the West away from the crises that now challenge its existence.* But there was an evil logic to the refusal to accept Lemkin's definition of genocide.

Culture is produced over evolutionary timescales. It originated with the investment of mental and material resources. Those collectively deployed resources are continuously needed to maintain the vitality of culture. Culture is something that we produce. The basis of that production is the economic surplus that a population is able to generate. The technical term for those resources is *economic rent*. This concept signifies the way we measure the value of the services provided by two distinct "commons": the commons of the natural universe, and the commons of our social universe. In *The Traumatised Society* I explain how the privatisation of those rents causes the destruction of a population's authentic culture. *The rent-seekers who came to control society could not allow their behaviour to be outlawed as a crime against humanity.*

Lemkin was unable to understand the underlying reason why his definition of genocide was unacceptable to the Western nations that shaped the human rights agenda. We are now able to do so. The story is horrifying, and painful for me to tell. The evidence, in brief, demonstrates that the Western mind-set was manipulated to protect the privileges of the cheats. Milestones in the mind-bending process include these two curiosities:

- The word *land* – representing all of the planet's resources – was omitted from the convention that purported to define every person's equal rights: the UN's Universal Declaration of Human Rights.
- The word *rent* – which classical economics identified as the revenue ideally suited to fund the public's shared services – was eviscerated as an analytical concept by what became the neo-classical school of economics.

The motives for these acts and omissions will unfold in my narrative. The evidence leads to a terrible conclusion. It does not take evil men like Hitler,

---

4   Lemkin (1944: 91).

Stalin or Pol Pot to commit genocide. In Lemkin's terms, *the democracies of the West were subjecting their citizens to cultural genocide, and they continue to commit this crime to this day.*

T HE task before us is nothing less than the reconfiguring of the Western mindset (Part 3). So fundamental is the necessary change to the way that we view the world, that we have to go back to the beginning.

My starting point is a unified theory of social evolution. We begin by elaborating a general theory of corruption (Part I). By identifying the core cause of the major cases of abnormal mass behaviour, we can isolate the one reform to the financial system that would mobilise people behind the determination to modify the flaws in the foundations of our communities.

Our task is not made easier by confusion over the best approach to viewing the world. Disputes over methods, such as whether the emphasis should be on nature or nurture to explain deep-seated problems, are distractions. Should we emphasise spiritual or secular principles? The monotheistic religions have spiritualised their teachings, while science, when its methods are applied to human affairs, is compromised by the suppression of a vital realm of reality from its database. Information that was available and understood a hundred years ago has been transformed into secret knowledge.

But the tragedies associated with the seizure of the Western world's financial arteries in 2008 give us reason to be optimistic. There is a growing consensus that a fundamental defect lurks somewhere deep in the system. Set against the new questioning of once cherished beliefs, however, is the barrier to straight thinking. The analytical framework that is needed to account for the myriad failures is not available.

But we are privileged like no other generation before us. We can equip ourselves with the knowledge to negotiate a new covenant to save our civilisation. That requires a negotiation which, as I explain in Ch. 1, must be in two parts. One is with whoever (or whatever) owns nature. The other is with whoever owns the commons created by our forefathers: culture. The act of genius of our ancestors was in the way they united the two distinct commons in a single practical formula: a stream of income that the classical economists called *economic rent*.

This volume is an investigation into how we have all been cheated out of our inheritance: an equal right of access to, and share in, the commons.

CHEATING is now the principal operating mechanism in society. I employ this word as an analytical concept, well aware that its confrontational nature will provoke resistance. Confrontation, unfortunately, is unavoidable if we are to begin the painful process of recovering our humanity.

Cheating is a word that combines two realms of reality. It refers to deeds by persons, but it also articulates a moral attitude. How we interrogate the cheating that distorts our communities will determine the future of the West.

I am concerned not with individual deeds of cheating, but with the institutionalised kind that is sanctified by law. It is easy to get angry about particular acts and, in doing so, misdirecting our attention from root causes. How, for example, should we respond to the revelations of corruption in the Western banking system? It has exposed itself as disreputable since the financial crisis of 2008. First there were the sub-prime mortgages which caused the crisis. Subsequently there were the disclosures of Ponzi schemes (especially in the Anglo-American countries). Revelations came thick and fast, including market-rigging dishonesty that cost consumers billions in over-priced products. Major banks like Barclays were exposed for manipulating interest rates. Then there was the mis-selling of complex derivatives to small businesses that threatened to cause bankruptcies. Bankers became Enemy No. 1. But were these no more than symptoms of a deep-seated flaw in the structure of society? Manifestations of a culture that rewards deviant behaviour that ought to be outlawed?

Cheating is now so deep-seated that it is the defining characteristic of Western culture. That is why it threatens the viability of the West. Explaining the future of civilisation in terms of a particular kind of cheating overturns conventional explanations for the global crises of the 21st century (one favourite scapegoat is "human nature"[5]).

I offer a mono-causal explanation for these crises. *The theft of a nation's economic surplus is the root cause of our major problems.* This surplus is the net income after remunerating labour (wages) and capital (profits, or interest). Net income is the rent that a nation generates as its taxable income. Rent is unique because it is the basis of the social evolution of our species. By understanding its social (for some, its sacred) character, rent lays bare the story of how early humans evolved from those who daubed abstract images on cave walls 40,000 years ago to the builders of urban civilisations. Without rent (which changed its material form with each phase of evolution), we would not have become the bearers of culture.

Rent is at the heart of the dialectic of power. It measures the energy that is pumped into making and sustaining complex societies. The direction of the flow of that stream of income tells us whether culture is flourishing or decaying, whether a civilisation is growing or dying. By chronicling the fate of rent, we begin to understand where a society may be located in the grand sweep of its history. And yet, rent is the one value which national statisticians and

---

5   According to John Coates, a research fellow at the University of Cambridge, the economic boom that led to the biggest bust since the 1930s was due to the fact that testosterone-fuelled traders in the financial markets were slaves to their hormones (Coates [2012]).

economists treat in a cavalier manner. This is not accidental. Obscuring the size and direction of flow of rent serves the interests of the rent-seekers.

The stakes are the gravest imaginable. When rents are misappropriated, the psycho-social health of the population is degraded and the reproduction of culture is prejudiced. There comes a point when, with culture and the natural habitat debased, civilisation slides into irreversible decline. But to grasp the profound significance of rent as a flow of income, and the cheating that is now associated with it, we need to clean up our language.

CHEATING was institutionalised by the rent-seekers of the past 500 years who developed the art of manipulating our minds. They *needed* us to lose track of what they were doing, and they were eminently successful in their mission. That is why, for example, economics as a social science is a discipline in crisis. It is no longer a tool for solving problems. Instead, it compounds our problems. In particular, it inhibits us from understanding that cheating is a routine process in the capitalist economy. No steps are being taken to erase that cheating, because it is not recognised for what it is – a corrupted culture that impoverishes the lives of everyone.

Economists disguise the cheating with words that sanitise and legitimise behaviour which would not be acceptable (say) on the sporting field. By deconstructing those concepts, we begin to glimpse the power of the forces that obstruct change.

I have the misfortune to be a symbol of the cheating that has now traumatised modern societies (three cases are documented in Part II). I am a reluctant cheat, I hasten to add, but one whose palm has been crossed with silver. I own a piece of residential land. My home has risen in value by leaps and bounds without my lifting a finger.

In yesteryear, the archetypal cheat was a member of the aristocracy. Today, "hard-working middle class homeowners" have joined their ranks. We do not *mean* to cheat anyone. We abhor cheating and are quick to censure those who do not abide by the rules of fairness. But the rules were rigged by the barons and knights of yore. The legacy is a social process that co-opts decent people into behaving as if they were congenital cheats. Coming to terms with that awful reality is the biggest moral challenge many of us must now face.

We cannot evade that moral challenge. For cheating has suffused our globalised society to the point where a piecemeal approach to analysis and remedy is futile, if we wish to meet the existential challenge.

The last time we humans faced such a crisis was about 25,000 years ago. Neanderthals were bigger than us. They used tools, like us. And there were more of them than us. So the odds were in their favour.

We wiped them out.

The technical term for what we did is *supplanting*. We took over their territories, drove them out, and watched while they grew extinct.

This time, the threat to humanity is from our own kind. And, again, the contest is over who controls the resources of nature.

We need to remind ourselves that cheating as a social process was the primary cause of the demise of the earliest civilisations. Why we have failed to learn from those tragedies is one of the questions we seek to answer. The evidence mounts to suggest that our abuse of both nature and society is leading *Homo sapiens* down a dead end. Our intellectual and political leaders wilfully ignore the survival rules that primitive humans brought with them out of nature. Our ancestors evolved by mimicking the laws of nature. This enabled them to create a new universe, the social universe.

Being human does not merely mean that we are more capable than other animals at using tools, or behaving socially, or communicating by means of sophisticated sounds and gestures. Our unique accomplishment was in combining these skills to adapt the laws of nature into rules to which people agreed to conform. They acted as if they were conforming to the laws of nature, but they did so within the context of a universe of their creation, a universe that was not accessible to other species. That made *Homo sapiens* unique.

The two universes, of nature and human society, are distinct but inextricably related. Early humans had to make them co-exist out of biological necessity. Today, we access the surreal world of virtual reality with the aid of our PCs, but there is no escaping the fact that our social universe remains anchored in the material universe.

WE NEED a fresh start based on multi-disciplinary studies. I call my formulation of that approach sociogenics. It combines the social sciences with biology. How does this differ from Edward Wilson's sociobiology? Wilson of Harvard University is a student of the social behaviour of bees and ants. Insights from these creatures, he argues, can inform our understanding of human behaviour.[6] His work of synthesis, *The Social Conquest of Earth*, insists that we must rely on science to understand the nature of humanity.[7] But his methodology, which highlights the notion of conquest, also leads to dangerously inappropriate conclusions about the nature of the threats facing our civilisation.

Social behaviour was paramount in the evolution of *Homo sapiens*. But the threat that we now face is not the result of social behaviour. All the major

6   Wilson (1975).
7   Wilson (2012).

pathologies that call into question the future of our species are the product of anti-social behaviour. If our forefathers had managed to preserve the social values that made civilisation possible, we would not now be wondering, with Wilson, whether our species is going to survive. We need to rescue the science of society (sociology) from the wastelands to which it has been banished, and synthesise its knowledge with biology to provide a more robust understanding of what it means to be human.

In my view, our civilisation has passed the tipping point into collapse. But we cannot blame Acts of God. The crises are not the result of "market failures". Nor can they be attributed to defects in "human nature". These are scapegoats which happen to serve the interests of rent-seekers. There is a job of work to be done to deal with the fall-out from the social and natural cataclysms which will recur with increased ferocity. We may be able to forestall the worst. But we will not make progress until we recover a sense of the meaning of humanity. The boy's-finger-in-the-dyke's-hole initiatives (such as the attempt to deal with the financial crisis by piling new debts on old debts), will not save the West.

The challenges appear insurmountable, but that is because the levers of power are operated inefficiently and unfairly. This dysfunctional behaviour is programmed by a pathologically disturbed culture that manifests itself in societal trauma. Fortunately, enquiring minds across the scientific disciplines and caring professions are beginning to pool knowledge. An example is the MRI brain scanning technique which, developed since the 1980s, is facilitating major advances in neurobiology and psychotherapy. This is deepening our understanding of intergenerational trauma. Trauma is a concept that now needs to be developed and applied to whole populations.

We can save our civilisation if we find the moral resources within each and every one of us to think straight and act courageously. We need to go back to the beginning, to recover knowledge that has been repressed. But which beginning? Biology, and the theory of evolution? Myths, and the findings of ethnographers and anthropologists? History, and the tablets and parchments excavated by archaeologists? An eclectic approach would combine all disciplines to animate a therapeutic process with the cathartic power to rescue our traumatised societies. That entails the engagement of everyone in an informed democracy. We need to forestall the temptation of granting power to the Strong Men who will offer to solve our social problems if we yield ourselves to their lethal embrace.

Part 1

A General Theory of Cheating

For only the eternal structural laws of the social life of man as such are of natural law, not the concrete architectural form.
                              Heinrich A. Rommen, *Natural Law*, (1998: 230)

Cheating is here used as an analytical rather than as a pejorative term. It signifies a social process which is not recognised as a threat to civil order. That is why it goes unchallenged. This cheating is now embedded in, and is undermining, the foundations of Western civilisation.

Statecraft is unable to respond to the cheating, because it was fashioned by the feudal aristocracy to enshrine and protect their doctrine of property rights. The free gifts of nature, and the culture that defines humanity, have been privatised. The legacy is a set of crises stemming from the abuse of the "commons".

When the community's revenue – the rents paid to use and sustain the commons – was hijacked, the rent-seekers incubated a process of cannibalisation that devoured natural habitats. They also transformed culture to accommodate their cheating, creating the pathologies that result in humanicide.

Chapter 1: God's Land Deal

I T was the first criminal act in history. *Genesis* reports the deed, but we are not told *how* Cain killed his younger brother. Did he pick up a rock that marked the edge of his field and smash Abel's skull? Or was a dagger concealed beneath his cloak, its sharp point plunged with mortal effect?

God's role is problematic. He sat in judgement on the offerings brought by the brothers. He approved of Abel's offering, but not Cain's. Why? What made the difference that it should incur the displeasure of God? Cain was mortified. God remonstrated with him. The next thing we know is that the brothers met in that field, and Cain had murder on his mind.

Abel's blood soaked into the soil.

This was not just a family tragedy. *Genesis* intends it as a warning. For the narrative is set in the context of God's reason for intervening in earthly affairs. *They* did not own the land. *He* did. That is what the Old Testament is about. God.

God and the Landless.

The social pressures that lead to murder may be inferred from the account of the deed. We learn nothing about the brothers, other than how they earned their living. This information is given its significance by the context. The Old Testament is the first formal contract to delineate the ownership and use of land.

God's offer of land came with a price tag: compliance with a moral code.

The Old Testament is a covenant. A theology of land.[1]

And so we learn that Abel was a shepherd, "but Cain was a tiller of the ground" (Genesis 4:2). Why *but*? What may we infer from the difference in the way they earned their living? Their household economies were worlds apart. They dramatised the interface between two universes: the natural and the social. Abel was from the old world. Cain symbolised the future. The differences between those two worlds were most starkly defined by the way land was possessed, and the way that the benefits were distributed.

Biblical scholars continue to dispute whether the narratives should be treated as history or as meaningful myths. Either way, the covenant is an inspired account of the psychology and sociology of land. It goes to the heart

---

1 Brueggemann (2002).

of the issue that might one day threaten the survival of the human species. Undisciplined, might civilisation grow into an all-devouring monster with the power to destroy life on planet Earth?

Frictions in the model of urban settlements were not being resolved by the people whose genius had made civilisation possible. The issues at stake were laid bare by the story of Cain and Abel. For what happened in that field is a metaphor for the social forces that were crushing the cities of the Near East.

Abel subsisted by hunting and by gathering food and fuel from nature. He could live comfortably, if the rains came, the grass grew and his flock could eat. He was at the end of a cultural continuum spanning the better part of 200,000 years.

Cain had moved on.

The secrets of nature were being unlocked. Those secrets would make it possible to transform culture. In the annals of our species, that transformation would eclipse in significance events like landing men on the moon. *Cain produced a surplus of food that could be traded and invested. That made possible giant leaps in the arts of governance and the formation of urban infrastructure.*

Civilisation.

The Bible is not interested in morbid family gossip. So why provide the account of Cain's crime in a text that elaborated a theology of land? The answer to that question, in my view, is that we are invited to reflect on the consequences of a social transition that threatened the tranquillity of ancient communities.

The shift from pastoralism to agriculture ruptured more than personal relationships. It triggered a systemic crisis. It shattered the terms on which people had co-existed, a breach in ways of living unprecedented in the history of our species. The big problem was that people had forgotten how to resolve conflicts over the possession of land.

God arrived to remind them. But would they listen?

Abel's nomadic lifestyle relied on practises sanctioned by an evolutionary process tracking back millions of years. Territorial behaviour, encoded in DNA, mediated the evolution of animals and vegetables. The territorial instinct was the organising principle that guided foraging and reproductive behaviour, and in regulating population size.[2] It was the mechanism that framed the evolution of our species. But if humans were to evolve out of nature, they had to adapt that instinct by developing a cultural equivalent. If they were to access new layers of existence, expanding their numbers and diversifying their cultures, a code of conduct was needed that was flexible, but resilient, and faithful to the principles of territorialism.

---

2   Hassell and May (1985: 21-22).

To co-evolve with nature, and to live in harmony with their fellow beings, a law was needed that synchronised spatial resources with abilities inscribed in DNA. Lawyers class the rules of this code under the concept of tenure. The rules had to be flexible but robust. Humans were unleashing themselves from the rigid laws of nature. If they were to create their own dynamic world, they would need to elaborate and honour a system of tenure that preserved harmony within their communities. The shift from gathering to growing food would create the greatest challenge of all. The confrontation between Cain and Abel represented the dangers in that transformation.

Still operating as a pastoralist, living off nature, Abel needed to roam the land with his flock. Cain, on the other hand, had learnt how to harness nature's powers to increase the productivity of his labour. That meant his household would enjoy a higher income. But to achieve the greater output, he needed to erect fences to protect his crops against foraging flocks. This collision of land uses signposted the most profound break between genetic past and cultural future.

In the pre-agricultural age, land was held and used in common. Rights of access were determined by carefully honed customs and practises. People enjoyed equal rights that were defined by kinship associations. Without those rights, the rites of courtship, marriage and the reproduction of the family would have been meaningless.

Agriculture demanded a new kind of tenure: a demarcation of boundaries. Private possession. This was necessary, if people were to invest their labour and capital to feed the present and fund the future. Primordial practises would be rendered obsolete.

Uncertainty remains about much of our evolutionary past. Archaeologists have not settled the question of when early humans came out of Africa and began using stone tools. Such tools discovered in present-day United Arab Emirates are dated to about 125,000 years ago. But we can be confident about certain aspects of our past. One of these is related to the changing role of land use, and the rights that regulated the relationships between people. Customs and practises were evolved to secure a sensitively balanced use of nature. Oral techniques transmitted knowledge down the generations. The moral in the tragedy of Cain and Abel, for example, appears not only in the Old Testament but other holy texts, and it is featured in mythologies of pre-literate peoples around the world.

And Cain talked with Abel his brother; and it came to pass, when they were in the field, that Cain rose up against Abel his brother, and slew him (Genesis 4:8).

That drama is enacted in similar contests over land which divide communities to this day. It is the template for Hollywood Westerns which relive the way cattlemen who roamed the open range tried to resist barbed wire fences, causing many a gunfight showdown (Box 1:1). So the challenge presented by God of the landless remains with us to this day: the search for the meaning of the Good Life without letting the blood of our brothers.

The systemic problem was incubated 10,000 years ago. Neolithic people began to transform fields by selecting seeds, channelling water and tilling the soil. But why would the capacity to nurture food out of the fields incur the disrespect of God? The clues are contained in Cain's offering to God. What was exceptional about it? Was it all the product of Cain's labour, or did God have a stake in it? Did God disapprove of the way in which the surplus was being *used*? Was Cain hoarding his extra output without sharing the bounty with others? Why *should* Cain share any part of what was surplus to the immediate needs of his family?

The Old Testament is a dialectic on moral governance and economics, at the heart of which is the issue of land. People willing to hear were left in no doubt about the terms on which land *gifted* by God may be occupied, but they would have to work out the practical rules to suit particular circumstances.

- Fenced off land was no longer available to those who had previously accessed it. Was Cain under an obligation to compensate the losers? What form could such compensation take?
- Should the surplus product be used for purposes other than current consumption? If so, how should it be invested, and how would this affect the rest of the community?

That something was terribly wrong in those emerging city settlements was evident from the abject poverty of able-bodied people, the bloody territorial conflicts that tore nations apart, the abuse of nature. People had lost the wisdom that had sustained their communities for tens of thousands of years. Civilisation was threatening to become a dead-end experiment.

The Metaphysics of Earth
The genius of early humans was displayed when they combined the natural and social universes.

When Neolithic people took the final step out of nature, they needed abstract images to help them to visualise a unique way of existing. They were shifting away from biologically-based instincts to a universe that was unique in the solar system. Without practical rules for regulating their behaviour, *there was nothing to stop them from pitting their lethal powers against each other.*

Box 1:1
Today's Cain & Abel Struggles

LAND disputes between cattle rancher and corn grower in the Wild West symbolise contests that divide communities on every continent in the 21st century.

- In Latin America, the Nukak Maku (first contacted in 1988), were driven out of their Amazon homeland by guerrillas who sought a refuge. The tribe faces extinction because, as nomads, their shrunken territory is insufficient to sustain them.

- In Africa, the Kalahari Bushmen locked themselves into an epic constitutional struggle over the right to remain in their desert settlements. The Botswana government wanted to control the diamond-rich desert.

- In Canada and Australia, aboriginal peoples remain in limbo land following the colonial displacement. Government apologies alone for past transgressions – displacement from their territories – cannot rescue the alienated first settlers.

The economic crises in the USA and Europe today can only be understood in terms of their origins in the land market.

Their solution was divine.

The title deeds to nature were assigned to deities. Super-natural forces regulated the flow of the energy circulating within nature. Gods lived in trees, were borne on the wind, brought the rains, inhabited caves, breathed fire. That determined the ownership rights. Mere mortals would settle for being the stewards of nature.

Two South African scholars, David Lewis-Williams and David Pearce, drew the links between the material and spiritual worlds. Economic activity and social organisation were articulated in

> an overall cosmology, a framework that simultaneously made sense of religious experience, belief and practice, as well as land rights. Religion, embedded in cosmology, validated land rights and the authority of those who managed the construction of monuments and their use.[3]

People would not fight each other for privileged access to nature's resources, because the resources belonged to the gods. Each individual was given the

---

3 Lewis-Williams and Pearce (2009: 197).

equal chance to contribute further to the biological, psychological and cultural welfare of those within the gene pool.

But what about the administration of those heaven-sent resources? Earthly representatives of the deities were needed. The bridge between the people and nature could be a tribal chief or a priest or a prince. They would act on behalf of supernatural authority to enforce behaviour which satisfied the common interest.

> *Changing concepts of land ownership therefore came with cosmological shifts and were represented in people's 'existential maps' – their monuments … political entities grew in complexity and ascribed their land rights to founding ancestors whose location, both conceptually and literally, was known and who legitimized those rights.*[4]

Before they could learn to paint on Sistine ceilings, write heavenly scores for orchestras or invent technologies to take men to the moon, our ancestors had to resolve the problem beneath their feet. Thanks to the invention of, and interventions by, the deities, there would be no systematic cheating, no profane contests to monopolise nature's resources, no depletion of the creative energies of people who wished to work for the mutual benefit of themselves and their neighbours. That sacred settlement was shattered by kings who administered the city civilisations.

Enter the blunt-speaking God of the Landless.

Interpreting the Mind of God
God first exposed his mind to mortal gaze with the expression of disapproval of Cain's gift. He was signalling a problem with the way the additional income was being used.

There *was* something wrong with the disposition of the product that the Cains of the new world were hewing from the land. God's business was to reveal the nature of the problem.

Interpretations of God's mind were provided by the first of the great Christian bishops. Their insights were complemented by first-hand observations of the civilisations of the classical world. The empirical evidence confirmed what they knew about the plight of people in the ancient world who lost their land and lapsed into debt bondage (Box 1:2).

The Christian bishops had front seats in the unfolding drama that became the decline and fall of the Roman empire. Men like Clement of Alexandria (c150-c215), Ambrose of Milan (337?-397) and Basil the Great (329?-379).

---

4 Lewis-Williams and Pearce (2009: 194).

Box 1:2
Debt Bondage & the Clean Slate

SOME people in the earliest civilisations fell victim to poverty (as when crops failed, and they borrowed money which they found they could not repay). To address the threat to the stability of the community, a practice known as Clean Slate proclamations was employed. Periodically, the land would be restored to families. This corrective measure was known as the Jubilee. It was proclaimed every 49 years or on the accession to the throne of a new prince. Debts were also cancelled, of the personal (but not commercial) kind.

This ancient practise is recorded in Leviticus, Chapter 25. God reminds Moses that "The land shall not be sold for ever: for the land is mine; for ye are strangers and sojourners with me" (25:23). To secure social stability, "ye shall hallow the fiftieth year, and proclaim liberty through all the land unto all the inhabitants thereof: it shall be a jubilee unto you; and ye shall return every man unto his possession, and ye shall return every man unto his family" (25:10).

One of them, John Chrysostom (347-407), lived almost long enough to witness their warnings come true. Rome was sacked in the year 410. They monitored the emerging poverty among Roman citizens, causally connecting it to the way land owners were monopolising the rents from land. Aided with the teachings of the covenant and the sermons of Jesus of Nazareth, they repeatedly warned that Rome was being degraded. Landlessness and poverty were induced by the misappropriation of land. Culture and the moral life were being depleted.

The observations on property articulated by the patristic teachers are now missing from pulpit preaching. Charles Avila recovered them while studying at a seminary in the Philippines. He had involved himself in the fight for peasant rights. This led him to a study of early Christian teaching. He drew the threads together in this summary of the state of the late Roman Empire.

> Thus the only object of the owners' drive for even greater wealth was an increase in the capacity for luxury, pleasure, and various forms of extravagance. The crafts and trades that developed among free workers were in luxury items like slaves and pomades, paintings and statues, lavish and showy construction projects, and whatever else the large landowners required for the new competition in pleasure, luxury, and ostentation.[5]

This lifestyle was unsustainable. When resources can be consumed without having to labour for them, the biological boundaries to limitless desires (labour

---

5   Avila (1983: 24).

power) are removed. Avarice prevails. And so, the land owners seized more of the peasants' land, to accumulate and consume yet more rents. Peasants were driven into the towns. The discontent of the unemployed was assuaged with "bread and circuses". The deterioration in the minds and morals of the population set the course for the implosion of a civilisation. Without a free peasantry that could stock the army, the Caesars had to rely on mercenaries recruited from the barbarian margins of the empire. Those barbarians would one day use their swords to take over the seats of power.

It was in the self-interest of the land owners to reverse the decline of their society, but this required reform of the tenure-and-tax system. They were not willing to heed the warnings of the bishops.

> One would have expected [the] decline in the slave economy to have brought about a renaissance of a stronger free peasant economy, dictated by a nation's self-interest. Yet it did not. The owners of the latifundia simply had no intention of giving up their absolute ownership of the land. To do so would have been tantamount to parting with their power and privileges voluntarily.[6]

The leadership of Rome lapsed into a state of trauma (see Ch.5). Once the city's culture had been corrupted by the privatisation of rent – the social revenue – all classes lost sight of the natural laws on which a viable community relies for survival and growth. The patricians gorged themselves on the rents and could not – would not – yield their power for the sake of national survival. The dispossessed lost the capacity to reclaim their natural right to share the rents which they helped to create. The end became inevitable.

Could the covenant with God have saved civilisations like Rome's?

The Covenant
The tablets which Moses brought down from the mountain were inscribed with the terms of the land deal. The children of Abraham were required to conform to a moral code. But the Old Testament was more than just about morality. It was a manual on how to construct a stable community. It provided a comprehensive sociological and psychological account of what happens when people fail to treat their common wealth in ways that work with the grain of social evolution. A synoptic treatment of that manual has been provided by Walter Brueggemann, a Professor of Old Testament at an American seminary.

---

6 Avila (1983: 25).

God as the voice of the landless assumed the mission to restore order. His wrath was directed at kings who managed the land for selfish reasons. The kings referred to in the Bible were those who presided over Israel and so had responsibility for the land.[7] Kings who mis-manage land are a disaster. By hoarding the economic surplus, they amass the means of coercion (horse-mounted troops), they lavished silver and gold on themselves and their homes, and turned people into serfs. That form of governance leads to landlessness.

To comply with the moral code, vigilance is necessary. Otherwise, there is landlessness. Solomon's abuse of power illustrates the way in which morality and culture are appropriated by those who abuse their positions of authority. Solomon enforced bondservice on people and created a bureaucratic state organised into tax districts. Monumental buildings were constructed to celebrate his greatness.

> *All this is capped by the building of the temple, the ultimate achievement of his reign. The temple serves to give theological legitimacy and visible religiosity to the entire program of the regime. The evidence is beyond dispute that he so manipulates Israel's worship that it becomes a cult for a static God, lacking in the power, vigor, and freedom of the God of the old traditions. This God, in contrast to the exodus deliverer, is a domesticated preserver of the regime. He dwells in silent, obedient, uninterrupted, and uninterupting security.*[8]

The rules for judging kings are set out, as in Deuteronomy (17:16-20). Kings did not have the right to rule as they saw fit, because God's care for the land was inalienable. In his discussion on "the royal road to exile", Brueggemann stresses that God holds the trump card. "No amount of royal finesse can change that. It is still covenant word and not royal hardware which governs land."[9]

Brueggemann summarises the ethic of possession in these terms: "Land is not, if viewed as gift, for self-security but for the brother and sister. Land is not given to the calculating, but to the 'meek,' that is, to the ones who do not presume".[10] But if the meek are not vigilant, landlessness follows.

Landlessness is portrayed with the imagery of wilderness – a formless void. Displacement "in that time and our time, is experienced like the empty dread of primordial chaos". Landlessness is "to be at the disposal of an environment totally without life supports and without any visible hint that there is an opening

---

7 Brueggemann (2002: 73).
8 Brueggemann (2002:80-81).
9 Brueggemann (2002: 94).
10 Brueggemann (2002: 73).

to the future". [11] To be landless is to be locked in a state of trauma, endured "as a place of murmur, protest, quarrelsome, dissatisfaction". [12]

Land can be restored to the landless.

> *That is what this God does. He speaks to restructure the relation of land and people. What had been threat becomes promise. What had been coveted now becomes gifted.* [13]

When God gifts land, order is restored. Food, and the minerals needed to construct urban settlements, are available, but more besides. There is a restoration of psychological health. Brueggemann notes that "The change is to be understood not simply in terms of geographic placement but in terms of an alternative consciousness in which sociological and cultural possibilities were transformed". [14]

Breaching the Covenant

Modern societies do not comply with the terms of the covenant. The Cain and Abel tragedy is ever present. So once again, their story becomes a point of departure for the re-examination of conflicts over the possession of land.

- The State of Israel believes that land in the Negev region could be put to better use by displacing the Bedouin who have occupied that territory for thousands of years.
- Islamic fundamentalists, disputing over their territories, invoke Allah as they strap explosives to their bodies to blow up innocent people in market places.
- Christians have their share of blood on their hands. We shall see from the cases discussed in this volume that European societies led the modern world into a surreal space between God and mammon.

Money is made out of *causing* mass poverty. Money is made by *abusing* the environment. Money is made through the *propagation* of instability in the economy. The financial interests which gain from this are mobilised to prevent change. [15] They expect their privileges to remain sacrosanct, whatever the cost to others, protected by multi-layered stockades. Do these barricades to justice inhibit us from even *thinking* about the root causes of the world's great problems?

---

11 Brueggemann (2002: 28).
12 Brueggemann (2002: 29).
13 Brueggemann (2002: 18).
14 Brueggemann (2002: 47, n.7).
15 The City of London spent an estimated £92m in 2011on lobbying activities to ensure that legislation was benign towards the interests of the City's financial institutions (Mathieson and Newman [2012]).

We need a route map back to *terra ferma*. To this end, we will examine the evidence to test this hypothesis:

> *Over the past 500 years, those who profited from the appropriation of the value that we all help to create, messed with people's minds, to prevent the losers from understanding the causes of the crises that afflict their communities.*

Did the rent-seekers skew language to invert reality? The word *capitalism*, for example, is at the heart of confusion in the public discourse. The meaning attributed to it seriously mis-describes the West's economy. Rent-seekers had good reasons to distract the population at large. But what about Karl Marx?

Marx fathered the most influential of dissenting doctrines. According to his account, modern pathologies were inevitable, inscribed in history. That thesis, however, also gave hope. Feudalism would be overthrown by capitalism, which would be overthrown by socialism to lead us to a new Promised Land. While such ideologies pre-occupy the young in universities, the villains roam free.

Marx's demonisation of capitalism contributed to the deepening of the crises that we now face, by obscuring root causes. But Marx was not alone in misdirecting attention. Sociologist Max Weber (1864-1920), in *The Protestant Ethic and the Spirit of Capitalism* (1904), characterised capitalism as the product of technology and the logic of bureaucracy. Awkwardly, the repeated booms and grievous busts that contradict the rationality emphasised by Weber also failed to authenticate his argument that capitalism was built on the prudence of the Protestant ethic.

Who benefits from the confusion? The impact of mangled language is displayed in economic policy, and the persistent failure to define remedies to the financial crises that exploded in the depression of the late 19th century, the depression of the 1930s and, once again, in the depression of the 2010s. *If we are to re-configure our minds to meet the challenges of the 21st century, we need to question forms of behaviour that are celebrated as virtuous features of the European model of social organisation.*[16]

Our intellectual leaders insist that there is no simple, single solution ("no silver bullet") to the world's problems. The sources of the crises are many and varied, requiring multiple corrective measures. Unfortunately, none of their time-tested remedies have worked. As for the competing theory that the

---

16 Calls for new ways of thinking fail to attract meaningful responses. Klaus Schwab, founder of the World Economic Forum (quoted in *The Times* of London, Feb. 2, 2012) declared: "We are in an era of profound change that urgently requires new ways of thinking". The world's economic and political leaders who were converging on Davos, however, did not offer imaginative solutions to the issue on which most minds were then concentrated: the financial crisis in the euro-zone.

ownership and use of land is at the heart of the world's pathological condition, that proposition is absent from the doctrines seeking to explain the pathologies of our civilisation.

We are all being cheated of the Good Life. If ours *is* an evidence-based approach to democratic law-making, there is no shortage of empirical evidence to confirm, from a scientific point of view, both the wisdom of the covenant, and the consequences of failing to apply it. Complex civilisations emerged, and then disappeared, and the abuse of the terms of the covenant was the common denominator in upwards of 20 cases of civilisations that died in shame. We have to dig in the detritus of their settlements to reconstruct a picture of how they lived and loved.

The evolutionary process is one of trial and error. Some experiments necessarily lead to dead ends. So we can understand that the ancient civilisations were vulnerable to errors. But with contact among them and the spread of knowledge, we might have expected the classical civilisations to have avoided the mistakes. We have no alternative but to go back over that history, to understand where they went wrong, if we are to understand why our 21st century civilisation, with its global reach, is also heading towards a similar fate.

The awesome idea of interrogating God[17] is an uncomfortable one for people of faith. Humanists, in any event, object to a faith-based starting point on the grounds that ours is a science-based society. For them religion is obsolete as regards the administration of civil society.

Humility may be warranted. We need to remind ourselves that pre-scientific humans achieved something that has remained beyond the competence of our science-based society. They created sustainable communities by solving the problem of the ownership of the commons. This enabled them to flourish for long enough to evolve the knowledge that made our lives possible. The secular approach has yet to match that accomplishment. And the secular veneration of "the rule of law" remains problematic (Box 1:3).

Do we have the wisdom to sift the threads of knowledge from the sands of time, to excavate the knowledge that would ensure the survival of our civilisation?

---

17 McIntosh (2012).

Box 1:3
Law as Secular Religion

Tom Bingham, a former Lord Chief Justice of England and Senior Law Lord of the UK, portrayed the rule of law as "the nearest we are likely to approach to a universal secular religion".[1]

The doctrine of the rule of law is strongly urged by the West on former colonial dependencies. Absent from such discussions is the acknowledgement that the rule of law remains a problematic feature of Western civilisation. Is this because the laws of the land are ultimately shaped to serve the exclusive interests of those who own the land?

Is that law subordinate to what people mean when they demand their "fundamental human rights"? Unfortunately, according to Bingham, "there is no universal consensus on the rights and freedoms which are fundamental, even among civilised nations".[2] Then it appears we even have to question the doctrine of "the rule of law".

---

1 Bingham (2010: 174).
2 Bingham (2010: 68).

Chapter 2: The First Law of Social Dynamics

L IFE originated as flickers of energy in the muddy margins of liquid pools some four billion years ago. Those flickers evolved into the concatenation of shapes and sizes, colours and sounds, that constitute the animal and vegetable forms of life. They became possible because of the co-operation that fructified the quantum of energy on Earth. That energy was nature's currency, its exchange between life forms the pricing mechanism. From this metamorphosed a volume of energy which was greater than the sum of its parts. Lions on the African savannah, tigers in the Asian rain forests, whales in the oceans, bears on the Arctic ice caps ... they all came from a process that *expanded* the quantum of life's energy.

Co-operation was not an optional extra. It was the necessary active principle guiding the selection and differentiation of species. Early humans were not exempt from the natural laws which made life possible. By the time humans of the Neolithic period had arrived, co-operation was embodied in complex customs and practises. These included the rules for specialisation in the production of goods which could be traded across long distances.

Language, which biologists discovered was crucial to the formation of the brain,[1] could not have been developed without the spirit of co-operation. To facilitate co-operation in all its forms – from selecting breeding partners to identifying gifted medicine men to doing deals with other tribes – early humans required rules of behaviour. They had to demarcate the rights and responsibilities of the individual and of the group. Those rules emerged out of biological history as the template that would inscribe the new possibilities for this unique species.

One of the requirements of the co-operative spirit was the development of a heightened sense of fair play. Without it, early humans could not have functioned coherently at the levels of biology (sex), society (kinship association) and ecology (resource maintenance).

A metrics was needed that worked with the grain of fair play. It was not possible for each individual to be judge and jury on what constituted acceptable

---

1 Dunbar (1977).

behaviour. Agreement was needed that would work across generations. One of the requirements of that metrics was the upgrading of nature's pricing mechanism.

Nature is defined by the exchange of units of energy between participating life forms. As early humans evolved, they adapted that pricing mechanism into a process that would work within their social universe. They agreed on the value that could serve as the "price" when products were exchanged. That price had to cover the energy invested in the re-shaping of raw materials into forms which delivered the kinds of utility that were not found in nature.

Prices had to be perceived as fair to all parties concerned. That obliged pre-literate societies to develop a sophisticated mix of property rights (individual and communal) to ensure that they could cover the costs and benefits of their activities. Costs fell on those who created them. Benefits accrued to those who worked for them.

Cheating was not an option.

The negative effects of activities were not to be displaced onto others. Behaviour that gave rise to anti-social behaviour was "fairly evident in small, household-centred communities. These externalities, in turn, led to the development of property rights as a way to internalize the costs and benefits created".[2] Terms like externalities need to be closely examined (Ch. 3), for they have become part of the art of deception in economics. For now, we will stick with the wisdom of the ancient peoples to whom we owe our existence.

The Metaphysics of Emancipation

Emancipation from the certainties of nature dictated the need for new reference points. Rules were required to ensure an appropriate flow of resources on which they depended for biological survival. Of paramount importance was the development of a metaphysics which would guide people in a way that filled the void in the emerging conscious mind.

The voyage of discovery was experimental: an evolutionary step like no other. It entailed two actions:

1. consciously *relearning* the ways of nature's seasons, *understanding them* through the mind. And
2. heightening the awareness of self: the potential in each individual, working co-operatively in community to determine new ways of living.

These two layers of meaning had to be harmonised. Symbols came into play in the unconscious collective mind, as psychiatrist Carl Jung represents

---

2 Cicarelli (2012: 91), citing Demsetz (1967: 350-353).

it: constructions that would smooth the process of adjustment to the new social universe.

To differentiate themselves from other species, our ancestors had to combine their dependence on the laws of nature with rules enabling them to carve out a unique form of social organisation. By a supreme act of genius, they mimicked the behaviour driven by natural instincts. They invented practises that harnessed the power of their innate creativity. This bought them the time needed to embark on a new voyage of discovery.

That break out of nature was dangerous. Early humans dared to challenge the laws of nature in their quest for a more fulfilling life. Extricating themselves from the certainties of nature's laws risked the wrath of Mother Earth. Survival was at stake. One bad mistake and *Homo sapiens* would be fossilised in the museum of failed experiments. Our ancestors persisted. Their journey was a layering of cultural innovations over biological inheritance. This turned humans into the most dynamic species on the planet.

Instincts of nature were employed as their first guides. Behaviour was adjusted by intuition to the circumstances of an emerging social universe. This process was facilitated by communicating with symbols. In the pre-literate phase, symbols articulated needs in relation to the potential offered by habitats. The Declaration of Detachment was the fluorescence of consciousness. Now, humans were obliged to exercise choice. The testimony of that transition is symbolically represented in the abstract images of other life forms on the walls of caves in France and Australia. From there, it was a matter of time, upwards of 40,000 years, before the literate stage made possible the science that would send rockets to the moon.

The proto-humans who had the arrogance to launch themselves into orbit outside nature knew that they had to appease nature. They would still need to draw on nature's energy. The evolutionary dynamics of the gene pool were aligned with the sensibilities of the emerging culture to harmonise two universes. The outcome was the synthesis that enabled humans to embark on their explorations into self-consciousness. The umbilical law that conjoined the social universe to Earth was the law of tenure.

A stylised representation of the 1st Law of Social Dynamics appears in Fig. 2:1. The arrangement for occupying and using land was a synthesis of the natural laws with the metaphysics that evolved into the sense of the spiritual. The integration of these two ways of viewing and ordering the world were expressed in concrete forms in the household economy of the individual, the social structure of the clan and tribe and the culture that was the content of ever expanding communities. These interacted with each other to provide the dynamics for the creation of the social universe.

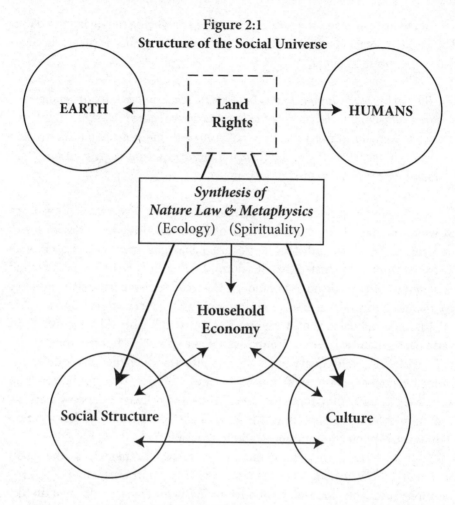

Figure 2:1
Structure of the Social Universe

So long as people kept the umbilical 1st Law in good working order, they would be safe. There would be food, clothing and shelter for those willing to work with nature to continue procreating. They learnt how to handle the challenges that came with consciousness. They employed first-person empirical methods to hone the social and moral rules that would guide them as they migrated through time and space. The outcomes were durable, and applied to everyone who contributed to the gene pool.

From Genetic to Cultural Code
Robin Dunbar, Oxford University's professor of evolutionary anthropology, has established that the optimum numbers for clusters of people, from early humans through to the villages of modern times, was 148 souls (the number has been rounded up to 150, and is known as Dunbar's Number). He found that brain size was correlated to the size of the social group.

At the primate stage, the greatest risk came from being caught by a predator. The implicit social contract that glued individuals together was calculated to defeat the common enemy.

> *But communal solutions of this kind mean that animals have to balance in a rather sophisticated way the benefits of unabashed selfishness (grab what you can at everyone else's expense) with the benefits that derive from co-operation as a group (which necessarily means being a bit more sensitive to others' needs and interests).[3]*

From primate groups through to early humans, and then on to the villages in which modern humans spent most of historical time, the effective mean number of 148 was sufficient to secure behaviour that served everyone's interests. Dunbar calculated that this optimum number persisted from the time of Neolithic villages through to modern Hutterite settlements and the military companies into which armies were composed in the 20th century.

The internal balance of the group was inextricably bound up with a third variable: the natural habitat. Groups occupied a space that fulfilled their ability to flourish over evolutionary timescales. Territories which the groups defended from intruders were proportionate to the numbers that could function effectively as users of nature's resources. Thus, the primary relationship in the evolution of our species assumed the form of a triadic symmetry: the evolution of brain size, population numbers, and territoriality.

In nature, each species interacts in ways which emancipate the latent potential in the genetic code. Adaptation is proportionate to the energy resources available in ecological niches. Early humans conformed to the demographic density principle. We now know that, when the spatial context is removed, their reproductive behaviour goes haywire. That much was clear from what they brought with them out of nature (Box 2:1).

The second group of laws, those honed by humans, yielded the social universe. Rules like "Thou shalt not kill" secured harmony within the breeding population. These met the needs of time and place, but conformed to the universal values regulating behaviour from Neolithic times to our age of virtual reality. Those values were compatible with the laws of nature. That is why we call those laws "natural". Transgression attracted punishments from peers within the community. The most heinous crimes could entail banishment. This would cast the individual back into nature, alone, excluded from the symbolic space that is the collective consciousness occupied by humans.

---

3 Dunbar (2011:12).

Box 2:1
The Dynamics of Ant Nests

NATURE ensures stability between host habitats and their populations. Ant colonies, for example, expand to an optimum size. If there are too few in the territory, "their behaviour is chaotic". By expanding to a threshold value within the living space, "the whole group becomes rhythmic. It is a bottom-up organizing process driven by ant-to-ant contact".[1] The nest's territory is regulated. "The colony has a sense of density and spatial order," reports Brian Goodwin of the UK's Open University.[2]

Many humans appear to have lost that capacity for order. In Britain in 2011, the Cameron government identified 120,000 problem families as costing the state £9bn in benefits, health care and anti-social behaviour. Louise Casey was appointed head of the Troubled Families Unit. She placed responsibility on the women for having too many children. Those mothers should be "ashamed" of the damage they were doing to society and stop having children.[3] No consideration was given to the responsibility of those who had re-ordered the spatial context into which the women were born and reared, whose subsequent behaviour was consequently chaotic.

---

1 Coveney and Highfield (1995: 272).
2 Goodwin (1994).
3 Winnett and Kirkup (2012).

Integrating these two sets of laws was the code that organically fused the natural and social universes. Its function was the efficient transmission of resources. In nature, territories were breeding spaces occupied by populations which conserved the resources on which they depended. The customs and practises of tenure were grafted onto, and modified, territoriality. This synthesis became the 1st Law of Social Dynamics. Without it, humans could not have maintained the stable conditions needed to evolve social substitutes for instinct-based behaviour. Rights and obligations were formulated that corresponded to the level of social development and the available resource endowments. This re-asserted what biologists call *homeostasis*. This is the tendency of an organism, or a cell, to regulate its internal condition to create and sustain a state of equilibrium. By learning how to evolve this principle into its cultural forms, *Homo sapiens* could propagate outside nature's comfort zone. Key to this process were the rules of tenure, which made it possible for populations to behave in optimal ways. That optimality was achieved under conditions of freedom. People needed to choose how to realise their potential as defined by the complex interaction of biological inheritance, their cultural resources and nature's endowments.

Shock of the Transition

Neolithic people paid a heavy psychic price. They endured the first collective trauma. Psychologically speaking, disconnecting themselves from nature could not possibly be a painless prospect. They were modifying behaviour so that they were not totally compliant with the certainties of nature's laws. This imposed the pressures that nourished the first expressions of moral reasoning.

To aid them in this journey through time and space, they needed the support of a complex social organisation. That change could not be accomplished without developing an ability to fructify the value of the energy provided by nature. As a prelude to this transformation, they evolved archetypal images in their collective consciousness. These served as guides as they ventured out of Africa and through the foraging stage of gathering food to the system that combined hunting and horticulture. A more sedentary way of life had to include a utilitarian association with particular plots of land. But the transition also required the retention of a shifting style of life within a larger territory.

The capacity to coax a surplus out of the land meant that new choices had to be made. This created a systemic crisis. What would happen to the surplus? This question presented the biggest challenge to the naturalistic ethics that humans brought with them out of nature. That surplus product, which was additional to the immediate biological needs of households units, could either be squandered, or invested in a new form of social organisation. The choices that were made led to the construction of the first civilisations.

How they removed the risk of conflicts over land was an act of genius. As we saw in Ch. 1, a divine force was mustered to mediate between the resources and their consumption by mortals. The agencies of the state (the earliest ones were administered by priests in temples) served the interests of the people. Community leaders, who specialised in elaborating the rituals of the gods and the routines of urban infrastructure, were supported by the people who worked in the fields. Everyone benefited from the distribution of the resources of nature, which were regulated in ways which served "the common good".

> *The only truly sovereign state, independent of all external control, is the state which the universe itself constitutes, the state governed by the assembly of the gods. This state, moreover, is the state which dominates the territory of Mesopotamia; the gods own the land, the big estates, in the country.*[4]

---

4 Jacobsen (1949: 200).

In Egypt, where the ruler was divine, the function of the state – mediated through the gods – was to own the land and the waters of the Nile. The state would defend, nurture, shelter and enlarge the population. In return, the people would worship the gods, whose controller "was the herdsman who kept them in green pastures, fought to secure fresh pastures for them, drove off the voracious beasts who attacked them, belaboured the cattle who strayed out of line, and helped along the weaklings".[5] The king of Egypt was one of the gods and was the land's representative among the gods.

The significance of this covenant with the gods is to be found in the sociological impact. The land could not be the subject of private dispute between individuals. The gods did not choose favourites. Land was accessible to all.

By evolving the cosmology of a divine world, ancient peoples carved a new space for themselves in a way which enabled them to create and expand the social universe. For so long as Earth was the domain of the divine power, mortals would not fight each other for privileged possession.

Abandonment of the authority of the gods proved to be fatal. This occurred as some individuals, who exploited their positions of authority, redefined their rights as superior to the gods. In substituting themselves for the divine rights of the Creator, they automatically redefined as inferior the rights of other people.

Every city civilisation in antiquity was confronted with the same dilemma: the need to neutralise the temptation to exploit nature for personal advantage and at the expense of the welfare of others. When populations succumbed and allowed minorities to assume proprietary control over the surplus that the community produced, the remainder of their city civilisation's history was a protracted case of trauma. People were forced to cope with the pathologies that stemmed from the breakdown in the sacred covenant. Thus originated the great blights on civilisation.

Institutionalised poverty.

Territorial wars.

Environmental degradation

The Duality of our World

The civilisations of antiquity were milestones in human evolution. Other species were sociable; some could use tools, demarcate territories, just like the primates from which our species emerged. None, however, could create a social universe, the space that ran parallel to the natural universe. But the crucial innovation was the wisdom that enabled them to pool the additional value, a value over and above what was needed to sustain families, to serve a wider social interest.

---

5 Wilson (1949: 88).

In doing so, they created settlements configured on laws that were unique in the natural universe.

The surplus could not have been created without the spirit of co-operation. It was dedicated to deepening humanity's journey into self-consciousness, a journey which found its expression in art, architecture and science. This history revealed the genius of people who worked on, and *with*, nature.

But time and again, the people who administered the earliest civilisations committed a fatal error. They sponsored – or failed to prevent – the abuse of the 1st Law of Social Dynamics. They allowed the social product to be diverted into private pockets. That behaviour was associated with coercion (slavery, or taxation) to raise the revenue needed to maintain the system. By degrading the social nature of their finances, a chain of events was unleashed which caused the implosion of the urban structure. It was the privatisation of the social income that divided society into two: those who *added* value to the wealth of their communities, and those who *extracted* value. That division became the basis for pathologically disturbed communities.

Towards a Healthy Society

Today, the notion of a *normal* society is rejected by post-modern philosophers. Everything is relative. There is no objective way of identifying the template elements of a healthy community.

But how can ours be a normal society if the general crises are systemic, originating in a systematised culture of cheating? If this deviant behaviour was one of the malformed pillars underpinning the structure of society, the rules that are natural to society had to be modified. They would have mutated into pathologically damaged social organisms.

Prior to the onset of civilisation, the cultures that evolved over thousands of years under conditions of freedom may be deemed to be *authentic*, if they are judged by the tests of time and the record of landmark achievements in the evolutionary process. These "natural" societies were grounded in rules and institutions that were not imposed upon them by external forces. People freely elaborated the rituals, economic practises and interpersonal relationships. These fulfilled needs within the parameters of what was possible, *and acceptable to them*, as defined by the codes of their combined biological and social systems.

If we move to recent times (the period between five and ten thousand years ago) we find that the embryonic phases of the earliest civilisations were in a strong sense authentic. As far as we can tell, people volunteered to pool their agricultural surplus to fund the investments in new ways of living. This made possible the cultural florescence that became the city civilisation.

But then, something went wrong. A new, an inauthentic, culture began to flourish and was imposed on people. We can infer this from the adoption of practises such as slavery, and from the poverty that stemmed from landlessness and crippling indebtedness. The character of urban civilisations changed, from open to closed systems, from sites of innovation to the enclosures (physically represented by walls around cities) that were constraints on the human spirit.

What transformed free communities into the degraded formations which ultimately collapsed? The major change occurred when the elites decided that they would discontinue serving the welfare of the population. Instead, they would arrogate the community's resources to themselves. What ensued was a two-phase process that degraded healthy societies into mechanisms of exploitation.

First, the internal colonisation of the commons by self-serving individuals. A well documented example from recent times is offered by the degradation of the clans of Scotland. Traditionally, the chiefs were stewards of the welfare of their kith and kin. Territories were held in common, giving access on the basis of need. Then (partly under the influence of the English aristocracy) the chiefs decided that they "owned" the land. It was not the physical space itself which they ultimately sought, but the stream of rents that could be extracted by transforming clansmen into tenants or by the replacement of people with sheep. By their assertion of exclusive rights over the territory, the chiefs-turned-proprietors acquired the resources to supplement their political and military authority. This, in turn, enabled them to reshape culture to accommodate the new socio-biological realities.

The second phase occurred as this anti-social system of land tenure matured. The owners felt the need to increase their flow of rents. This propelled the colonisation programme. The land of others was appropriated; in the process, fashioning hybrid cultures that reflected the hierarchy of dominance. The landless were subordinated to the landlords in an economics of apartheid.

The culture that matched these relationships was synthetic. Both the exploited *and the exploiters* were forced to adjust their thinking and behaviour to fit into structures and social processes that were pathological. Culture had to be redefined. Histories were re-invented. The interventions in people's minds (primarily involving the suppression of memory), combined with the denial of the deeds that deprived people of their land rights, led to the formation of new national identities. These hybrid identities and cultures were composed, in part, of folk lore and fabricated myths.

Sociogenics: a Synthesis of Knowledge
In evolutionary terms, humanity lost its way. The route back to growth is a new approach to knowledge. The fatal threat to our civilisation (and now, according

to some scientists, even to our species) is to be found somewhere in the triadic relationship between nature, society, and the individual.

Current approaches to the search for answers have not proved effective. One reason is the segregation of the social and natural sciences. When attempts are made to apply biological models scientifically to human problems, we find that the practitioners are resorting to pseudo-science. A multidisciplinary synthesis is needed. The objective is to expose the fissures through which malevolent forces seep into society to warp behaviour and trigger disasters.

Recovering knowledge of how societies are divided is the single most important challenge for anyone wanting to serve the best interests of both themselves and their communities. To achieve this, we need a new approach to viewing the way the world works.

Sociogenics is concerned with the sociability of humans as created by biological as well as cultural forces. A first step is to re-assess the activities that differentiate *normal* from *pathological* behaviour. Most urgently, we need to identify behaviour that undermines the psychic and biological welfare of humanity. By "going back to the beginning" and thinking afresh, we may re-learn important lessons from (say) the marital practises of Neolithic people.

To flourish and elevate their social systems, pre-literate peoples created increasingly complex patterns of allegiances. They achieved this by synchronising cultural practises with biological imperatives. Exogamy is the practise of seeking mates outside one's kinship group. Anthropologists have observed this practise among nearly all pre-literate societies.[6]

Exogamy served two purposes. Biologically, it promoted genetic diversity. Inter-marriage between distant groups secured vitality for the gene pool, and so it adhered to one of the key principles of the evolutionary process: *adding value through co-operation*. Concurrent with that biological drive was the social benefit of deepening the range of contacts. You learnt to trust people you knew. The extension of trade was one outcome: the exchange of goods and the evolution of the market mechanism. People increased each other's material welfare by specialising in the production of goods based on the endowments of their habitats. This is expressed by economists today as the principle of comparative advantage. Each group does what it is best at doing, and the ensuing exchange results in satisfaction that is greater than the sum of its parts. Mutual benefit arises simultaneously in both the biological and social spheres, consolidating itself around a moral life. This nourished something which was unique in nature: humanity.

These step-changes in activity and spatially dispersed relationships did

---

6   Posner (1980: 41-42).

Box 2:2
The Mission of Humanity

HUMANITY, as here employed, goes beyond the dictionary definition. Our humanity is not fixed. Humanity includes the potential latent in each of the two commons which, taken together, constitute the essence of *Homo sapiens*.

The biological potential is inscribed in DNA. The social potential is inscribed in culture. When these are combined, there are no outer limits to this potential. First, humans participate with other life forms to expand the riches in the natural universe. This is the evolutionary process, in which co-operation includes other living forms that share the habitats.

Also through co-operation, the social universe is continuously expanded, which therefore extends what it means to be human. The more humans experience the joys that come with the conscious awareness of what can be achieved (in spheres as diverse as philosophy, art, crafts or sport), the more is culture enriched. This expansion is achieved by increasing productivity. But all of this comes at a price: we have to work for it.

not result in the manic way of living to which modern people are shackled. Neolithic people combined work with leisure to secure the greatest contentment for everyone. Their choices were exercised on the basis of considerations drawn from biological, social and aesthetic imperatives. That balance of life defined humanity (Box 2:2).

Choices had to be made. The evolutionary pathway is defined by reason and morality. Aboriginal peoples "consciously chose their ideal of living well and all that that implied – under-production, more leisure, and a near uniform quality of life on a *per capita* basis – even when other options were clearly attainable".[7] A daily routine of three to five hours work was sufficient for food production. The density of populations was regulated to ensure a healthy balance with ecological niches. Marriage practises and fertility rates were *not* determined by blind obedience to the law of nature. They were based on an emerging understanding of what it would take to enjoy the Good Life.

Hunting and gathering was not a passive way of life. It required the combined intelligence of mind and aesthetic sensibilities. Amerindians, for example, knew that they increased the productivity of nature by the controlled use of fire. Burning the undergrowth increased the population of herbivores and other animals, and so increased the numbers of people who could occupy the territories. "[M]anaged fires could create more than they destroyed."[8] So "living in balance with nature" was a dynamic exchange in which *humans added value*

---

7 Sahlins (1974: 34).
8 Cicarelli (2012: 94).

to nature. To secure balance, they devised and applied a structure of use rights and practises that enabled everyone to perform his or her task in fulfilling the biological, social and spiritual needs of the population. Tools were privately owned. Land, however, was unique. Secure possession came with obligations. Land had to be used; otherwise, it would revert to use by others.

> *Possessory rights lapsed if cultivation ceased or was suspended even for a single growing season.*[9]

Use rights were sophisticated and synchronised with the grain of evolution. Trading goods across long distances was conducted both by barter and the use of "money" (Amerindians used wampum both as a measure of value and to fulfil other socio-psychological needs). The surplus product, where it was available, was shared for the benefit of the community.

But how does a sociogenic approach help us with the problems of the 21st century? One of the grievous crises, today, is the failure of the social sciences. These are fragmented into "schools" which represent the preferences of practitioners. They cloak personal prejudices in scientific garb. This makes it difficult to test the wisdom of the advice from "experts". A sociogenic approach identifies the measures and principles on which we might rebuild communities that deliver benign outcomes. One challenge, for example (elaborated in Ch. 5), is to differentiate between two broad categories of doctrines.

1. *Pro-creative narratives* These help people to deploy their energies in ways which advance the quality of life. The doctrines help to establish order and to channel energy in goal-achieving ways.
2. *Coping strategies* These are responses to socially significant shocks. Eugenics is an example of trauma thinking. It was the ideology adopted by a social movement (starting in the US) to cope with the social pathologies of a century ago.

Ideologies emerged thick and fast over the last several hundred years. Their value – as measured in terms of their problem-solving achievements – was in inverse proportion to the density of the analysis they offered. They did help people to cope with the stresses inflicted by modern life. That was both good and bad. They ameliorate painful conditions, but they also distract from the fundamental issues that *might* lead to the restoration of healthy ways of living.

---

9   Cicarelli (2012: 91).

That coping strategies should be viewed as temporary expedients is emphasised by the British population's state of psychological dis-ease. Soporific doctrines (like socialism) do not eliminate the consequences of social trauma. Three generations have been exposed to the cradle-to-grave securities offered by the Welfare State. And yet, according to Richard Layard, director or the London School of Economics' Centre for Economic Performance, mental illness accounts for 40% of all illness. Six million people suffer from depression and anxiety disorders, accounting for 40% of all absence from work through sickness. These psychological problems also account for most of the economic losses arising from people working below their capacity.[10]

Can we afford further distractions from coping doctrines, or should we now search for root causes? All depends on our capacity to recover our primordial knack of spotting the cheats in our midst.

---

10 Layard (2012).

Chapter 3: Cheating as Social Process

THE civil servant of Her Majesty's Government knew what he would do with people who cheated the public purse.

The cheats Terry Moran had in mind were costing Britain's Welfare State more than £1bn every year in fraudulent claims. So, he told a conference of Whitehall officials: "If I had my way I would put their photograph on every lamppost in the street where they live".[1]

The budget *was* vulnerable to abuse by people at the bottom of the income scales, who claimed the need for welfare support from taxpayers. Those cheats, however, were getting away with peanuts. Lynch mob strategies are not directed at the people who deprive society of countless billions. Just how many billions are at stake we cannot tell, because the mis-appropriated money is disguised by legislation and the ideological camouflage devised centuries ago by the landed aristocracy.

No country in the world is exempt from the cheating that is conducted as a social process. The scale is measured by the rents people pay for the use of the common services provided by both nature and society.

Rents are measured in the land market. The freedom to bid for the use of common resources enables people to identify the good effects which they expect to derive from those services. In assessing the amounts they are willing to pay, they subtract the value of negative influences on the localities where they need to live or work. The net effect of these two forces is the rent that people are willing to pay. In technical terms, the market is the mechanism by which the *externalities* are summed into a cash price.

Rent thus represents, in cash terms, the good and the bad effects of the way people live and work and affect each other. The good values measure the activities to which we all contribute, and which we wish to share. In the modern state, an example of how this value is created is the provision of a new railway system. Unless it is a reckless project that few want to use, it will *more than* pay for itself. We discover this, by measuring the uplift in rents in the locality of the stations served by the railway. If the rents are diverted away from funding the transit system, those who funded the railway are cheated (Box 3:1).

---

1 Hope (2012).

Box 3:1
Underground Cheats

London needed a new underground train service in the 1980s. The Canadian entrepreneurs who were constructing tower blocks for a financial centre in Docklands were willing to foot the bill, but the Thatcher government declined.[1] Taxpayers were consequently obliged to invest £3.4bn in the Jubilee line. It was a good deal – the net return (after paying off Labour and Capital) was around £14bn!

Eleven new stations were opened. Journalists, bankers and brokers could now reside near The Globe, the Shakespearian theatre just a few minutes walk away from the Tate Modern art gallery, and enjoy an easy commute to Docklands. The demand for residential properties was brisk along the length of the railway. But because the government did not collect the added value created by the investment of public money, that value – in the form of land rents – went into the pockets of people who happened to own tracts around the railway stations.

1 Harrison (2006: 64-82).

Unlike low-income individuals who cheat the public purse by lodging false claims for benefits, those who pocket the nation's rents are engaged in an epic racket. Their mission is the privatisation of *economic rent* (Box 3:2).

Because this cheating is sanctioned by law, it is no longer recognised as immoral. Because the consequences of its transformation into privately consumed income are not discussed, people have lost track of the psycho-social impact on them and their communities.

The conversion of community-created value could not have been sanctioned during the formative stages of our species. The real-time audit of how individuals in pre-literate societies behaved was automatic. It stemmed from the structure of the community. Close encounters ensured that every person was acquainted with activities that might affect his or her wellbeing. Anthropologists have observed, and evolutionary psychologists have confirmed, that "everyone literally knew everyone else, so social persuasion was sufficient to insure compliance with established norms".[2] Evolutionary psychologists have demonstrated experimentally the significance of the facility for spotting cheats (Box 3:3).

Cheats *had* to be prevented from short-changing their kith and kin. Evolutionary success depended on vigilance by everyone. By enforcing fair play, the opportunities for physiological and cultural development expanded

2 Cicarelli (2012: 98).

Box 3:2
The Definition of Economic Rent

People want to live in a territory that is protected by an army. A secure nation encourages people to invest their capital for the future. The net gains from that productivity surface as an additional layer of value due solely to the provision of public services.

Nature's contribution is the resource endowments available within each habitat. These range from deep sea harbours to subterranean minerals to the electro-magnetic spectrum used for cell phones. There is no cost of production, so the revenue is a pure surplus.

Society's contribution takes the form of the collaborative efforts that are shaped by the population's ethical consciousness that prescribes ways of working together for the mutual benefit of everyone. We all participate in that process

The value flowing from all these sources merges in the land market as the rents people pay for the use of these services. Rent is the excess over the part of the income paid to Labour as wages and to Capital as profits.

exponentially. The social universe was theirs for the making. The imagination was released, taking flight to the outer edges of minds that were expanding as early humans deepened the moral and technical challenges they set for themselves. And with every successful experiment, new possibilities opened up in the arts of body decoration, the sense of spirituality, the achievements from craftsmanship. As early humans gazed out towards the stars, they visualised limitless possibilities for creating a new social universe on earth. There were no limits to the boundaries of what they could achieve. But all of this was on one condition: *no cheating!*

Spotting the Cheats
Amerindians were typical of aboriginal peoples the planet over.

The purposeful moderation of Amerindians stressed communal responsibility, respect for individual liberty, and the cultivation of friendship over personal aggrandisement.[3]

A premium was placed on leisure. Nature was generous, and the people structured their economic tasks so that they could balance lifestyles to secure material well-being and maximise free time to enjoy life.

---

3 Cicarelli (2012:105).

> **Box 3:3**
> **Altruism & Cheating**
>
> The mind is an information processing mechanism that enables the individual to decipher the meaning in all kinds of signals, both verbal and of the non-verbal kind (such as facial expressions and gestures). American psychologist Leda Cosmides and anthropologist John Tooby examined cheating in the context of evolutionary biology. They show that the mind has a switch which can be turned off. Cheats will not be identified unless the information is provided in a relevant form. This is less a problem in hunter-gatherer groups, where practises of a non-benign kind were visible and could be challenged.
>
> But they warn that subtle cheating could have grievous consequences. If not controlled, research shows that it could challenge the evolution of the altruism that is a bedrock of group dynamics. Without group stability, people would not have co-operated. This would have prejudiced the evolution of the social universe.
>
> _____
>
> Cosmides and Tooby (1992).

Everyone was expected to work and usually did so in communal groups, be it 100 or so men engaged in an organised hunt, a group of women tending to their personal gardens or the tribal plots, or both sexes working together on tasks, dependent on gender co-operation. Universal contribution to the work effort was expected although exemptions were made for the infirm, the very young, and the aged.[4]

Amerindians conformed to the natural law. When they divided the product of their labour, they "embraced the Golden Rule, treating others as they would like to be treated, understanding that this ethic applies to the basic wants and needs all people share and not to personal idiosyncrasies or deviant behaviour".[5]

In small bands, people procreated and developed the capacity to migrate into new ecological niches by harnessing the principle of co-operation. Biological security was essential during the hunting and gathering phase of evolution. If someone sought to avoid personal responsibilities, such behaviour could jeopardise the group's existence. The size of the population ensured the intimacy that exposed those who sought to cheat their way through life.

Most people would love to lounge around the camp fire and wait for others to hunt, endure the risks and bring back the meat for the evening feast. Such behaviour could not be tolerated. Censuring the cheats served a dual purpose.

_____

4   Cicarelli (2012: 89).
5   Binmore (2005: 129-130).

Biologically, the group would not be put at risk by individuals who sought to live parasitically on others. Socially, the sentiments serving as the glue of the group – such as trust and acts of reciprocity in times of need – were not jeopardised by individuals who refused to fulfil their roles in the life of the community.

The socio-genic necessity of outlawing cheating is evident in all walks of life. Fairness is most volubly enforced by spectators in sport. If a player is observed to cheat, the howls of disapproval emitted from the stands registers the collective disapproval.

Feedback devices ensured stability over tens of thousands of years. When early forms of social organisation became redundant, their obsolescence was the result of discovering more productive ways of living. These required new arrangements to ensure people's freedoms. The pre-condition was the adoption of customs and practises which mimicked the key laws of nature. Spotting the cheats was a self-correcting mechanism.

Civilisations, on the other hand, have been lucky to survive a thousand years. As a life support system, urbanisation on the scale that required massive investment in infrastructure was fatally flawed. My general theory of cheating accounts for the tragedy that is embedded in civilisation. It explains all of the dysfunctional forms of behaviour which combine into crises on a scale that leads to collapse of the system. Cheating on a socially significant scale corrodes the structural foundations of civilisation. The kind of cheating with which we are concerned exercises the power to block the feedback mechanisms (such as moral codes) that would otherwise deliver stability.

The urban settlements that flourished in Mesopotamia were necessarily liable to profound disturbances. The invention of writing, the discovery of new ways of counting, were revolutionary in their impact. To secure the time necessary for people to get used to such innovations, the system needed robust feedback mechanisms. To override them, something extremely powerful had to be at work. Behaviour that can block regulatory devices must be capable of mustering an awesome power of destruction. That power is the cheating that captures the energy of society and converts it to private use. Once the social system has been captured, cheating becomes an integral part of everyday life.

- When cheating is institutionalised, society is no longer a benign formation. The structure that is supposed to support the population becomes anti-social.
- Once society is anti-social, new generations are inducted into the cheating process without being aware that they are acting against their own interests.
- Cheating assumes a life of its own, penetrating deeper into the system. If society is not rescued in time, it ultimately devours itself.

Such a society is overwhelmed by negative practises which dissipate the energy on which civilisation depends. Identifying the onset of that process is a matter of life and death.

When Neolithic villages expanded into towns and then cities, the traditional ways of securing compliance with norms of good behaviour were replaced by the impersonal laws of civil society. These were initially informed by the natural laws of justice. As such, they were the software that made possible the complexities of urban living. For cheating to flourish, it would first be necessary for the law-making process to be captured. Laws would have to be modified to validate the cheating. Those renegade laws would then have to be enforced against the victims. So the beneficiaries of the cheating process would also have to capture the means of policing the system.

When this operation is successfully executed, the outcome is a transformation in the nature of power. Formerly, that power made it possible to mobilise resources for the common good. Resources could be invested in the mega projects that were beyond the ability of individuals, hamlets or villages to undertake. The hydraulic infrastructure of the arid regions miles away from the rivers Tigris and Euphrates – the canals that carried the water to transform wastelands into fertile fields – required the deployment of benign power. The outcome was a rise in the well-being of the whole population.

But once the cheating took hold, power became pernicious. It would simultaneously corrupt the ecological and the social spheres of life. People lost the capacity to realise what was being done to them, and to the natural environment. This is what occurred when the manipulators of people's minds engaged in one of the most cruel acts imaginable: selling sub-prime mortgages to landless migrants in America in the 19th century, raising their hopes that they would finally be able to rebuild their lives in harmony with nature.

Myths & Mind Manipulators

Myths take a long time to form and embed in the collective consciousness. Their purpose is dual: collate a great deal of information (the store of knowledge function) and to guide behaviour (the rules of conduct function). Appropriately structured, myths are crucial to security and prosperity.

What happens when society's myths are appropriated to serve private interests? Disaster ensues. One myth employed by the cheats is grounded in the claim that there is a plentiful supply of land freely available to those who would reclaim it from nature. An example is the way in which the notion of the "land of the free" was manipulated to extract rents from the arid environment of the Great Plains.

Previously, settlers avoided the territory west of Kansas and Nebraska, deterred by an unreliable rainfall. Their judgement was faultless. But as the eastern acres were enclosed, the pressure was on to exploit the opportunities to speculate in land further westwards. But how to overcome the Great American Desert, as it was called in the mid 19th century? A new myth was needed, that would re-calibrate the collective consciousness of the aspiring settlers. Thus was born the theory that settlement itself would cause the rains to fall and the grass to grow.

The geologist who surveyed Nebraska in 1867 was Ferdinand V. Hayden. He formulated the thesis that planting trees on each quarter-section would affect the climate, increasing the moisture and fertilising the soil. This would increase rainfall across the territory, extending across the dry belt to the foot of the Rocky mountains. Hayden made his intentions clear – he wanted to please the people who wished to develop this territory – and he was willing to bend the science to suit this agenda.

Collaborating in Hayden's mission was Samuel Aughey. He became State Geologist, and Professor of Natural Sciences at the newly-established University of Nebraska. He, in turn, was associated with Charles Dana Wilber, a speculative town builder and amateur scientist. Henry Nash Smith traced the myth of the rain makers and concluded: "Near the culmination of the great boom period of the eastern plains these two men joined forces in extending the myth of the garden beyond the Missouri". The myth coincidently served "the economic interest of every landowner in Kansas and Nebraska ... Aughey and Wilber were speaking for their people on all levels of imagination, ingrained habit, stereotyped response, and the most rigorous calculation of potential profit from unearned increment". [6]

The methods of science were manipulated by people who were willing to cheat both nature and society. The potency of the myth was disseminated with Wilber's terse epigram "Rain Follows the Plough". This was

An inspired slogan which makes the oldest and most sacred of agrarian symbols the instrument whose magical stroke calls down the life-giving waters upon the land. Although it was Aughey who furnished the technical dressing for the argument, it was Wilber who grasped its imaginative overtones. [7]

By manipulating the minds of the landless, Wilber extracted a fortune by selling worthless land to gullible rainmakers. The land itself was abused by being subjected to uses for which it was not fitted. In the fullness of time, to enable the settlers to remain on this territory, the landscape would have to be reshaped and irrigated at heavy cost to both nature and society.

---

6 Smith (1970: 181-182).
7 Smith (1970: 182).

The ruthlessness of the rent-seekers was elegantly examined by Adam Smith in *An Inquiry Into the Nature and Causes of the Wealth of Nations*. His treatise analysed productive activity as it was disclosed by the distribution of income. He identified behaviour that was the socially sanctioned cheating process.

The Wealth of Nations

Adam Smith had learnt from the French Physiocrats that, if he wanted to understand the way a nation's wealth was produced, he would have to disaggregate the flow of income into its component parts. The three classic categories were: rent, wages and profits. These streams of income were collected by landlords, employees and the owners of man-made capital. But there was something exceptional about some of the claimants: land owners did nothing to add to the stream of the nation's revenue.

Smith identified the cheats with brutal honesty. Landlords, he wrote in Book 1, Ch. 11, are

> *the only one of the three orders whose revenue costs them neither labour nor care, but comes to them, as it were, of its own accord, and independent of any plan or project of their own.*[8]

Of its own accord? Independent of any plan? By the time the moral philosopher began to write his masterpiece on political economy in the 1770s, the landlord class had the benefit of 200 years of planning and law-making to legitimise the appropriation of part of the nation's income. *They were the cheats who got away with living off others by annexing the state's political power.* The cheating mission was skilfully executed over time and coercively embedded to ensure its acceptance in perpetuity (the English case is explored below, in Ch. 6).

Smith analysed some of the social and economic consequences. He observed that landlords were "too often defective" in their knowledge of what it takes to act in "the general interest of the society". Their indolence,

> *which is the natural effect of the ease and security of their situation, renders them too often, not only ignorant, but incapable of that application of mind which is necessary in order to foresee and understand the consequences of any public regulation.*[9]

This characterisation of landlords was courageous, for Smith lived in a society dominated by that class.

---

8   Smith (1776: 276-277).
9   Smith (1776: 277).

It did not matter that the indolent cheats were ignorant, however, and that their minds were insufficiently disciplined to understand the impact of public policies. Such inadequacies would not be at their expense. They had incubated a culture that consolidated itself in ways that protected their vital interests in perpetuity. So there was little need for the individual within that class to apply his mind to anything other than indolent pursuits. After all, they had designed taxation to ensure that the growing share of the increased income that was delivered by improvements in productivity would be paid out as rent. This is how Smith put it: "All those improvements in the productive powers of labour, which tend directly to reduce the real price of manufactures, tend indirectly to raise the real rent of land".[10]

There was little that the value-adding producers could do about this anti-evolutionary behaviour.

> As soon as land becomes private property, the landlord demands a share of almost all the produce which the labourer can either raise, or collect from it. His rent makes the first deduction from the produce of the labourer which is employed upon land.[11]

Smith exonerates the market. The source of conflict stemmed from property rights, as formulated by government. The appropriators could collect the rent because they deemed themselves to be the owners of earth. By excluding others from access, they enforced a process that would not have been tolerated in Neolithic communities. There was no end to the ingenuity of the cheats.

Smith drove home his argument that landlords made no contribution towards the formation of rent. He cited the case of kelp. The landlord

> sometimes demands rent for what is altogether incapable of human improvement. Kelp is a species of sea-weed, which, when burnt, yields an alkaline salt, useful for making glass, soap, and for several other purposes. It grows in several parts of Great Britain, particularly in Scotland, upon such rocks only as lie within the high water mark, which are twice every day covered with the sea, and of which the produce, therefore, was never augmented by human industry. The landlord, however, whose estate is bounded by a kelp shore of this kind, demands a rent for it as much as for his corn fields.[12]

---

10 Smith (1776: 275).
11 Smith (1776: 73).
12 Smith (1779: Bk.I, Ch.. XI, PT. I).

Financial Times reporters recalled that Winston S. Churchill, speaking in the House of Commons in 1909, branded the "land monopolist" as rendering "no service to the community, he contributes nothing to the general welfare, he contributes nothing to the process from which his own enrichment is derived".[13]

Karl Marx would have concurred. In *Critique of the Gotha Programme* he explained that the power to exploit workers was contingent on the negation of their right of access to land. He wrote: " … the monopoly of property in land is even the basis of the monopoly of capital … " In other words: erase the monopoly power associated with the privatised ownership of land, and the power of capital withers with it.

To understand the nature of power, note Marx's further observation: "In England, the capitalist is usually not even the owner of the land on which his factory stands". The owner of capital, as Smith made clear, added to the value that was created by working people. But factory owners were obliged to pay rent to the land owner.[14] Entrepreneurs, too, were exploited, along with those who laboured for their wages.

By the time Smith wrote his monumental work on the economics of the emerging industrial era, cheating was routinised throughout Europe. The cheats had hijacked their societies by claiming to own nature. The terms which defined the incentives to produce and exchange goods and services were corrupted. Now, every advance in the arts and technologies which increased the productivity of labour was an opportunity to siphon off part of the product for the benefit of the cheats. The example of the education of new generations illustrates the pathology of income distribution in this system.

Commentators who were anxious about the financial crisis of 2008 urged governments to invest more resources in education to increase productivity. They failed to disclose that this would redound to the advantage of the cheats. How the increased output from improvements resulting from education is divided is represented in Fig. 3:1.

Part of the value is "externalised"; that is, it is not paid to the people who produce the goods and services traded in the markets. This added value could be used in one of two ways.

1. It could be collected to fund the cost of education (from whence it came). If that happened, government would not have to tax people's earned incomes in order to fund schools and the teaching staff.
2. It could be pocketed by those who claim to own the land. In that case, government would have to tax people, to fund the education system.

---

13 Giles *et al.* (2011).
14 Harrison (1979: 211).

Figure 3:1 Investment in Education

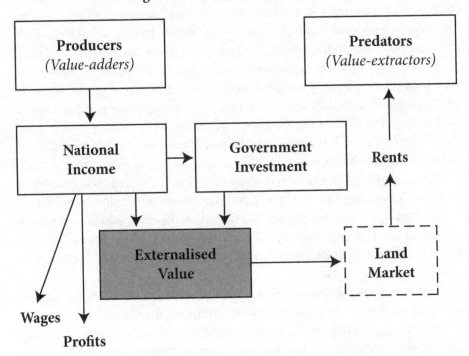

The word "externalised" is important, as much for what it does not tell us about the cheating process. Anyone could be forgiven for not recognising it as something that implicated them, as home-owners, in the cheating process. This is how one textbook defines the word:

> Externalities *are social costs that are not taken into account by the firm because they are not internal to the firm. The central authorities can levy taxes equal to the excess of social costs over private costs and thus force the firm to take account of these costs. When the state does this, it is said to be* internalising an externality.[15]

Now we shall de-code the jargon.

As people work and invest, they not only generate sufficient value to support their households, and reproduce the capital they need to finance their enterprises. They also generate an additional value that could be reserved for the benefit of everyone in the community. After all, it *was* the product of cooperation! But the people who produce the extra value do not collect it as

---

15   Lipsey (1979: 436). Emphases in original.

their rightful income. The value is "externalised" and ends up, primarily, in the pockets of land owners.

Those externalities are not treated as moral lapses, or the result of Machiavellian manipulation of the pricing mechanism. Rather, they are noted as imperfections in Adam Smith's "invisible hand",[16] the result of market failure. This de-personalises the behaviour and allows the cheats to escape censure.

In reality, externalities are *not* "social" costs. They are private costs that are imposed on others.

- Good, or positive, externalities are values produced by people who, by their productivity, create more than they take home in their pay packets. That extra value is measured in the land market.
- Bad, or negative, externalities, are costs (a favourite example is pollution) which are shifted on to others. The people or corporations who incur those costs are by law allowed to avoid them.

Does this tell us something significant about a rule of law that legitimises this behaviour?

If you walked into a supermarket and "externalised" the value that belonged to the shareholders, by walking out with a trolley full of goods without paying, you are cheating the owners. You might earn a period in gaol. But when such behaviour is camouflaged by clunky terms like *externalisation*, the significance of the action is depersonalised. The word fails to convey that (i) I create a *loss* for which I expect *you* to bear the burden; or (ii) you add value to the sum total of wealth of the nation which you are prevented from claiming. *Instead*, that value goes into *my* pocket. These are processes of cheating, whichever way you look at it.

Another jargon term that is calculated to deceive is *rent-seeking*. The concept features prominently in *The Price of Inequality* by Joseph Stiglitz, the Nobel prize economist.[17] He argues that the Western economy will not survive if it continues to generate the income inequality caused by rent-seeking. Stiglitz defines rent-seeking as corporations with financial clout manipulating markets or legislation to their advantage, to appropriate revenue that rightfully belongs to others.

The confusing thing about this use of the word *rent* is that the concept is not employed to refer to the rents that are paid for the occupation and use of natural resources, or which we pay for the use of the cultural commons. How did this happen? A century ago, neo-classical economists distorted the meaning of the word. It was redefined to refer to "a set of activities through which monopolies

16 Samuelson & Nordhaus (1985: 46).
17 Stiglitz (2012).

expend valuable resources not to produce goods but to obtain, strengthen, and defend their monopoly positions (and to gain long-lasting profit)".[18] We sense that there is something wrong with such language, which may be because we are distracted from the site of the real crime.

Distorting the Markets

When the tax regime is biased to favour land as a tradable asset, we would expect investments to be biased towards activities that included a high content of land (capital gains are taxed at favourable rates compared to the fiscal burden on incomes of employees). This, in turn, would result in the under-employment of people. The ripple effects would include the formation of defensive organisations that impose additional costs. Intolerable consequences include organised criminal networks.[19] If cheating is a globalised phenomenon, we would expect poverty to be trans-national, on a scale that defies all attempts to eradicate it.[20]

How would we expect the cheating process to affect behaviour towards nature? Superior rights would tend to erode respect by nurturing an attitude of detachment. Land would be treated as a commodity rather than esteemed as exceptional.

The cumulative impact of cheating as a social process would manifest itself in many other ways. We would expect to discover problems such as:

- *blurring* of the boundaries between public and private space ;
- *narrowing* of choices over the path of social development. And
- *diminishing* the contentment of the population at large.

To assess the character of cheating which yields such confusions, we need to clarify many issues. One is to draw a distinction between capital gains derived by cheating, and the good fortunes from the intervention of Lady Luck or from risk taking. Windfall gains derived either directly from the ownership of land, or indirectly, by manipulating government, do not fit into the categories of either luck or risk.

1. Land is defined by economists to include all of nature's resources. In the medium to long term there is little risk or luck attached to income from owning it as an asset. In times of high inflation or uncertainty, it is the one asset that provides a "safe haven" for money.

---

18 Kohler (1992: 720).
19 Harrison (2010a).
20 Harrison (2008).

2. Rents (these do not include the "rents" paid for leasing automobiles or apartments) are at the expense of others. This is not so with (say) the lottery, in which people buy tickets on the understanding that they will probably lose.

3. When super profits are made from investing in a risky business, the gain is derived from delivering a service that some people want and (for whatever reason) are willing to pay a price above the long-run competitive rate. The transaction is one into which all parties voluntarily enter.

In the labour market, the transaction between employee and employer is affected by laws enforced by government and its agents. The wage that is paid may be determined either by private negotiation or the minimum rate sanctioned by law. The contract of employment specifies those arrangements, and is enforced by the legal system.

In the capital market, I, as the contributor of resources, am bound by laws that may make me responsible for the health and safety of the users of my capital. Such considerations are laid out in laws and contracts, and enforced by public agencies.

In both the labour and capital markets, government actions are transparent. *In the land market, government discriminates in favour of one of the parties: the owner of land. That discrimination is covert: the redirection of some of the value created by working people to those who do not make a contribution towards that value. Furthermore, the transfer is concealed, not laid out in contracts for the consideration of all parties concerned. The government transfer of people's incomes to land owners is not sanctioned by those who lose out, it is hardly ever discussed in the media, and it is not taught to students of economics.*

A blanket of silence envelopes part of The Transaction. The role that the land market is made to play is not scrutinised by scientists or moral philosophers. As for political leaders, they observe *omerta* (the mafia oath of silence) on how their expenditure of taxpayers' money enriches the few at the expense of the many.

The Slush Fund

Money is indirectly channelled to the cheats via a complex system of legislation and funding that camouflages the identities of those who pocket the cash. In the agricultural sector, for example, the general taxpayer pays rents to landowners through farm subsidies. In Europe, about 40% of the EU budget is transferred to farmland owners. Such transfers are publicly justified in terms of the need for "food security"; even when, as under the Common Agricultural Policy, Europe produced mountains of surplus food.

- Families on low incomes receive a subsidy to cover the cost of housing. The main beneficiary is the land owner.
- Governments establish Enterprise Zones to create jobs. Employers are relieved of the obligation to pay the property tax. The owner of land within the zone raises his rents to capture the fiscal concession.[21]

This cheating should be measured just by cash costs inflicted on the taxpayer. It distorts what Adam Smith called the "natural course of things".[22] A forensic examination of the body politic would trace the fingerprints of cheating at all levels of society.

- *Culture* When rents are privatised, corruption becomes endemic. The elite re-shape culture to their advantage. The reciprocal effect is the pathological response provoked by the need to survive. The formation of aggressive trade unions is one example.
- *Psychology* The damage infects a population's feedback mechanisms. Instead of co-operation in the production of wealth, people adopt negative postures that damage productivity.
- *Law* The judicial process assumes adversarial rather than conflict-resolution approaches. The same thing happens in inter-personal relations as others seek to emulate the cheating by transgressing moral codes.
- *Community* The pursuit of capital gains from land disrupts the spatial distribution of population. Withholding land from use in the expectation of higher future gains, even when such sites are needed for housing or employment, causes sprawl. This adds to travel costs, pollution and the waste of public funds that have to be invested to provide services to the outlying districts.

Morality is also compromised. Because of the human cost of the distortions to the economy in the 20th century, governments responded with "affirmative action" to try and mitigate the damage. Corporations learnt how to manipulate public opinion and the political process by claiming the need for subsidies. They did not disclose the honest reasons for their claims. They fabricated stories that debilitated public discourse. The costs were inflicted on nature and society.

All of this was the logical consequence of the doctrine of property rights written into the West's version of the social contract. With a few honourable exceptions, the authors of the various drafts of that philosophy failed to insert

---

21 The Thatcher/Reagan exercise in enterprise zones and the way these raised land values is discussed in Harrison (1983: 264-6).
22 Smith (1776: bk.1, Ch. X).

clauses to secure every person's natural right of access – on equal terms – to life-sustaining nature.

John Locke was the single most influential of the contract theorists. His *Essay Concerning the True Original, Extent and End of Civil Government* is known as the *Second Treatise on Civil Government* (1690). This started by affirming everyone's natural right to "life, liberty and estate [land]". And yet ... Locke was in the business of rationalising the privatisation of land for the benefit of those who already monopolised it. He authored the constitution (for Carolina) which legitimised the land grab in America, on terms that did not protect the interests of the first settlers. On behalf of those who were enclosing the land, in England and the New World, he chose to stress the bountifulness of nature. He ducked the problem of how to reconcile everyone's interests when the supply of land ran out in places where people needed to live and work. So he deployed anecdotes like his version of Cain and Abel. He claimed, in Ch. V (§38):

> *Thus, at the beginning, Cain might take as much ground as he could till and make it his own land, and yet leave enough to Abel's sheep to feed on: a few acres would serve for both their possessions.*

And yet, the terms on which that ground was taken led to murder.

By such reasoning were the peoples of the West folded into the culture of cheating. The cumulative effect was humanicide.

Chapter 4: Humanicide

GENOCIDE is derived from the Greek *genos*: race. It is "the deliberate and systematic destruction, in whole or in part, of an ethnic, racial, religious, or national group".[1] The atrocity in Rwanda in 1994 was a case in which the colonial legacy culminated in the attempt to exterminate one tribe by another.[2] The bodies could be counted and the guilty brought before the International Criminal Court in The Hague.

Ecocide is the destruction of a natural habitat. British lawyer Polly Higgins proposes that the UN turn the assault on nature into a prosecutable crime.[3] The charge would relate to a specific event. At present, corporations may be prosecuted for oil spillages from tankers that devastate wildlife, but corporate bosses who commission the demolition of rain forests escape indictment.

Humanicide is the ultimate crime. It entails both genocide and ecocide. It bears witness to a crime that almost defeats the imagination. It is the act that abnegates the essence of humanity. It is not a single deed with a finite consequence which can be prosecuted in court. It is a continuous process of evisceration that systematically removes freedom and the conditions for a healthy community. *Humanicide bequeaths the deadened spirit of a population whose future is negated by the containment of the creative genius that is latent in every individual.*

The crime is initiated when people are displaced from their natural habitats and annexed to a pathological form of property rights. This deprives them of the rights they hold in common. Cambodia is a contemporary case of this crime in the making.

In Cambodia, the land benighted by the evil of the Pol Pot regime, an estimated 1.7m people lost their lives (20% of the population) during the genocide of 1975-79. But the cultural deprivation did not stop when the villains were arraigned in The Hague. Today, visitors to Phnom Penh may observe in real time how people are unable to recover their culture and re-create communities

---

1 Funk (2010).
2 Harrison (2010a: 75-80).
3 Higgins (2012).

> ## Box 4:1
> ## Russia: A Dose of Shock Therapy
>
> Beginning in 1991, Western advisors lost little time urging President Boris Yeltsin to apply "shock therapy" by privatising Russia's urban land and natural resources. The assault on what was already a fragile state, as the fabric of the Soviet state was dismantled, was accompanied by a savage decline in life expectancy.
>
> For men, the average lifespan in 1987 was 64.9 years. In 1994, it had crashed to 47.5 years. For women, the drop was from 70 years to 65.3 years, a loss of an average of five years of life.
>
> A concurrent reaction was the drop in fertility. The population peaked in the first year of shock therapy (148.6m people). The nation lost 5m people over the following decade. Living standards crashed and hopes that *perestroika* would offer a better life withered.[1]
>
> ---
> 1 Harrison (2008: 25-26).

that would fulfil their needs. The living nightmare is documented by Dirk Löhr, a professor at Trier University of Applied Sciences.[4]

The Cambodian state, which holds most land and makes it available on leases, fails to recover the whole of the economic rent for the national exchequer. This creates the financial incentives that lure capital out of the urban industrial sector into the acquisition of rural land leases. Only about 10% of the land is being used to grow food. Speculators bank on making larger capital gains in the future. Peasant land holders engaged in land speculation, too: they were tempted to sell their land and migrate into city slums.

Löhr reports that Cambodia's land price bubble was partly fuelled by the inflow of "hot money" created during the US real estate bubble that burst in 2006. Instead of extending credit to entrepreneurs to invest capital in urban enterprises, banks extended loans to land speculators in response to the higher capital gains. Human rights organisations noticed that "land grabbing and forced evictions have escalated significantly over the last 10 years in Cambodia".[5]

The beneficiaries of the fiscal failure of governance are identified by the status of land owners. The main land owners are businessmen (31%), followed by high-ranked officials with the title His Excellency (23%), a further 23% were *okhna* (the title given for financial contributions to political parties of more than US$100,000), high-ranked military officers (generals, 15%), and members of the National Assembly (8%).

---

4 Löhr (2012, 2011, 2010).
5 Löhr (2012: 6).

Far from nurturing the population back to health from the atrocities of the Khmer Rouge, the tenure-and-tax laws are systematically traumatising the population.

The rules of tenure are supposed to be neutral, leaving people free to choose the cultural formations that best meet their needs. But when the power of tenure is monopolised, this results in two fatal outcomes. The immediate impact is on institutions. These are compromised, re-shaped to reinforce the privileges of land owners. Then, as the pathological forces are unleashed, social evolution is constrained in ways which compromise behaviour. People begin to act in ways that are not sustainable. Sex and procreative activity is one realm of behaviour which is damaged. The dynamics of maintaining demographic balance with the natural habitat is jeopardised. Populations may implode or explode, depending on the particular circumstances. This happened when Russia switched from totalitarian control of its natural resources to the capitalist model that assigned exclusive ownership of enormous rent-generating resources to a class of oligarchs (Box 4:1).

The process of excluding people from the commons of their culture and their homeland space constitutes the killing of what it means to be human. That killing is a composite of the biological (the destruction of people, to clear the land for new settlers) and the psychological (the impoverishment of the mind and soul, degrading the human spirit). The outcome is a population in a state that is less than its human potential.

The Metrics of Humanicide

To grasp the scale and nature of humanicide, we need a new concept of growth.

As measured by economists, growth is confined to the value of goods and services as defined by government statisticians, with the emphasis on the accumulation of material wealth. The growth of what we mean by humanity encompasses something that cannot be given a numerical value. It includes the expansion of moral capacity, the deepening of aesthetic sensibility and the extension of social solidarity.

In fits and starts, humans evolved by pushing outwards the boundaries of what they could achieve. We may not be able to catalogue in an inventory all of their accomplishments, but we know it for what it is: the realisation of the human spirit in action. This condition was hard won out of nature. Barriers that block the process are a crime against humanity.

A stylised representation of humanicide is provided in Fig. 4:1. It is located in a timetable that fits recent English history, the paradigm for what is now happening in every country in the world.

Figure 4:1 Trends in Cultural Development

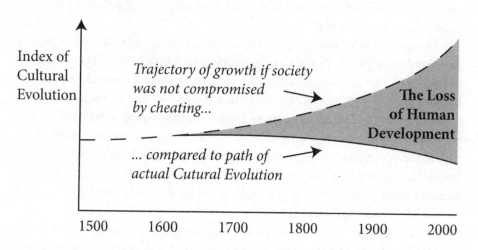

The systematic privatisation of the commons began in the 17th century. This forestalled the optimum evolutionary path that was emerging. The English were forging into an Agricultural Revolution, to be followed by the Industrial Revolution. These giant leaps in productivity would generate increasing amounts of resources over and above what was needed to sustain household economies. That additional income was available to be invested in a renaissance in the rural communities from whence it originated. England would have experienced a remarkable flourishing of the moral and artistic life as hamlets and villages expanded the educational and recreational opportunities for everyone who helped to produce the rents. Instead, the material means for those life-enhancing experiences were channelled away from the hamlets and villages by the land lords.

The English and their culture were debased at all levels: material, social and spiritual. An example of profound significance is the way the emerging factory owners, who would be demonised by Marx, were not able to innovate an authentic entrepreneurial culture. To secure access to the law-making process, they had to ape the culture of the aristocracy.

> *To make himself a gentleman, therefore, the merchant who had accumulated his wealth in the cities … bought land as a matter of course.*[6]

---

6 Toynbee (1890: 62-63).

The rent-seeking culture corrupted the potential for social evolution. This was cultural cannibalism on a fatal scale, the consequences of which disfigure global society in the 21st century.[7]

We cannot know how much the social universe lost. The sustained onslaught destroyed what people would have accomplished if they had not been scattered on to the byways, many driven to the four corners of the world. We cannot imagine the achievements if the population had been free to engage in creative projects funded out of the community rents. We cannot imagine the symphonies unwritten, the paintings not brushed on canvas, architecture that would have elaborated vernacular buildings, sporting feats that could have inspired. All lost because the rents were captured and congealed in the mansions of a handful of families, their monumental follies secluded behind high fences and the broad swords of county sheriffs.

Fig. 4:1 can do no more than inflame our imagination about the size of the gap between what actually happened over the past 500 years, and what might have been achieved. From the time of the civil war in the mid-17th century the gap between the potential and the actual accelerated. The rent-rich grew richer even as they slept (John Stuart Mill[8]), the poor poorer as the power to realise the expanding horizons of their humanity ebbed away. The void represents the negation of the spiritual and material condition of the people and the fabric of their communities. What is recorded in the history books is not the authentic experience of a free people. It is the record of the pathology of a population compressed within the confines of an inhuman culture.

In attempting to comprehend the loss, we acknowledge that the actual trajectory of growth (the lower line on Fig. 4:1) was pitted with peaks and troughs. Resort to the slave trade was a step down in the human condition. The abolition of that trade was a catch-up step. The oscillations in social evolution, as distorted by the terms of the tenure that prevailed, deviated downwards as the feudal class claimed an increasing portion of the nation's rents. Quantification may not be possible, but we can be certain that the shortfall in the realisation of the population's potential was significant, that the void grew over time, and that this outcome was the wilful crime of a class that put its interests before those of the people of the commons.

Culturally, the English now linger centuries behind what they would have achieved had they been free to retain the output of their creative genius and invest those resources for the welfare of every individual. Fleetingly, achingly,

---

7   One manifestation in the transformation of entrepreneurship was the corporation that came to acquire legal status as a "personality". Corporations can be sold in the markets for the highest profits without qualm: there was little prospect of their evolving as *social* institutions, partners with society in the production of wealth for the good of both shareholders and their communities.

8   Mill (1891: 523).

> **Box 4:2**
> **Culture at the Coal Face**
>
> Listen to the English miners of Yorkshire playing exquisite symphonies on their brass instruments. Listen to the Welsh miners' male voice choirs singing opera in the village halls of the valleys. Burley men with calloused hands, their lungs filled with the dust from the coal excavated from the bowels of the earth, but moved on Sundays to form their unions to bear witness to the beauty of the human spirit.
>
> Reflect on the sacrifices that we currently endure because the vitality of generations of those labouring men and women was destroyed, their children left uneducated, families fragmented as the jobless migrated to foreign lands. One outcome is known as "cannon fodder". Young men of the Welsh valleys and Yorkshire dales, unable to find peaceful employment, joined the battalions that were sent to defend the colonial territories appropriated from other people.

we are given a glimpse of the creative spirit of those people in the beauty that springs from the souls of the commoners who, for generations, were driven from the fields to earn their living below ground (Box 4:2). What England endured applies to the whole of the human race today, with the exception of the few tribes surviving in the deepest rain forests who have yet to be contacted.

Pandemic

The dis-ease infected every corner of society. Each European nation (with exceptions in the continent's northernmost periphery) has its own history and timetable. I will draw my illustrations from the United Kingdom. These emphasise the banality of the actions that spread the mortal virus deep into the body politic.

- **Economy** Governments employ taxes which damage productive activity. Those taxes circumscribe the quality of people's lives and impoverish their communities. The UK lost wealth and welfare equal to one year's national income over the 10-year period in which Tony Blair presided as Prime Minister.[9]

The deprived neighbourhoods of Ulster, Britain's remaining Irish outpost, are testaments to the human costs of governance that was bent to worship at the high table of the noble cheats in their mansions.

---

9 Harrison (2006b: 43-44, 155).

Tony Blair received his popular mandate to form a government in 1997. Financial reforms were introduced in 1998. Between 1999 and 2008, the number of suicides increased by 64% in Northern Ireland, according to the Public Health Agency. Most suicides were among young men between the ages of 15 and 34. The heaviest concentration of suicides was in the disadvantaged areas of north and west Belfast. In 2009, the number of deaths registered as suicide was 260; the figure for 2010 was expected to exceed that number. Explanations for these tragedies were several, but references to unemployment were unconvincing: the Ulster economy boomed as Blair's property bubble drove land-and-house prices skyward. Despite the apparent prosperity, however, and the relative peace in the post-Good Friday era, despair was endemic. The suicides were a continuation of the deaths that result from armed combat. Stephen Platt, a Samaritans trustee and professor of health policy research at the University of Edinburgh, assessed the data in these terms:

> The suicide rate in Northern Ireland appears to have increased after the end of the period known as the Troubles. Previous studies have shown that suicides decrease during periods of war because people feel a sense of integration in their communities while uniting against an adversary. When war ends, this feeling falls away to the detriment of mental health.[10]

Before the Troubles (which began in the 1960s) there was despair – and suicides. These were replaced by overt killing during the phase of guerrilla warfare. Then, peace, and the return to self-harming techniques. Young people could not cope with the pressures of life. What kind of society was this? The coherent explanation emerges when we take into account the failure to apply the 1st Law of Social Dynamics.

Tony Blair's skills as a politician were inadequate to deal with the impoverished condition of the people in the housing estates of West Belfast. Here were herded the offspring whose Celtic forefathers had lost their ancient land rights. Each generation intuitively understood that its prospects were perverted by a deep-seated deprivation. For their cousins in the Republic of Ireland, the apparent safety net was emigration to the United Kingdom. That is what happened when the Republic's land bubble burst. The exodus of young people restarted. The Dublin-based Economic and Social Research Institute estimated that 100,000 people would emigrate over the two years 2011-12. This is equal to 1,000 a week, or 2% of the total population, equivalent to the UK losing 1.5m people in two years.[11] But for the youths from the Twinbrook

---

10   O'Hara (2011).
11   Fitzgerald (2011:13).

Figure 4:2 Spatial Distribution of Life Expectancy in the Capitalist Economy

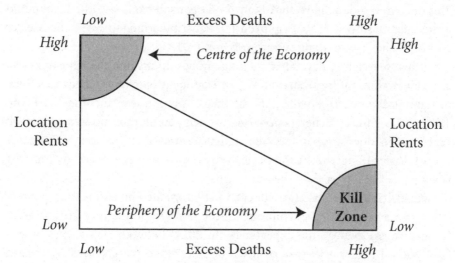

and Colin districts of West Belfast, they were *already* in the United Kingdom. Psychologically, there was no escape for them to a land that might offer better prospects. So many of them are just killing themselves.

- **Society** Government tax-and-tenure policies rupture people psychologically from their social environments. One example is the realisation by young people that their place of birth is hostile to their need to work and procreate. The damage is measured by differential rates of mortality. They do not commit suicide. Nonetheless, neighbourhoods, and whole towns, suffer the deprivation of people who die before their natural time is up.

The killing is on an epic scale. The deaths are not random. They are systemic, the result of a spatial dynamic in which the organising principle is the distribution of income as determined (ultimately) by taxation. One indicator of the influence of this policy is the early deaths of hundreds of thousands of people in the rich nations who live and work in Kill Zones (Fig. 4:2). For people who live in high-rent locations, average life expectancy is high. The reverse is true for people in the Kill Zones. Taxes fall most heavily on people who live in the margins of the economy where productivity is lowest. Here, the tax burden is felt most intensely, the consequential stresses most extreme, rendering people most vulnerable to life-threatening behaviour in its myriad forms (such as smoking, over-eating, under-exercising).

The working assumption of politicians and social scientists is that premature deaths are the result of poverty. From this, it follows that if an enlightened government transfers money to people on low incomes, this will erase poverty. This doctrine guided the Welfare State for 60 years. It has not worked, nor could it, because the fiscal tools employed to redistribute income were themselves part of the poverty-making syndrome (Box 4: 3).

When a systemic flaw survives long enough to assume the appearance of normality, communities have to try and adopt prophylactic measures. One of them is the doctrine which claims that a "progressive" income tax is fair. The logic is simple: richer people ought to pay more than poorer people. In practise, this does not happen. The statistics reveal that "progressive" income taxes transfer money from the poor to the rich.[12] That is a major reason why rich people live longer than the poor.

Superficially, the statistics appear to support the perception that poverty is the cause rather than a symptom. In the London borough of Westminster, the gap in the average life expectancy (in 2011) between rich and poor was 16.9 years. In the north-eastern town of Darlington the gap was 14.6 years. The presentation of facts in this way is arbitrary: defining mortality in terms of a single monetary continuum. But when we plot average life expectancy on a graph, we lay bare a spatial component to the mortality figures. Average life expectancy is 84 years in Westminster. This figure then regresses steadily along the road to Wallsend in the North of England, where the average lifespan drops to 77 years. Move further northwards to Scotland, and the average drops even further in pockets of Glasgow.

How can this profile in the distribution of life expectancy be explained? The most comprehensive measure, which sums both negative and positive influences, is provided by the rent of land. Mortality rates shadow the trend of land rents.

David Ricardo, in *Principles of Political Economy and Taxation* (1817), provided a rigorous account of the formation of rents. These were highest at the centre of economic activity. They declined in line with the distance from central locations. Variations might be attributable to soil fertility (the uses-of-land variable). Another explanation was transport costs. These had to be deducted as a cost of production from total revenue, leaving less to be paid as rent (the spatial variable, as elucidated by Johann von Thünen in *The Isolated State* [1826]). Land commanded the highest rents at the centre of a community where people concentrated and engaged in the most productive activities, and where transport costs were at their lowest. At the margins of society, where population tends to be dispersed and engaged in relatively higher cost enterprises (if only because of the longer distances to market), the surplus that can be paid as rent is at its lowest.

---

12 Harrison (2006a).

Box 4:3
Poverty Now and Then

Medical scientists at the University of London used the type 2 strain of diabetes to measure the vulnerability of Londoners to poverty. The hot spots in 2010 matched the areas of poverty that existed in London in the 1880s. Douglas Noble, a public health doctor and lecturer at The London Medical School, Queen Mary, University of London, who co-authored the study, said: "It was no surprise to see that diabetes risk is high in areas where poverty was high. What was surprising was that some of these pockets of deprivation and ill-health have persisted for over 100 years".[1]

The Welfare State, which was unable to erase the cheating culture, had also failed to eradicate poverty. The astonished researchers could not make sense of the spatial dispersion of that poverty. The fiscal process and its spatial consequences are described at length in *Ricardo's Law*.[2]

1 http://www.qmul.ac.uk/media/news/items/smd/63821.html
2 Harrison (2006a).

Similarities in the profiles of the spatial distribution of rent and life expectancy do not prove a causal relationship. The correspondence in the graphic trend lines may be no more than a coincidence. To establish the connection, we need to consider the psycho-social consequences of depriving people of the equal right to share in the nation's rents.

People living on the periphery need not endure lower living standards than those at the demographic centre of the country. In a market economy, competition of the healthy kind ensures that wages and profits across the regions tend to be equalised through migration of people and capital. The locational differences in productivity are measured by rent. Thus rent may be channelled through the public purse and distributed on an equal basis. Life chances would be transformed for those who, today, are disadvantaged by the fiscal regime. This is because people at the economic centre, enjoying greater benefits, would pay correspondingly more into the public purse. But everyone would enjoy equal access to rent-funded public services. The result would be a spatial rebalancing of the economy and of society. No region would enjoy privileged access to the value contributed by the commons of nature and society.

Under these equalised conditions, the remaining differences that arise in life expectancy would be due to personal factors (some individuals are willing freely to engage in self-harming activities that foreshorten their lives). Such behaviour is the responsibility of the individual, not of society. *But the wholesale foreshortening of the lives of about 500,000 people across the NATO countries alone, every year, without a shot being fired in anger, is not explicable in terms of idiosyncratic behaviour.*[13]

Male babies born in the seaside town of Blackpool on the north-west coast of the England can expect to live 11 fewer years than male babies born in the London borough of Kensington and Chelsea. There is nothing in the DNA of boys born in Lancashire to distinguish them from those born in the millionaire communities located close to Buckingham Palace in London. But socially created rents are not shared on a *per capita* basis. This gives an advantage at birth to children born in rent-rich locations.

The fiscal discrimination is aggressively enforced by government. Because rents are privatised and receive privileged treatment in the fiscal system, governments have to fund public services by taxing earned incomes. Those taxes fall disproportionately heavily on people in the lowest income brackets, and on the relatively lower productivity regions at the margins of the economy. This unequal burden is compounded by government spending. Expenditure on infrastructure like roads and transport follows the contour of Ricardo's graph, as do the measures for expenditure on research on health, on the homeless, and on other elements of deprivation.[14]

Some of the components of the good life are summed in the Halifax Quality of Life Index. This tracks the regressive decline in standards of people who live further away from London and the south-east of England. The survey examines all 405 local authority districts in the UK. The top ranking districts are located in London and the south-east, with the highest life expectancy in Kensington and Chelsea (85.1 years) followed by the neighbouring borough of Westminster (83.8 years).[15]

When we combine the pathological costs of a dysfunctional tax-and-tenure system, we perceive the depth of the psychological and social deficits. The stresses bear down on people in a graduated way, reflecting the unequally distributed rents. Psycho-social stresses are imposed most heavily on the most vulnerable sections of the population who live in the Kill Zones. Unemployment shadows the Ricardian rent gradient. So do rates of deaths from cancer, and psychoses that will never be erased until society itself is restored to health. Is it any wonder that people constrain the human spirit through fear of too close an association with neighbours (Box 4:4)?

For an expert assessment of the number of people who fall victim to the perverse land-and-tax nexus, I sought the testimony of Dr. George J. Miller. He

---

13 This estimate is by the present author, based on extrapolating from data available for countries like the US and UK.
14 Harrison (2006a: 80, 106, 133). Valuable analysis of the spatial distribution of the condition of the people of Britain is contained in the works of Danny Dorling (2010, 2011a and b), and the illustrated maps in Dorling and Thomas (2011).
15 Halifax Press Release, December 24, 2011.

> ## Box 4:4
> ## Space for the Inner Life
>
> Artistic creativity flourishes when nourished by free association with others, Scottish philosopher John MacMurray (1891-1976) emphasised in *The Self as Agent*.[1] Without spontaneous, artistic creativity, "we are not ourselves; there is something the matter somewhere, though the blame may not be ours".[2]
>
> > *In fact, the great hindrance to art is fear and its outward manifestation, the demand for security. We are afraid of ourselves, and so afraid to be ourselves. We are afraid of the spontaneity of others, therefore we build up, individually and socially, a great network of defences against the desperate spontaneity and creativeness of the personal ... these secret fears in the mass are the root of the injustice and squalor of our civilisation ... the absence of art is the absence of spontaneity, of proper humanity; the penalty for it is an inner stultification, a loss of spiritual integrity, a slowing down of the pulses of the inner life.[3]*
>
> MacMurray hoped that people would "start rebuilding a human life from the beginning. If we are to make peace in the world, we must make peace with our own souls".[4]
>
> ---
>
> 1 MacMurray (1957).
> 2 MacMurray (1935: 158).
> 3 MacMurray (1935: 158).
> 4 MacMurray (1957: 159).

estimated the number of people who died in England and Wales every year due to causes that could be attributed – either directly or indirectly – to the impact of taxation. At the time, Miller was a member of Britain's Medical Research Council's Senior Clinical Scientific Staff, and Professor of Epidemiology at the University of London Queen Mary and Westfield College. His calculation was 50,000 excess deaths: the number of people in England and Wales whose premature deaths would be avoided if Britain administered a justice-based fiscal policy.[16]

There is no acknowledgement in the literature of the social sciences that the private ownership of land is the infectious source of pathologies that cause deaths on this scale. The exception is the monumental study by George Miller. He chronicled the link between land rights, poverty and ill health in Britain over the past millennium in *On Fairness and Efficiency: the Privatisation of the Public Income During the Past Millennium*.[17] Miller's peers, including advisors to the UK government with whom he was on first name terms, studiously ignored

---

16 Miller (2003: 56).
17 Miller (2000).

his warning that this pandemic was the result of tax policies administered by governments elected by the people. Decades earlier, the fiscal remedy that would equalise people's life-chances had been described by a medical scientist (Box 4:5).

The Corruption of Personality
It is not just institutions that are perverted by private property rights in the commons. Personality is also distorted.

In its most primitive form, property rights that initiate humanicide were elaborated in the law of primogeniture. Adam Smith castigated the laws of succession to land.

> *They are founded upon the most absurd of all suppositions, the supposition that every successive generation of men have not an equal right to the earth, and to all that it possesses; but that the property of the present generation should be restrained and regulated according to the fancy of those who died perhaps 500 years ago.*[18]

Smith understood that the monopoly of land was the tool for monopolising people. To cling on to that power "it was thought better that [land] should descend undivided to one … [E]very great landlord was a sort of petty prince. His tenants were his subjects. He was their judge, and in some respects their legislator in peace, and their leader in war". Such was the tyranny associated with the monopoly of land that

> *he made war according to his own discretion, frequently against his neighbours, and sometimes against his sovereign. The security of a landed estate, therefore … depended upon its greatness.*

Thus was established the tyranny of the rule of the law which we have inherited. But it was not just the structure of politics that was distorted when the feudal aristocracy began to accelerate the process of hijacking the power embedded in the possessory rights to land. Land owners also curbed the fruitfulness of nature. Smith observed that seldom was a great proprietor a great improver of his land. Rather than plough the rents back into improving his estate, he would use his profits to buy more land. Not for him the taxing task of generating value for money.

---

18   Smith (1776: Bk. III, Ch. II).

> **Box 4:5**
> **Search for the Sinless Tax**
>
> Dr. S. Vere Pearson published a warning in the *British Medical Journal* on January 24, 1926 on the connection between preventable diseases such as TB and "social ills". Medical scientists were aware of the social nature of many diseases. But they ignored Pearson's warning that public welfare was prejudiced by the fiscal regime that shaped the distribution not just of income but also people's health. He called for "the discovery of a sinless tax which cannot be passed on to the poorer workers and cannot burden production. As doctors it beholds us to study these questions".
>
> The optimum conditions for the health of both the population and the economy arose with a shift in taxes away from people's earnings and on to the rents of land. Pearson spelt this out in *London's Overgrowth and the Causes of Swollen Towns* (1939). The eyes and ears of the medical and political establishments remained closed.

To improve land with profit, like all other commercial projects, requires an exact attention to small savings and small gains, of which a man born to a great fortune, even though naturally frugal, is seldom capable. The situation of such a person naturally disposes him to … [t]he elegance of his dress, of his equipage, of his house, and household furniture, are objects which from his infancy he has been accustomed to have some anxiety about.[19]

In Scotland, Smith noted that perhaps one-third of the country was entailed in the laws of inheritance which cramped the personalities who inherited the estates. But what of the fate of the outcasts? The poor law of 1579 defined them as vagabonds – "idle persons", apparently, who are up to no good (unlike the idle landlords who could afford to devote their lives to preening themselves in the latest fashions from the salons of Paris). For the vagabonds, that 1579 law was explicit about the punishment for idleness. The first provision was that "all strong and idle beggars between the ages of 14 and 70 should be apprehended and tried, and, if convicted, scourged [whipped] and burned through the ear with a hot iron".[20] No such penalty was exacted against the nobility. Their idleness, indeed, was admired as a mark of the gentleman.

The narcissism of the First Son spawned the pathologies of the Second Son. Many of them migrated to seek their fortunes, killing indigenous peoples whose territories they turned into plantations. The people who were caught up in the

---

19 Smith (1776: Bk. III, Ch. II).
20 Ferguson (1948: 168).

sugar plantation culture of the Caribbean suffered the moral and sociological consequences that arise when people are displaced from their land. When the home economy repels second sons and the landless, what choice do they have? The colonial project was the safety valve for such a society.

For the people of the British Isles, the islands of the Caribbean were an economic escape hatch. The soil proved suitable for the production of sugar. More than 90% of those who boarded ships bound for Barbados in the 1630s were aged between 15 and 24. Almost all of them were males, giving rise to an unbalanced demographic composition among the homesick settler population. Those who cornered the land engaged in speculation, selling and re-selling tracts for increasing prices. Those who did not toe the line were "arrested and imprisoned or pilloried in the hot sun, with a favourite twist being to nail the victim's ears to the stocks". With 16 men to every woman, the moral life proved impossible. Visitors complained of the "incest, sodomy, and bestiality prevalent on the island".[21] The frustrations of white settlers were visited on black slaves.

The corruption of personality was the direct consequence of abnormal conditions created by pathological property rights. The effects were not confined to first generation victims. Land speculation in, and rent hoarding from, the sugar plantations, reverberated back to England where sugar barons invested their money in landed estates, further displacing people from the land. As Matthew Parker shows in *The Sugar Barons*, the evidence on which Adam Smith based his strictures against the characters who presumed to be the owners of land was well founded. Many sugar barons failed to nurture their plantations, leaving them to middle men who underused the land, neglected the capital investments on the land, and brutalised the African labourers who tilled the land. There were exceptions, but the culturally determined rule of law was established. It was inhuman, and its corrosive influence prevails to this day. But thanks to the passage of time, so inured are we to the influence of this form of ownership that we are little moved by the tragedies when they are encapsulated in large numbers, such as those representing the decimation of the Amerindians during the land grabs that began in the 16th century.

The horror statistics are mitigated by the language of historians. The "discovery" of America by Christopher Columbus, for example, was "the most dramatic and far-reaching cross-fertilisation of cultures in the history of the world".[22] There was little *cross*-fertilisation, but much one-way transmission of deadly viruses, biological and cultural. The demographic collapse registers the impact on populations that had adapted to life on the continent to which they had migrated in ancient times, but they could not withstand the European

21   Parker (2012: 27-28).
22   Driver (1969: 554).

Table 4:1
The Demographic Impact of Cultural Contact in the Americas

Region	Pre-contact Population (consensus estimates)	Size of Surviving Population
United States	2.5m (1492 level)	500,000 (late 17th century)
Mesoamerica	25m	5m
Hawaii	300,000 (1778)	40,000-50,000 (decline within 25 years)

Source: Cicarelli (2012: 84), who reviews the estimates and identifies the consensus numbers from the authorities cited.

onslaught (Table 4:1). The size of pre-contact populations remains uncertain but the scale of the killing is not contested.

The contrast in the quality of life of Amerindians before 1492, and the life that unravelled thereafter, could not be greater.

Social scientists and anthropologists continue to argue over how to view pre-contact communities. One group, called the formalists, apply the assumptions of neo-classical economics. The precepts of their model impoverishes perceptions of the aboriginal way of life by minimising the qualitative differences between their communities and the capitalist model that was imposed on them.[23] To legitimise this comparison, neo-classical ideologues had to eliminate land as a distinct life-force. They achieved this by conflating land into capital. This had the benefit of soothing the psychic distress that would otherwise disturb scholars who analyse the European impact on Amerindians. Thus, the "savages" of North America were said to occupy a level of development equivalent to that of the peoples of England in the time of Julius Caesar. This is puzzling. For, despite the technical accomplishments of Europe, we learn that in the 1500s

Life expectancy among indigenous Americans at the time of contact was about 35 years, roughly the same as that of the Europeans.[24]

Furthermore, 500 years *before* the Scottish Enlightenment of the 18th century, the Cahokians, who occupied a vast area on the banks of the Mississippi, lived in towns that were at the crossroads of a vast trading network. They constructed flat-topped pyramids, and occupied "a metropolitan area with a population equal to that of contemporary London at the time, and a standard of living higher than that in any part of 13th century England".[25] The Amerindians enjoyed

---

23 Cicarelli (2012: 80).
24 Cicarelli (2012: 88).
25 Cicarelli (2012: 106).

a quality of life that was just as good, if not better, than that of the people of the British Isles. And they accomplished this without stealing the riches from the lands of other peoples.

This history is a painful one to address. But without honesty, how can we be sure that the analysis presented by the experts is a faithful representation of the conditions that led to our current condition? An example of the idealisation that distorts much of social science is offered by the work of Daron Acemoglu and James Robinson, respectively of MIT and Harvard. They characterise the treatment of indigenous peoples in a curious way. We saw from Table 4:1 that the population of North America collapsed by about 2m people. Amerindians, according to Acemoglu and Robinson, were "sidelined". This notion clears the way for those two scholars to celebrate the outcome by saying that it "created an egalitarian and economically dynamic frontier".[26] The reality was a frontier created by the frenzy to extract resource rents for the benefit of the few. That reality is not palatable to social theorists who cope with the facts by using language which camouflages the truth.

Humanicide, as the abnegation of the unique qualities of our species, when globalised, leaves no basis for concluding that our social universe can continue. Is our world coming to an end? There is no Reset button that can take us back to the beginning. But the evolutionary process means that we are capable of adjusting to new conditions, *capable of making our world* in the words of archaeologist V. Gordon Childe.[27] What is preventing us from re-setting our minds? Are our societies too traumatised to act in time to prevent the cataclysms that some scientists say are looming?

---

26 Acemoglu and Robinson (2012: 37).
27 Childe (2003).

Part 2

Apartheid Economics

The extermination of a nation's collective memory and its ability for self-reflection is like a living organism's rejection of its own immune system.
Ai Weiwei, *The Guardian*, May 28, 2011

Humanity, united in a global community of nations, faces the threat to its existence from forces within. A population of 7 billion people is locked into a single fate as the social universe crumbles under the stresses caused by economic and environmental crises. Are the leaders of nation-states, and the agencies that select them, fit to guide their peoples through a very dangerous century?

The scientific, political and spiritual communities *want* to deliver free and fair – and safe – societies, but they are failing in their duty of care. Our daily lives are compromised by the privileges of those who profit from the chaos of mass poverty, unemployment, the erosion of asset values, and the other pathological problems of our age.

Nation-states are out of control because their leaders are compromised by a trauma that inhibits clarity of thought. To change course, we need to identify the reasons why the decisions that affect the fate of nations are tailored to serve the interests of a minority. The objective is to reclaim control over our futures.

Chapter 5: The State of Trauma

T HE draughtsmen working in Parliament were not engaged in a grand conspiracy. They did not *intend* to brainwash the yeomen of England.

Their proposals for an Act of Parliament were confined to re-designing the layout of the village of Helpston, to maximise the rents of landlords. They succeeded. Earl Fitzwilliam achieved a 30% return on the money he invested in enclosing those fields.[1] The procedure was defined as "Inclosing Lands in the Parishes of *Maxey with Deepingate, Norboro, Glinton with Peakirk, Etton, and Helpstone* in the County of *Northampton*" (1809).

The unintended consequence was injurious to the evolutionary process that had come to define humanity. Such laws of enclosure crushed the customs and values of people who had innovated through the ages, so that they might push humanity to the next stage of social development.

The technique for closing down Project Civilisation was brutal. The minds and emotions of the men who tilled the fields were reconfigured. Just like switching off the software in your PC. It took longer to mangle people's minds. But that outcome was inevitable once the coerced realignment of the landscape was completed. Within 10 years, Helpston's ancient way of life was eviscerated. Parliament had once again fulfilled its mission, adding one more victim to the catalogue of damaged communities. Between 1700 and the onset of the Napoleonic wars, the population of freeholder farmers of at least 160,000 souls was practically wiped out.[2]

William Pitt the Younger did commission an enquiry into the ownership of land. It was required to determine "What advantages have been found to result from inclosing land, in regard to the increase of rent – quantity or quality of produce – improvement of stock, etc". Pitt was the Prime Minister who introduced the Income Tax in 1799, just as the most savage effects of enclosure were being felt by villages like Helpston. The terms of reference of that enquiry did not include the social or the psychological costs that would be inflicted on the people who were ripped from their homeland. The condition of the nation was assumed to be synonymous with the personal interests of

---

1   Bate (2005: 52).
2   Toynbee (1890: 59).

the few people who owned Britain. What was good for the landlord was good for the landless.

Some people did not agree with this doctrine of statecraft. They still enjoyed access to the commons of England, their sensibilities not yet blunted by the claustrophobia of enclosure. One of them recorded the joys of being nurtured within the commons. He was born before the landscape was ripped apart around his village. It was a very hot day in the month of July 1793. Ann Clare gave birth to twins, a boy and a girl. John grew up to become the poet who would record the rich texture of life in the years immediately preceding the enclosure of Helpston. That qualified him to articulate the social desolation of the years that followed Parliament's decision to inflict the loss of the commons on his neighbours.

Clare's biographer, Jonathan Bate, offers a glimpse of the scale of the loss when he describes the organic relationship between the people and their habitat.

> In Clare's world, there was an intimate relationship between society and environment. The open-field system fostered a sense of community: you could talk to the man working the next strip, you could see the shared ditches, you could tell the time of day by the movement of the common flock and herd from the village pound out to the heath and back. Once a year everyone would gather to 'beat the bounds', that is to say, walk around the perimeter of the parish as a way of marking its boundaries. The fields spread out in a wheel with the village as its hub.[3]

Helpston's topography and traditions had evolved on the principle of spatial openness. Its circular pattern located household dwellings at the centre – the heart – of the community. The annual festivals marked the seasons, ensured social solidarity and enriched the memories of the villagers. Children played in the meadows and climbed ancient trees. The mind and emotions of John Clare were indelibly marked by the joyousness of that life. His formative years were shaped by the personal relationships, his aesthetic senses tuned to the rhythms of the seasons.

Then the law ordained change. Not a controlled adjustment with the consent of the people, so that they might enrich the strategy for increasing the nation's income while synchronising the changes into their patterns of life. Promoted as "progress", the fields were enclosed and the circular configuration ripped apart in favour of a linear landscape. The three large open fields around which crops were rotated and livestock moved were no more. The parish was divided

---

3 Bate (2005: 47), drawing on the analysis in Barrell (1972), who describes the spatial configuration of the traditional village.

into rectangular blocks. These, in turn, were sub-divided by their owners and the space *enclosed*. As Clare grew from adolescence to adulthood, between the years 1809 and 1820 when the final enclosure was awarded, his childhood world was no more. Where people once roamed, now there were restrictions. Families which for generations had traversed the landscape as free people, were now outlawed from the places that were cherished by their forefathers. But this was more than an exercise redefining property rights and economic practises. Minds and bodies were compressed in an unrelenting process of confinement.

The Clare family's closest friends, the Turnills, "were forced from their home without compensation at the time of the enclosure; as far as Clare was concerned this was proof that the new regime gave unrestricted power to the large landowners".[4]

> *For many villagers, enclosure was experienced as an engine of social more than economic alienation ... symbolic of the destruction of an ancient birthright based on co-operation and common rights. The chance of Clare's time and place of birth gave him an exceptional insight into this changed world.*[5]

Clare recorded rural life as it flourished in the years before the enclosures. He then chronicled his anger at the destruction that unfolded before his eyes. Whit Sunday would never be the same again. He had witnessed how young people met at a fountain to drink sugared water as a good-luck charm. When the spring was enclosed, the custom was abolished. Annual events like the holiday on Plough Monday were cancelled. Clare's pen poured acid on the "tyrants" who wrecked ancient ways of living. Historian E.P. Thompson recognised Clare as a protest poet who registered the rupture at the interface between the commons of people's culture (the parts of their lives that they shared) and the commons of nature (the resources that they shared).[6] In *Remembrances*, Clare wrote:

> *Enclosure like a Bonaparte let not a thing remain,*
> *It levelled every bush and tree and levelled every hill*
> *And hung the moles for traitors –*
> *though the brook is running still,*
> *It runs a naked brook, cold and chill*

He ended up in an asylum.

---

4 Bate (2005: 49).
5 Bate (2005: 49).
6 Thompson (1993).

Attacking the Immune System

By the time of Pitt's premiership, towards the end of the 18th century, England's culture was bipolar.

The separation of a population from its natural and social commons under the laws of the land created stresses of a schizophrenic character. These were evident in the decision-makers, who had to balance the need to satisfy their "stake holders" – the land owners – with the need to keep the system operating. Rents had to be generated. The tensions were palpable in the paradoxes that tested the mental and moral landscapes. In the case of Britain –

- *Philosophically*, the political class presented itself as the champion of freedom (vigorously attacking the French mobs – "revolutionaries" – that were proclaiming *liberty*); while suppressing the liberties of populations in the colonies they administered.
- *Economically*, the entrepreneurial class insisted that its model delivered rewards for those willing to work; a doctrine at odds with the repression of the living standards of citizens who no longer had a stake in the land of their birth, many of whom were beggars.
- *Scientifically*, the aristocracy encouraged inventions in technologies that mobilised the power embedded in nature's hydro and carbon resources, which they possessed; while destroying ancient community practises that fuelled the creativity of the people.

As such polarities were driven deeper, the nation's immune system was systematically dismantled.

In the animal world, organisms deploy biological mechanisms to protect themselves from disease. Malevolent viruses and parasites must be blocked from living off their life-giving energy. No matter how primitive the organism, it has to evolve immune systems. Bacteria protect themselves with enzymes. In the vegetable world, a waxy cuticle is layered over leaves as defence against infections.

In humans, individuals secure their well-being by (for example) a diet of fresh fruits, vegetable, and foods rich in certain fatty acids. Neglecting a balanced diet exposes the individual to influences that may contribute towards premature mortality.

Societies employ the most complex of all immune systems. Barriers to threats are composed of chemical signals supplemented by tools drawn from culture and from the natural world (from which we continue to draw much of our knowledge, including our identities). Defensive strategies are grounded in the accumulated information base which is mobilised to ensure survival. *If the immune system is damaged, a community may expose itself to mortal risk.*

Parasites seeking to live off a new source of living energy, whether from the most primitive of organisms or a human population, *must* try to dismantle the immune system. In the animal world, immune systems have to acquire the ability to detect pathogens that deploy detection avoidance strategies.

Human parasites that want to drain the life-giving energy of human populations can succeed only if they launch continuous attacks on their quarry. They need permanent access, if they are to feast on the accumulated riches of society.

Humans were naturally adept at spotting the cheats who wanted to take advantage of them (Ch. 3). To overcome such mechanisms, human parasites have to overcome layers of obstacles. These include:

- *Institutional*: organisations charged with sounding early warnings of danger.
- *Neurological*: chemical signals that decode the presence of threats.
- *Psychological*: sensory and ethical aptitudes that heighten awareness.

When one or a combination of these barriers is damaged, a population becomes fair game to predators. The richer a community – the more rents it has accumulated and converted into capital and culture – the greater the incentive to feed off its life-blood. When a population is forcibly detached from its natural environment, for example, it loses one of its most important sources of information. The population is traumatised, and its immune system consequently malfunctions. That leaves the way open for predators to move in and feast.

Trauma has been studied in relation to individuals rather than whole societies. The evidence, however, is an important starting point for generalising the insights that lead to an understanding of how an apparently well-educated, sophisticated community may have rendered itself vulnerable to vultures. Psychologists have established that trauma may have both organic and in-organic effects.[7] Physiological impacts may be registered on the brain and personality.[8] Violence that entails loss, if unresolved, may transmit its effects inter-generationally.[9]

Of special importance are the insights arising from dislocation and isolation. American psychiatrist Judith Herman cites the effects of prolonged captivity on people (such as women subjected to extended periods of battery). One of the reactions is "learned helplessness", which translates into the erosion

---

7 Kolk *et al* (2007: 48-49).
8 Schore (2003: 109); and Kolk *et al* (1996: 291-6, 350-351).
9 Hesse *et al* (2003: 57).

of personality.[10] Psychological "infantilism" is another response to prolonged periods of captivity (as when police officers are taken hostage), resulting in less than efficient survival strategies.[11] The evidence shows that people deprive themselves of opportunities to mitigate the effects of the traumatising shock or violence to which they were subjected.

The psychological consequences are magnified a million fold when a whole community has been subjected to violence of the kind that overwhelms its immune system. And the trauma is deepened as the parasitic effect is extended. *That happens when a population is emotionally and physically dislocated from its natural environment, confined by the laws of the land, marooned in limbo land, and coerced over the course of generations into accepting its condition of deprivation.* Learned helplessness becomes a way of life. Institutions and laws repeat the violence, transmitting the trauma through the generations. This may occur (say) through the state of collective arousal that is not allowed to ease off. If displacement causes the permanent unemployment of a significant proportion of the population, this conveys a state of anxiety from one generation to the next.

The trauma may manifest itself in many forms.

- *Loss of memory:* Nature provides an important part of our knowledge base; without it, populations lose part of their capacity for remedial action.
- *Loss of confidence:* Erosion of group identity depletes the psychic power to act. False identities are fabricated (responding, say, to appeals of "patriotism").
- *Loss of community:* Networks of support systems are fragmented (the extended family, neighbourhood groups).
- *Loss of income:* Material resources are not produced, eroding the funding needed to vitalise the cultural commons.
- *Loss of dignity:* Pejorative labels, when attached to a deprived community, diminishes the capacity to challenge the exploiters.

A population's immune system is shot to pieces by the systematic abuse that arises when a significant proportion of its rents are sucked out of it. Being schooled into accepting this fate is designed to deprive people of the capacity to recognise the cheats in their midst. They are condemned to live in a permanent state of dis-ease.

---

10 Herman (1992: 90).
11 Herman (1992: 47).

The Pathology of Land Loss

The enclosures tormented John Clare. The emotions surfaced over a protracted period, and they could not be treated by any known form of therapy. He had no doubt about the profound implications arising from the loss of land. The stresses sapped his body as he struggled to deal with the conflicts in his mind.

- He showed deference to the local grandees, but was "bitterly satirical towards the newly prosperous, socially aspirant farmers who benefited from the enclosure at the expense of the rights and customs of his own class".[12]
- He recorded cherished memories of the open landscape that he roamed as a child, while suffering the indignity of "working with a team on the labour of enclosure [in which] his poetic freedom was reigned in".[13]
- He was grateful to the rent-collecting Marquess of Exeter who granted him an annual stipend of 15 guineas for life, while feeling mortified by the indignities of his friends who were barred from their fields, ejected from their homes.

Earning a labourer's wage to re-shape his beloved landscape to accommodate "the law of enclosure and the profiteers who benefited from it"[14] inspired his poetry of protest, but it also tested his psyche. He was a loyal patriot. What did it cost him to love England while hating her laws of the land? Clare's father was one of the victims. His landlord raised the rent of the family home, the cottage with the garden whose apple tree helped to pay the rent. Clare Snr. was forced to seek Poor Law Relief (five shillings a week), which mortified him. In 1818, when Clare was "discovered" as a poet, the family owed two year's rent.

The deterioration in Clare's mental health cannot be ascribed to any one cause. His biographer Jonathan Bate reports that Clare suffered from an array of physical and mental symptoms. In America today his condition would probably be diagnosed as post-traumatic stress disorder. His frequent headaches may have been the result of stress, but they might also have been caused by a clot from a fall from a tree. Bate suggests that Clare's symptoms conformed to the classic pattern of manic depression or "bipolar affective disorder".[15] He suffered severe bouts of depression in the early years of adulthood; that is, after the enclosures had torn up the world into which he had been born and bred. For many years before his death of "apoplexy" in 1864 he was confined in asylums.

12 Bate (2005: 58).
13 Bate (2005: 75).
14 Bate (2005: 106).
15 Bate (2005: 412).

Is Clare a metaphor for a society whose immune system had been dismantled? He crafted poems to preserve the memories of the childhood places "that were disappearing as enclosure changed the face of the land".[16] Did the inner anguish of his emotions affect the balance of his mind? The commons defined his identity, set the boundaries to his personality. When the commons were gone, why wouldn't his personality unravel? *There is no analytical framework in psychology or sociology, then or now, to analyse the pain of land loss on a population.* But the enclosures did subject the people of the commons to a terrible violence. By the end of the 18th century, the nation had been compressed into legal and social abnormalities that re-defined people's status with each other and with the land. The main element of that status was expressed in a four-letter word: loss.

Land loss is a continuous assault on a population, a prolonged and invasive violence. Does this create a state of trauma *en masse*? Clare lamented in 'The Mores':

Inclosure came and trampled on the grave
Of labour's rights and left the poor a slave ...
And birds and trees and flowers without a name
All sighed when lawless law's enclosure came

Lawless law. The rule of chaos. The price exacted by the cheats who broke through society's immune system was heavy. But what is the mechanism that has to be dismantled, if the immune system is to be rendered helpless?

Villages of Lost Souls
The traumas that concern psychologists who treat patients on a one-to-one basis stem from "an extraordinary event or series of events which is sudden, overwhelming, and often dangerous, either to one's self or significant others". Trauma is "an emotional state of discomfort and stress resulting from memories of an extraordinary, catastrophic experience which shattered the survivor's sense of invulnerability to harm".[17] The rupture of people from their lifeline to the commons is of a different order of magnitude. The effects are felt at two levels.

- The protracted disengagement from land fosters anxieties which become deeply embedded as fears that corrode the archetypal forms that give content to the collective unconscious; the ballast to the mind that enabled

---

16 Bate (2005: 106).
17 Figley (1988: 85).

pre-literate people to navigate oceans of time as they pushed the boundaries of human experience ever further outwards.

- The onset of inter-generational shocks such as the relentless rise in rents and taxes, the cyclical loss of employment, and awareness that the nation-state is not a safety net wrapped around everyone.

Each generation became a victim of the malevolence sanctioned by the rule of the landlords. To understand that kind of trauma we need to turn to field-workers like Claude Lévi-Strauss (1908-2009), who contributed to the emergence of anthropology as a disciplined method for investigating the human condition.

Lévi-Strauss argued that the "savage" mind had the same structure as the "civilised" mind; and that human characteristics did not vary across continents. In his quest for evidence, he came to realise that it was necessary to distinguish surface appearances from inner realities. He wrote in *Tristes Tropiques*: "The nature of truth is already indicated by the care it takes to remain elusive".[18] His field work in Brazil in the 1930s focused on the Bororo, one of the tribes of the linguistic group known as Ge. They occupied the plateau between the Araguaya and São Francisco rivers. For an estimated 7,000 years, these people lived contentedly in this part of South America. We may assume that their institutions, values and behaviour constituted a cultural formation that was in some meaningful sense *normal*.

Then the aliens arrived. They spoke in tongues (Spanish and German). Their brutal techniques displaced the Bororo (the name means "village court"). When Lévi-Strauss arrived on the crime scene, few settlements displayed anything that resembled the ancient way of life. By living in the village of Kejara, he recovered valuable evidence of the secret that had sustained them through millennia.

By this time, relationships between the Bororo and the settlers had been stabilised by Italian missionaries. The Salesian Fathers represented a society established by Don John Bosco. He had worked among the poor in Turin, and by the 1870s his Society of St. Francis de Sales had been approved by the Pope. The new order rapidly established itself in France and as far away as Argentina. Their mission was to help the impoverished. For the Bororo, the Fathers came as peace-makers.

The Fathers diligently documented the ancient culture. But they did so with a purpose, observed Lévi-Strauss. Their mission was to spread The Word of God. To achieve this, they had to execute a life-changing transformation in the way the Bororo lived. So the Fathers "pursued the systematic obliteration

---

18 Lévi-Straus (1955: 57-58).

of native culture".[19] Genocide does not capture the essence of their crime. They did not want to kill the people. Humanicide. They achieved this remarkable feat of destruction by exposing the foundations beneath the architecture of Bororo culture.

They began by studying the floor plan of the villages and interrogating their complex practices – kinship patterns, marriage conventions, gender rules – and their relationship with their natural environment. This provided the clues the Fathers needed if they were to replace the Bororo belief system with Christianity.

As with Clare's Helpston, in England, Bororo villages were organised in a circle. This spatial arrangement integrated the psychological and physiological needs of the people with their ecological niche. The dwellings were configured like a cartwheel. In the centre – the hub – was the men's house. Here, the social and religious life was pursued by males in the dwelling from which the women were banned. The women lived in homes arranged in a circle. The village was divided into sections which ordained who could marry whom, the rights and obligations of each member of the community, and how the public ceremonies would be orchestrated for everyone's benefit. By decoding the spatial rules, the Salesian Fathers exposed the minds and the souls of the Bororo. Their spatial cosmology was the key to the balanced order which regulated the size of the population and the flow of nature's resources. The pattern was based on the principle of efficient access to the animals and vegetables which flourished around them. The spatial configuration embedded the principle of equality in their personal disposition towards their home territory. They affirmed their *mores* through their artwork, samples of which Lévi-Strauss took back to Paris to inspire artists like Picasso.[20]

The Salesian Fathers diligently compiled the archive of evidence that revealed those practises. Lévi-Strauss acknowledged his debt by stating that "they went to a great deal of trouble to understand, and preserve the memory of this complex pattern. Anyone visiting the Bororo must begin by studying their researches".[21]

The Fathers were in the business of wiping clean the minds of the Bororo. Their objective was to replace ancient beliefs with a religion which bore no functional relationship – for them – to their socio-ecological environment. How was this deed executed?

The circular arrangement of the huts around the men's house is so important a factor in their social and religious life that the Salesian missionaries in the Rio das Garças region were quick to realize that the

---

19 Lévi-Strauss (1955: 216).
20 Wilcken (2010:16).
21 Lévi-Strauss (1955: 221).

Box 5:1
Who was Nasty and Brutish?

English philosopher Thomas Hobbes soothed troubled minds with his claim, in *Leviathan* (1651), that people living in the state of nature endured lives that were "solitary, poor, nasty, brutish, and short". This, evidently, was not what freeborn Englishmen had to endure!

Hobbes wanted a theory that explained the nature of power in civil society. "The state of nature" was his analytical device. He drew on reports about indigenous peoples who were being supplanted by Europeans, whose tribes *had* been reduced to a nasty state. As for brutishness, was that not more appropriately a description of the behaviour of European intruders?

Denial was essential if the European mind was to be cosseted, self-esteem protected from the nightmare of how aboriginal peoples in America, north and south, were being cleared to make way for Europeans, many of whom had been cleared from their homelands.

surest way to convert the Bororo was to make them abandon their village in favour of one with the houses set out in parallel rows.[22]

Town planning. That's how the priests re-configured the minds of the Bororo.

Once they had been deprived of their bearings and were without the plan which acted as a confirmation of their native lore, the Indians soon lost any feeling for tradition; it was as if their social and religious systems (we shall see that one cannot be dissociated from the other) were too complex to exist without the pattern which was embodied in the plan of the village and of which their awareness was constantly being refreshed by their every day activities.[23]

By disconnecting the people from the circular configuration of their settlements, their minds and souls were wrenched apart. Gone were the rules of residence. The moieties to which each individual belonged began to lose significance. The marriage patterns that secured stable demographic balance, the invisible paths that linked the homes of the women with the ceremonial space … all shattered. Property rights thrown to the wind, respect for each individual's access rights to nature's resources shrugged aside in the chaos. Knowledge of ecological zones was depleted, because the spatial reference points were

---

22 Lévi-Strauss (1955: 220-221).
23 Lévi-Strauss (1955: 221).

dissolved to accommodate the wishes of the agents of the European mind-set. Through evolutionary timescales the Bororo had embedded their rights and obligations in that spatial life-cycle. Once that psycho-social construct was shredded, the dwellings now lined up in straight rows, communities were rendered dysfunctional.

Europe's philosophers used travellers' accounts of the villages of lost souls in the Americas to assert that this was what you get from living in a "state of nature" (Box 5:1).

The lesions in these communities are the indicators of deep-seated dis-ease. Today, the remnants of the Bororo struggle for survival on land 300 times smaller than their original territory. The decimated population is estimated to be a little more than 1,000 souls surviving on the margins of Latin nations that supplanted them. Alcoholism is rife. Contests continue over the ownership of land, with anthropologists like Sylvia Caiuby Novaes confirming that the surviving Bororo rituals are still regarded as transgressions that offend the settler culture.[24]

British environmentalist George Monbiot suggests that John Clare's experiences were identical to those of indigenous peoples who were torn from their land under colonialism: "His identity crisis, descent into mental agony and alcohol abuse are familiar blights in reservations and outback shanties the world over. His loss was surely enough to drive almost anyone mad; our loss surely enough to drive us all a little mad."[25]

Coping with the Trauma

The Salesian Fathers halted the violent contests between European settlers and the indigenous tribes, but by demolishing an ancient culture they cleared the way for further intrusion into the lands of the Bororo. By dissociating the people from the living texts on which they relied for their bearings – the natural guides through the cycle of birth, marriage and death – the intruders could capture more land. Furthermore, they could do so at a cheaper price in terms of investment in weapons and loss of life. The Bororo had been disabled. Their power to resist was diminished to the point of total vulnerability. The economics of apartheid was seeded in the centre of the continent by men who meant well but who also knew what they were doing.

How does a population cope with this kind of trauma? To embrace a whole population, what form would a coping mechanism assume?

Scholars celebrate the Western mind-set as a *coalescence* of ideas that emerged in periods which they identify as Enlightenments. Could the reverse

---

24 Novaes (1983).
25 Monbiot (2012).

be closer to reality? Is the European mind the product of the *dissolution* of knowledge of both the empirical and moral kinds?

When we survey the grand sweep of intellectual history since the time of Christopher Columbus, we can trace the logic which transformed worldviews. Doctrines were adopted that did not stimulate progress of the evolutionary kind. Their purpose was therapeutic, the ideas structured to enable people to come to terms with their impoverished condition. To understand this history of ideas, we need to remind ourselves of how capitalism is structured.

In capitalism, populations are divided into two classes: those who add value, and those who extract value. The dissonant social structure *had* to be brought back into some semblance of stability. Unable to combat the injustice head-on, the people who were dispossessed of their commons developed mind-sets that rationalised their predicaments. The pain, the shame, the horror of their anarchic state – cut loose from ancient hamlets and villages … their minds had to be shrouded to bring relief.

The loss of the commons meant the loss of memories and identities. To make it all tolerable, powerful new images were needed. The emerging doctrines were not intended to reform. They were designed to cope with the shock of the savage displacement.

Figure 5:1
Structural Deformations & Comfort Doctrines

Primary shock	16-18th centuries: Agrarianism	19th century: Industrialism	20th century: Corporatism	21st century: Virtualism
Land Loss	Millenarianism	Left: Socialism	Fascism	Nihilism
		Right: Conservatism	Libertarianism	(Terrorism, Anarchy)

Humans are resilient in the face of natural disasters. To ensure survival, they adapt and recover composure when threatened by earthquakes and droughts. Man-made disasters, which dismantle a population's immune system dictate the need for strategies which compensate for the nightmare. This is schematically traced in Figure 5:1 (using, in the main, English history for illustrative purposes).

When the sacred lands of the monasteries were appropriated by Henry VIII in the 1530s, and patricians began to enclose the commons, people had little choice but to seek solace in rewards to be gained in the future. Those rewards could not now come on Earth, so they would have to be sought in heaven. Landless agrarian masses began to transform their spiritual and folk beliefs in the direction of millenarian mind-sets. Dissenting groups challenged the authority of the church. Peasant revolts throughout Europe confronted states, but they were no match for the metal-plated patricians astride their stallions. People like Thomas Muntzer recruited acolytes as Anabaptists, the Mennonites and Quakers provided alternative visions of the sacred life, and Pilgrims sought salvation in the New World.[26]

The urban/industrial nexus stimulated a new phase in the construction of coping doctrines. Mind-sets splintered and gravitated towards outlooks animated by materialism. This was the product of a complex dynamic. What had now become the dominant culture of the cheats prescribed an amoral vision of the universe. There was to be no rescue by the God of the Landless (Box 5:2). The people were now physically and mentally distanced from nature. Their landscapes were secularised, whole villages destroyed and their inhabitants expelled into industrial towns. As the stresses intensified with the shocks of business cycles, further refinements were necessary to cope with the voids in their lives. Two streams of doctrines emerged to reflect the social psychoses.

The outcasts sought refuge in radical left-wing visions. Marx promised salvation once the exploited working classes had mobilised to overthrow capitalism. A concurrent set of coping doctrines was required to support the agents of the new culture of enterprise. This stream of conservative imagining culminated in the post-classical schools of economics which erased land from economic thinking and idealised the market.

Policing these adjustments to a collective consciousness in chaos were the institutions that protected the privileges of the cheats. But with the onset of the depression of the 1870s, the grotesque instability in the social system threatened the tenuous structure. Further refinements to belief systems were required. The Left splintered and, in part, turned to fascism (national socialism). A corresponding fragmentation occurred on the Right, with ideologies posing as scientific thinking. These included the theories that were invented by economists who converged on the University of Chicago. They rationalised the private ownership of land and rent as compatible with – rather than antithetical to – the commercial economy.

By the late 20th century yet further adaptations would be necessary. Capitalism was rapidly fragmenting. The Age of Cyberspace enabled people to seek solace in surreal reality. Nihilism surfaced both on the streets and in the closets of minds.

Intermittent challenges to the rent-seekers were deflected to protect their privileges. But why, in those societies that insisted they were working for the good of the whole population, that people were treated as equals before

---

26 A revealing insight into doctrines as coping mechanisms would be the comparative study of the beliefs and practises of Afro-Caribbean slave populations. Voodoo and other quasi-naturalistic beliefs and rituals need to be compared to the cosmologies of African tribes in the regions from which these people were kidnapped and sold to plantation owners.

Box 5:2
The Limits of Coping Mechanisms

The Reverend Thomas Malthus (1766-1834) did not preach the theology of land. His pulpit was secular. His expertise in economics was rent, and he trained civil servants in the art of administering the colonies. He provided one coping doctrine that has proved durable. In 1798 he published the first edition of *An Essay on the Principle of Population*.

Malthus appeared to make sense of the helplessness of large numbers of people in the midst of English plenty. He provided an arithmetical formula that rationalised mass poverty. Poverty was due to the irresponsible sexual behaviour of the poor. The rich were relieved of their culpability, and the poor were made to feel guilty. To the extent that the doctrine achieved general acceptance, the population learnt to live with the restrictions imposed on it by the economics of apartheid. To this day, the Malthusian theme of "over-population" serves as balm that helps to soothe the European conscience.

the law, did the outcasts fail to recover their rights? This is the story of how modern nations innovate ways to cause grievous mental and bodily harm on a continuous basis. The way in which trauma is entrenched to divide the population permanently may be illuminated by the case of the United States of America.

Entrenching the Trauma

The English aristocrats who established the first colonies in America created the blueprint for property rights and the power structure which remains in place today. The economics of apartheid which defined colonies like Virginia are celebrated as proof of the virtuous origins of America.

America is the product of a constitutional neurosis. Formally, it places the liberty of *We, The People* at the heart of its belief system. But the authors of the revolutionary documents which sanctioned the rupture with Britain had a practical problem. They owned the land of America, and they were not going to yield their privileges to anyone. So, while paying lip service to the natural law theories of John Locke, they perverted the sentiments to camouflage the practical reality.

Locke had written that, under natural law, everyone had a right to "life, liberty and estate [land]". The Founding Fathers could not commit themselves to this doctrine. They invented a new one. They upheld the right of every individual to "life, liberty and the pursuit of happiness". By means of linguistic gymnastics the rule of their law became the brand that served the class interest of the land owner. But this placed trauma at the heart of the American dream.

How could the doctrine of the "land of the free" be squared with the economics of apartheid?

The first plantation owners had driven the indigenous peoples from their territories, and stocked their estates with slaves who had been kidnapped in Africa. The Africans were observed to be "degraded and depressed".[27] The psycho-social pathologies of the 17th and 18th centuries were transmitted into the 20th century in a way that sustained the trauma at the expense of the mental health of both the victims and their oppressors. The history of that relationship is traced by American civil rights lawyer Michelle Alexander in her book *The New Jim Crow*.

The first doctrinal challenge came with the civil war and the freedom of the slaves. But legal emancipation did not include reforms to property rights. "[T]he Reconstruction Era was fraught with corruption and arguably doomed by the lack of land reform," notes Alexander.[28] Apartheid (separate development) continued to shape America's destiny. "[T]he separation of the races had begun as a comprehensive pattern throughout the South, driven in large part by the rhetoric of the planter elite, who hoped to re-establish a system of control that would ensure a low-paid, submissive labour force."[29] Racial segregation in the North was matched with similar systems for controlling the emancipated slaves in the South to enshrine a national doctrine that rationalised control over the economic outcasts.

The landless European families that sought refuge in America were not congenitally racist. But it was necessary to inculcate in them the attitudes that would deflect attention away from the realities (not the least of which was the denial of land to many of them). The patriotic myth insisted that America was the "land of the free". The land *was* free – to those who were first able to grab it (if we do not take account of the costs inflicted on the supplanted tribes). Subsequent settlers were tenants of the land owners. So racism became functionally necessary to enable the white outcasts to cope with the tensions in a pathologically deformed society. As one historian noted: "As long as poor whites directed their hatred and frustration against the black competitor, the planters were relieved of class hostility directed against them".[30]

African Americans were not given a chance to develop their human potential. But then came the civil liberties movement of the 1960s. Laws which discriminated against people of colour were deleted from the statute books. Could this society finally be transformed? President John F. Kennedy

---

27 Cited by Alexander (2012: 187).
28 Alexander (2012: 29).
29 Alexander (2012: 30).
30 Wilson (1978: 54).

offered the charismatic leadership that was needed if America was to embark on a new course. He was assassinated in 1963. His brother Robert proved equally determined to push America closer to its constitutional ideals. He was assassinated in 1968. If the African American population was to be pulled out of its depressed state, it needed a moral voice. This was provided by Martin Luther King Jr. He, too, was assassinated in 1968.

America was at war with itself. At stake was the soul of a nation. If the feudal privileges of the English aristocracy were to be retained, the outcasts would have to be contained. Michelle Alexander traces the fight back, engineered under the guise of the War on Drugs. If people could not be legally segregated on the basis of racist ideology, they could be incarcerated in the name of the rule of law.

Today, more people are languishing in jails in America than in any other country. A gulag of prisons (some of them privately owned) flourishes across the continent to hold about 500,000 people for drug offences compared to about 41,000 in 1980.[31] Alexander analyses in painful detail the way in which this "war" was a device to hunt down African Americans. The war was prosecuted so that more Africans could be criminalised for offences for which white citizens were at least equally culpable. By the end of the 20th century, more than two million people in America were incarcerated. In 2007, over seven million people were behind bars, on probation or on parole. The population of America is about 5% of the world's total. Yet she incarcerates on a scale that represents 25% of the entire world prison population. The bias against people of colour is indelibly scored into the judicial system.

> *The nature of the criminal justice system has changed. It is no longer concerned primarily with the prevention and punishment of crime, but rather with the management and control of the dispossessed. Prior drug wars were ancillary to the prevailing caste system. This time the drug war is the system of control.*[32]

Segregation is the process that transmits trauma inter-generationally, the displaced people's futures blighted by the marks of poverty (Box 5:3). Lives are forever compromised by the right of employers to discriminate against people with prison records. So there is little or no upward or outward mobility. The exceptions do not contradict the rule. African Americans are ghettoised.

America, like most of Europe's nations, needs a therapeutic shift towards normal, healthy conditions. What would this mean?

---

31 Alexander (2012: 60).
32 Alexander (2012: 188).

Leaderless World: A Prognosis

Tʜʀᴏᴜɢʜ colonialism, the culture of rent-seeking now dominates the way people view the world. The values that embed the culture of cheating frame the standard model for assessing political action.

Under these conditions, the future can only be bleak. We need to determine the degree to which our leaders are capable of dealing with the global crises which will seal the fate not just of Western civilisation, but of humanity itself.

The test we set is the capacity of agencies in the realms of politics, science and religion to select leaders who are able to act for the common good. The primary challenge is to determine whether those leaders, who shape people's popular opinions, understand what created the fault lines in our social universe. "Contrary to popular perception, we haven't cheated our way to affluence," asserts author and BBC presenter Evan Davis.[33] That complacent view emphasises the need for an informed debate among people who are not wedded to the authorised versions of how we got here, how our identities were shaped, and the prospects that will seal all our futures. With moral and intellectual compasses deranged, our societies are so traumatised that we have difficulty deciding who to trust.

Of one thing we can be sure. The power structures are not calibrated to objectively meet people's needs. The people are voiceless. How this arose has been documented in the case of the United Kingdom. Parliament represents the interests of an exclusive brethren united by privileges of the rent-seeking culture.

John Clare symbolised that voicelessness. There is no ambiguity about the forces that operated to inhibit him from giving voice to the condition of the millions who were rendered outcasts in the land of their birth. His anger at the way the people of the commons were unceremoniously ejected from their habitats was expressed in his poems. But those poems were either modified or not published during his lifetime. His patrons, the aristocrats who lived off the rents, guided him to alter the phrases he crafted. One of his trenchant documentations of the alienation stemming from land loss, which he called *The Parish*, was not published in its full form until 1985. He wrote it in 1823. In his preparatory note to that poem he wrote:

This poem was begun & finished under the pressure of heavy distress with embittered feelings under a state of anxiety & oppression almost

---

33 Davis (2012).

> **Box 5:3**
> **Poverty as By-product**
>
> Is the United States united? In the richest country in the world, about 50m people live on the bread line. Vast swathes of unoccupied territory alongside millions of families who draw food stamps supplied by government to keep body and soul together.
>
> Is the United Kingdom united? The Institute for Fiscal Studies (IFS) predicts that, by 2020, the number of children living in relative poverty will reach 3.3m. That is almost one in four children. According to the director of the IFS, the government does not have a plan to achieve its own legally-binding targets.[1]
>
> In political debates about poverty, there is no acknowledgment that the routine production of poverty is intrinsic to the mix of property rights and the corresponding tax policies which protect the income received by land owners. Poverty, apparently, comes from nowhere.
>
> ───────────
> 1 Johnson (2011).

amounting to slavery – when the prosperity of one class was founded on the adversity & distress of the other.[34]

Clare was locked into a Kafkaesque nightmare. Is it any wonder that he was heading for the asylum? His acute distress, the confusions arising from the way his poems were manipulated by patrons who did not want his views to disturb the convivial control of society by the landlords, stifled his personality. The psychological cost was immense.[35] He was the voice of the people who had been dispossessed of their commons. Poets were needed because pulpits were silent. The bishops who spoke for God of the Landless had retired to the benches in the House of Lords. It had been a long time since St Gregory the Great (the Pope during the years 590-604) had declared:

> *Those who make private property of the gift of God pretend in vain to be innocent, for in thus retaining the subsistence of the poor they are the murderers of those who die every day for want of it.*[36]

───────────

34 Attack (2010: 52-53).

35 The patronising treatment he received from the peers of the realm is most elegantly summarised by Rosemary Attack, who writes: "The suppression of this poetry was the rejection of one of Clare's most important roles in English social life and history, written about, but not for, the appropriating classes. This was probably one of the many contributory causes of the severe mental distress experienced by Clare through most of his life. He was patronised and his work suppressed by the same people" (Attack [2010: 42]).

36 Cited in Douglas (1976: 11).

The majority of people had been turned into social hostages, many of them a crust of bread away from having to throw themselves on the mercies of the parish workhouse (as nearly happened to Clare's parents). Many became "disappeared" – despatched to penal colonies for stealing bread or rabbits.

Statecraft in the 19th century was the mature expression of the cheating culture. The parasites had dismantled the last layers of society's immune system. The intellectual communities, representing the natural and social sciences, could not give free expression to the fundamental problem. So the masses had to settle for the coping doctrines that were safe: those doctrines that would not disturb the world of the land lords who caused the social pathologies.

The people were leaderless. The primary function of those in power was to remain alert to threats to their privileges. The state of trauma had cheated the people out of their land, and out of their culture. They were deprived of their culture when they lost the rents that were needed to maintain the vitality of their social lives.

Leaderless, because allegiances are divided by the economics of apartheid.

Chapter 6: The Depletion of Society

WHAT happens when a society consumes more than it produces? If it does not balance its books by reducing consumption, it has four choices. All of them are grounded in the culture of cheating.

1. Producers can be made to work harder to increase output: the Treadmill Effect.
2. Stealing from others to cover the deficit. Responding to the Depression of the 1870s, Europe's imperial powers began to ransack Africa: the Colonising Effect.
3. Borrowing, to consume more today by shifting the costs onto future generations: the Debt Effect.
4. Consuming the capital of past labours: the Depletion Effect.

By the mid-19th century all four strategies became standard policies of statecraft for most European nations. That meant they were moving slowly but surely towards the collapse of their form of social organisation. That collapse would first surface as a financial crisis from which there could be no escape. The financial façade, however, concealed the political, moral and intellectual infirmities induced by the state of trauma to which they had been reduced. The West is victim of the virus that has eroded people's capacity to add value to the wealth of their nations. This diagnosis will be tested against the evidence for the United Kingdom. Two propositions will be examined.

- A nation that undermines its immune system loses control over its destiny.
- A nation that undermines its economic foundations locks itself into a downward spiralling vortex.

To address these propositions, we need to determine why many of the rich science-based nations of the West are apparently unable to produce as much as they need to consume. The apparent shortfall is measured by socially significant levels of poverty. When a large proportion of a population is apparently unable to meet household needs, does this mean the nation is incapable of producing as much as people need to consume? Or is the apparent shortfall the result of the working population being deprived of a significant part of the income it generates?

The evidence reveals that the deficit is *not* one of *under-production*. Working people are short-changed. To appreciate how this crime can be executed against a nation, we have to step back a thousand years to the conquest of England by William, the Norman duke who would be king. We cannot understand the nature of the crisis of the 21st century without taking into account the events that have unfolded since 1066.

William adopted the statecraft employed by Anglo-Saxon kings. He found that they had developed a process of consultation in which four representatives from each village assembled in regular county meetings (moots) to keep the monarch informed of what was happening in their communities. William evolved this structure into a consultative process that became the modern Parliament. But something changed along the way. *The House of Commons did not become the Parliament of the people of the commons.* The character of the power structure is revealed by the finances of the nation.

At the beginning of the Norman reign, monarchs administered England out of the rents of land (Fig. 6:1). Rents were, and remain, the natural source of revenue for the state. They were the amount that could be taxed out of the economy, without injuring the welfare of the people. The legal terms on which land was held reflected that financial reality. The tenure of the barons and knights who received rents was conditional on their discharging services to the state.

Over the 11th to the early 15th centuries, monarchs convened Parliaments primarily to consider the raising of revenue. The doctrine emerged that those who were affected by a new tax had to give their consent in Parliament.

Through the 14th and 15th centuries, Parliament evolved to include representation from both the shires and the towns. After 1332, the burgesses – two from each town – sat in what became the House of Commons. In 1407, the king formally affirmed the right of the Commons to initiate all grants of money. The state continued to draw its revenue almost exclusively from the rents of land. Revenue that did not come directly from the Land Tax (which was based on the assessment of the land's value), was drawn from rents via various occasional charges on land holders.

The first major event that sealed the fate of the people of the commons took place in 1429. Hitherto, elections were arranged through the County Court. All free men had the right to vote for their representatives. That rule was changed when the barons intervened to exclude people of "low estate".[1]

---

1 This history of the way in which the House of Commons was shaped is drawn from Parliament's website: www.parliament.uk

Fig. 6:1
Land Rent as % of Public Revenue (1066–1842)

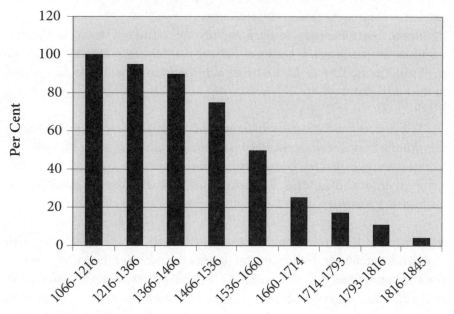

Source: Cobden (1842).

From then on, only substantial freeholders of land worth 40 shillings had the vote. This restricted the franchise to a small group of land holders. Their intent is revealed by the way rent, as a proportion of total state spending, began to decline. According to Parliament's account of this episode:

> From this point the knights of the shire largely came from and primarily expressed the interests of the landed elite, known as the gentry, and were often brought into Parliament by the influence and efforts of the peers in the Lords.

This was the beginning of the *coup d'état* by the nobility. Landed estates were supposed to be held in return for services rendered to king and country (such as defence of the realm and the administration of justice). *Rent was society's revenue, and was used to fund those services that everyone needed but which they could not provide by themselves.* That was the doctrine which the nobility had to erase from the statecraft of the emerging modern state. They wanted to privatise the nation's revenue. To achieve this crime, they had to control the power of taxation. The first step was to reduce revenue from the Land Tax.

But to maintain the flow of funds to the state (owners needed *their* properties to be protected against foreign aggressors, for example), they would have to substitute exactions on the incomes of peasants. To execute this mission, they needed to control the House of Commons.

But to hijack the rents of the kingdom, the aristocrats would also have to neutralise the burgesses in the towns, whose fiscal interests lay with preserving the Land Tax. So their noble lordships launched the campaign to rig elections in the boroughs.

> *Just as peers and landowners influenced the selection of knights of the shire, so they were also invading the boroughs, and tried to get their own followers elected, even if they had no connection with the place ... over the centuries aristocrats increasingly influenced elections, sometimes choosing members for both seats themselves.*

What became known as rotten boroughs "allowed aristocrats to place their non-resident followers in Parliamentary seats". The share of the nation's revenue from the rents continued to diminish. The fiscal coup was consolidated by the land grabs that began with Henry VIII's Reformation.

England's monasteries and abbeys were demolished in the 1530s, their sacred lands sold to courtiers at knock-down prices. The revenue from land in the 16th century was reduced to half of the total as Parliament invented new ways of squeezing the working population with taxes on commerce. The fabric of English society was ruptured in all its aspects, including religion. Henry anointed himself head of the Church of England. This ensured that the theology of land would not be preached from the pulpits.

In the 17th century, rents supplied just over 20% of the state's revenue, and by the time of the political upheavals of the 19th century the Land Tax supplied a trivial 4% of the nation's public revenue. Richard Cobden (1804-1865), a manufacturer and one of Parliament's few champions of economic justice, denounced the theft of the state's rents as "a fraudulent evasion" of the duties of those who held land.[2]

The landlords funded public services by innovating fiscal devices such as the ale and salt taxes. These fell primarily on the peasants.

- **The ale tax:** In *Rights of Man* (1791), Thomas Paine fulminated against landlords who commuted their feudal services to the Crown; and burdened the peasants with a tax on ale. Their lordships brewed *their* beer on their

---

2 Cobden (1842).

Box 6:1
Tyranny of the Narrative

Rent-seekers have to camouflage their actions by re-writing the language of economics. New myths, or narratives, were constructed. As a result, minds were closed to people who want to challenge the authorised versions of what passes for reality. Douglas Keenan, a mathematical scientist who worked for an investment bank in London in 1991, was shocked by the taste of such rejection.

Keenan discovered that interest rates were being manipulated by banks, and that this was common knowledge in the early 1990s. So when the scandal of rate rigging became public knowledge 20 years later, he offered to give evidence to the House of Commons committee that was set up to investigate the practise. The outraged public was being led to believe that the rigging began in 2008 (or 2005 at the earliest). Keenan knew otherwise. He offered to provide evidence under oath to the Commons. His testimony was rejected because, he was informed, it "contradicts the narrative".[1]

---
1 Keenan (2012).

estates, so they escaped *their* tax. The peasants had to buy their ale (the alternative to drinking contaminated water). They were trapped.

- **The salt tax:** Sir Robert Walpole (who became the Earl of Orford) was Britain's first Prime Minister (between 1721 and 1742). He reduced the land tax to one shilling and imposed a tax on salt. The burden fell regressively on the working population.

Other notorious fiscal devices included the Window Tax, which turned disease-ridden tenements into traps that killed their occupants.

By such tactics, the landlords' Parliament evolved the doctrine of "broad-based" taxes, to which economists subscribe to this day. Fiscal philosophy was manipulated to persuade people that taxing anything that moved would result in the best of economic outcomes (land, of course, does not move). The Big Lie.

The 'Free of Rent-Seeking' Rate of Output

Production of wealth in Britain, over the past three centuries,was below its Free of Rent-Seeking Rate (FRSR). It was not possible to recover the natural long-run rate of output, once the social immune system was badly damaged. Britain's leaders could not even understand what was weakening the productive capacity of the economy. This was one consequence of the way information was compromised by the rent-seekers.

Rent, which measures a nation's taxable capacity, ought to be tracked with care. Instead, with the exception of Japan, statistical offices of nation-states studiously avoid measuring what goes on in the land market in contrast with the diligence that is applied (say) when measuring income in the labour market.[3] So the single most comprehensive indicator of a nation's health is ignored for macro-economic purposes. This deprives governments of the most sensitive of early warning signals. This would not be tolerated in a society whose immune system was working properly. The outcome is that governments may reject vital information that is needed for good governance (Box 6:1). That happened to me in 1997.

In *The Chaos Makers* (1997), I explained that the global economy was heading for a depression.

> *By 2007 Britain and most of the other industrially advanced economies will be in the throes of frenzied activity in the land market to equal what happened in 1988/9. Land prices will be near their 18-year peak, driven by an exponential growth rate, on the verge of the collapse that will presage the global depression of 2010. The two events will not be coincidental: the peak in land prices not merely signalling the looming recession but being the primary cause of it.[4]*

In that year, Tony Blair's New Labour party enjoyed a landslide election victory. I wrote to the new Prime Minister, with personal letters also addressed to his Chancellor of the Exchequer (Gordon Brown), the First Secretary to the Treasury (Alistair Darling), the head of the Downing Street Press Office (Alistair Campbell, with whom I had briefly worked in Fleet Street), and Peter Mandelson MP, New Labour's chief political strategist. I explained that they had 10 years in which to redesign fiscal policy and avoid what would otherwise be an implosion of the economy. They failed to take action. The recurring mantra of New Labour's stewards of the economy was that they had abolished cyclical boom/busts.

In 2005, I repeated my warnings in *Boom Bust*. Blair's government was fuelling the economy to cause maximum damage to people's welfare. Evidence of the delusion that gripped Her Majesty's Government and the Treasury appears in Fig. 6:2. This was published on the website of the UK government's Valuation Office, the agency responsible for reporting the price of real estate. Land prices would continue to forge upwards into 2013. There were no storms on the horizon: people could carry on digging themselves deeper into debt by

---

3 The doctrinal warping of scholastic minds to contribute to what became the neo-classical school of economics is documented by Gaffney (1994).
4 Harrison (1997: 27).

Fig. 6:2
UK Land Prices (2008-2013)

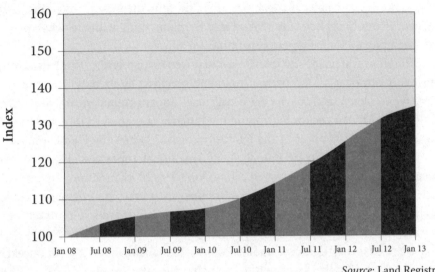

Source: Land Registry

bidding up the price of houses.

The government's predictions were false. I was correct. I forecast that house prices would peak at the end of 2007 as the prelude to a depression. Here was a laboratory-like test of the real economy. My information was available to the government for the 10 years of Blair's premiership. But like a rabbit staring transfixed into the headlights of an on-coming car, the law-makers appeared not to understand what I was telling them, so they were incapable of taking preventive action.[5]

The British government was not alone in closing its mind to the root cause of the financial crisis. The most thorough assessment of the economic trauma that followed the seizure of the banking system in 2008 was conducted on behalf of the US Congress by the National Commission on the Causes of the Financial and Economic Crisis. The Commission rejected the conventional wisdom that "no-one could have seen this coming, and thus nothing could have been done".[6] But by repetition, such falsehoods are turned into truths.

Hysteresis: Degrading Productive Capacity
There is an old saying: "If you don't use it, you lose it". Athletes understand that, if

---

5   Harrison (2010b).
6   Financial Crisis Inquiry Commission (2011), whose Chairman, Phil Angelides, warned: "Despite the expressed view of many on Wall Street and in Washington that the crisis could not have been foreseen or avoided, there were warning signs. The greatest tragedy would be to accept the refrain that no one could have seen this coming and thus nothing could have been done. If we accept this notion, it will happen again" (FCIC Press Release, January 27, 2011).

muscles are not regularly exercised, they lose their peak performance. The same applies to social and moral sensibilities. Individuals – and whole populations – may suffer if their natural capacities are allowed to atrophy through disuse or misuse. Economists have discovered that the same thing happens when people are unemployed for long periods of time.

The technical term – *hysteresis* – is borrowed from physics. Think of a coiled spring. It can bear a load within the range specified by its natural properties. Remove the load, and the spring recoils back to its original state. No damage is done, and it can continue to serve the function assigned to it by the laws of nature. But what happens if the load is excessive? When the load is removed, the spring is found to be damaged, its functional capacities distorted. The metal is contorted and the spring can no longer fulfil its function. That is what happens when an economy is over-burdened with taxes that damage people's ability to work. Many are rendered unemployed, and there is a contraction in the economy's long-run ability to produce income.

The anti-evolutionary character of the taxes sponsored by rent-seekers may be gauged by the damage it does to the natural instincts of parents. They want to bequeath a better life to their children than the one they experienced. The development of a creative society is underpinned by that aspiration, which motivates people to work better today and invest for tomorrow. A balanced family life fructifies into a flourishing neighbourhood, community and nation.

Ours has become the first generation in modern history to flout that sociogenic process. Young people leaving school and university today face a future that is inferior to the one enjoyed by the generation that was born after 1945. Economists have documented this reality in cash terms. When people are forced into unemployment for a year or more, they lose their former earning capacity. Income over the following 20 years is below what it would have been had their period of idleness between jobs been shorter. Because of the obsolescence of skills, or drop in motivation, an extended period out of the labour market prejudices people's life chances.

The contraction in the capacity to generate income is embedded through many routes, but most of them track back to the use and abuse of land and rent. An example from the US identifies the lower earning power of adults who were raised in one-parent families compared to those raised in "intact" families.[7] A major reason for the fragmentation of families is the stress created by distorted labour markets. Other reasons stem directly from land speculation, which distorts land markets and raises the cost of residential properties beyond the reach of low-income families. For Ireland, the cost is measured not just in terms

---

7 Mohanty and Ullah (2012), who provide the evidence to show that children from intact families (1) acquire more years of schooling, and (2) lead happier lives, which affects earning power in adulthood.

Box 6:2
Ireland: No Home for Children

The families of Ireland were shattered over the course of 200 years, as British landlords sucked the rents out of the island. A land-rich territory was prevented from supporting its own children. Generation after generation was forced to migrate. Nothing changed when, with independence, the Republic of Ireland retained the financial policies inherited from Britain. Frank Flannery, a former political party official, pointed out that corruption comes in more forms than just brown-envelope bribes paid to politicians. "[A] better definition of political corruption is the inappropriate use of power and authority for purposes of individual or group gain at public expense."[1]

The years of apparent growth (1992-2008) were a tragedy in the making for children born in those two decades. They were told that their homeland had become the Celtic Tiger, a safe haven for the children. Then the land-led boom turned to bust. In 2011, according to the Central Statistics Office, 76,300 people left Ireland in search of work. The land is blamed by politicians who decline to accept responsibility. "We can't all live on a small island," Brian Lenihan Snr., a former Minister of Foreign Affairs, had once declared.[2]

---

1 Breadun (2012).
2 Coronella (2012).

of lost income, but lost generations of children (Box 6:2).

Land-led booms and busts create cycles of lost income. Cumulatively, these deprive nations of unquantifiable amounts of wealth. The rate of this loss is accelerating for many Western nations. The depression of the 2010s rendered 50% of school leavers and university graduates unemployed in countries like Spain, Greece and Italy. In Britain, one-in-three of the unemployed had been out of work for 12 months or more, and a record number (1.4m) forced to work part-time, according to the Office for National Statistics (March 2012). As a population ages and the young lose the productive capacities of their parents, the gap in the incomes needed to fund people's basic requirements grows wider. In 2012, Britain's university graduates faced the prospect of starting salaries that had fallen back in real terms to 2003 levels, according to a study by Incomes Data Services. There were nearly 50 applicants for every graduate vacancy, with employment and salary prospects on a downward trend.[8] Employers complain that they have difficulty encouraging the young to conform to the disciplines associated with apprenticeships. And according to a European Commission study, a decline in educational achievements further undermined Britain's

---

8 Peacock (2012).

long-term economic prospects.[9] One outcome is the heightened risk of anarchy in the streets (Box 6:3).

The Nation's Trust

The proposition that Britain is a nation in trauma will be met with scepticism, despite the evidence. Outward appearances suggest that the English are content with their past (not so with many of those with Celtic ancestry). Many of the country palaces of the aristocracy have become the property of the National Trust. This affords people the opportunity to visit the monumental mausoleums constructed with the rents squeezed out of the peasants. Many visitors to the palaces are pleased to learn that some mansions are still occupied by the descendants of the barons and knights who cheated people out of the commons of England.

The nation has been socialised into accepting this history with equanimity. The process by which this was accomplished is illustrated by the attitudes and actions of John Ruskin (1819-1900), one of Britain's greatest art critics. His sensibilities betrayed him when he wrote about politics. In *Time and Tide* (1867) he dissected the appalling condition of the working people in Victorian society. He brusquely dismissed Adam Smith's "invisible hand" free market ideology as "the pious mysticism of the business man's philosophy". Ruskin "roundly denounced its falsity".[10] He was not able to differentiate the functions of value-adding producers from rent-seeking predators.

The state must nationalise land, he wrote, but on one condition. Reform should not destroy the landed families.

> [I]n the case of the great old families – which always ought to be, and in some measure, however decadent, still truly are, the noblest monumental architecture of the kingdom, living temples of sacred tradition and heroes' religion – so much land ought to be granted to them in perpetuity as may enable them to live thereon with all the circumstance of state and outward nobleness; but their incomes must in nowise be derived from the rents of it, *nor must they be occupied (even in the most distant and subordinately administered methods) in the exaction of rents. That is not nobleman's work. Their income must be fixed and paid by the State, as the King's is.*[11]

Ruskin wanted to preserve the landed aristocracy in financial aspic. His attitude

---

9   Aldrick (2012a).
10 Hobson (1920: 93).
11 Ruskin (1867:§151). Ruskin's emphasis.

Box 6:3
Urban Anarchy & Mind Control

When the residents of deprived English communities rioted in the 1980s, the Secretary of State for the Environment, Michael Heseltine, wrote a report to explain the civil disorder. Between then and the urban riots of August 2011, Britain endured two property boom/busts. Millions endured the humiliation of losing their homes and jobs. The income gap grew wider as the rich grew richer.

According to Prime Minister David Cameron, the riots in the summer of 2011 were triggered by (i) 120,000 problem families who lived in the inner cities, and (ii) the deterioration of society's moral fabric. Lord Heseltine (elevated to the peerage in 2001) argued that inter-generational unemployment and drug-related crime could only be overcome by the appointment of local leaders "if we are to create one society, not two".[1] With such notions did the elites comfort themselves. They displaced class responsibility for the state of the nation by implying that traumatised local communities were failing to throw up their own leaders. Meanwhile, children whose parents were rich enough to send them to private schools performed better than the rest in occupational and sporting attainment.

---

1 Heseltine (2011).

was coloured by the experiences to which he was exposed as a child. He "retained through life a singular tenderness of feeling for the local gentry whose stately homes he was wont to visit as a child with his father, driving about in a gig to take orders for 'sherry'. His imagination wove a romantic history around their origin, which later on he sought to extend to the rest of the 'upper classes'".[12]

Generations had been disfigured by the appetites of the aristocracy. Ruskin's proposal would ensure that their culture would be preserved. Entranced by the patricians and their stately homes, Ruskin failed to understand that capitalism was composed of two distinct cultures. The Predator Culture was antithetical to that of the Producers. The market model which Ruskin attacked was the vulgarised version of what Adam Smith advocated. Smith stressed that his model of the market was under-pinned by a pricing mechanism that organically bound the natural and social universes into a symbiotic whole. The Land Tax, he wrote, was the "peculiarly" suitable source of state revenue.[13] Rental payments, in his formulation, complied with the norms of morality: payments were tailored to reflect the benefits that owners received from the state.

The influence of Ruskin's socialised mind was transmitted into the 20th century through the work of Octavia Hill (1838-1912), one of the co-founders

---

12 Hobson (1920: 185).
13 Smith (1776: Bk. V, Ch. II, Pt. II, Art.I).

of the National Trust. She was dedicated to improving the condition of working people, and she had a profound understanding of how lives were shaped by the absence of access to nature. She had no illusions about the way in which the culture of 19th century Britain was brutalising the masses that were compressed into urban tenements: "There are two great wants in the life of the poor of our large towns … the want of space, and the want of beauty".[14]

With financial support from Ruskin, Octavia Hill initiated what became the social housing movement of the 20th century. Other initiatives were aimed at exposing people to "beauty". But her major legacy is the National Trust. This was established to acquire open spaces and the "heritage" properties, mainly the aristocratic palaces whose inhabitants re-worked nature and society around their narcissistic personalities. The mission of the National Trust was not intended to be transformative. The great houses would be preserved in as close to their original condition as possible so that people may gawk at them on their day trips. There was to be no rupture with the past, no rehabilitation of the people. How could there be when one of the chief supporters of the National Trust at its inauguration was the Duke of Westminster, the owner of one of the largest estates and a centurion of the rent-seeking culture?

Octavia Hill helped to consolidate the character bequeathed to the nation by those individuals who had cheated the Anglo-Saxon race, and the Celtic tribes of Scotland, Wales and Ireland, of their destiny. For Hill, progress would come not through government action but through the re-moralisation of individuals (their assumption of mutual responsibilities to each other). But her vision could not be achieved while the population remained severed from its natural habitat, still under the spell of the class that had consumed the lives of their ancestors.

The People Fight Back

In 1879, a journalist in San Francisco wrote a book called *Progress and Poverty*. It became the first global best-seller on economics. Henry George took the British Isles by storm with his public speeches.

George combined Christian precepts with classical economics to explain that the recovery of people's rights could be achieved through taxation. If rents were pooled, this would automatically trigger healthy adjustments throughout the community. The social, spiritual and material life would benefit from the removal of the monopoly power that reposed in the hands of those whose names were on title deeds.

On the back of the popular demand for tax reform, at the beginning of the 20th century the Liberal Party barnstormed to power. Winston Churchill spoke

---

14   Quoted in Clayton, (2012: 26).

Box 6:4
Abuse of the Democratic Mandate

Armed with a popular mandate, the Liberal government enacted the People's Budget with the intention that rents would support people who were out of work, and to fund pensions for the aged. The aristocracy fought a rear-guard action, successfully thwarting the democratic will. They used the courts to block the valuation of land, on which the tax would be based. The People's Budget was not implemented. Again, in 1931, the tax shift was enshrined in law by Chancellor of the Exchequer Philip Snowden (1864-1937). He had attended one of Henry George's public meetings. Again, the law was not implemented.

How different might Britain have evolved in the 20th century if the democratic will had not been abused by the rule of law? The Mother of Parliaments twice asked people to give their lives in world wars. That same Parliament was not willing to enforce its own laws on the one issue that was central to the welfare of the people.

eloquently in pubs and town halls to explain how shifting the tax burden off wages and back on to the rents of land would put history into reverse. This was the chance to recover from the trauma of the enclosures and the imposition of burdensome taxes. The Finance Bill that heralded social transformation became law and was known as The People's Budget (1909). It died an ignominious death.

The motives of the politicians who refused to enforce the law were disclosed in the actions of Neville Chamberlain (1869-1940). He succeeded Snowden as Chancellor in 1931. In 1934 he deleted Snowden's Bill from the statute book (Box 6:4). In that year, at the height of the Great Depression, Chamberlain introduced The Special (Depressed) Areas Act. This established a £2m fund to relieve the stresses of those who lived in areas of high unemployment. The Labour Opposition criticised the sum as insufficient. Chamberlain replied that it would be "absurd to set aside an extravagant sum which could not be wanted".[15] This "niggardly grant" contrasted with Chamberlain's subsidies to land owners. Those who grew beet sugar received more than £9m between 1932 and 1934. Wheat growers received more than £11m. Dairy farm land owners received over £3m. Cattle farmers received £3m. These subsidies would not have reduced the cost of food to the general population or raise the wages of farm labourers. They were captured as rent.

The fate of the 1909 and 1931 Acts defined the limits of what Britain means by the rule of law. There is one law for those who rule the land, and another law for those who were dispossessed of their land. The will of the people was

---

15 Hannington (1937: 20).

not allowed to prevail in the Parliament of the Peers when it comes to matters relating to land tenure and taxation.

Some hope of reform followed the Second World War, which weakened the aristocracy. The socialists grabbed their chance. They came to power determined to apply the socialist model to the recovery of rents. Their policies were not practical; they did not run with the grain of the market economy.[16] So it was back to business-as-usual for land speculators by the 1970s.

Socialism as a coping doctrine found its expression in the way that Labour governments mimicked the host culture. In the mid-1950s, working class communities in the northern counties of England were classified as D-villages. They were to be demolished. The people would be re-located in new towns, and the land returned to agriculture.[17] If this Labour policy had succeeded, the working class culture which had been fashioned within the interstices of the capitalist economy would be wiped out just as Anglo-Saxon villages were erased by the aristocracy in the pre-industrial age. Gone would be the community spirit, the brass bands and the social solidarity that made life tolerable for the men who earned their living as miners.

The D-villages had been declared "unfit for human habitation". The inhabitants did not agree, and they fought back with some success. But the real victor was the culture that continued to co-opt the politicians who claimed to represent the labouring people of England. During Tony Blair's administration, many working class communities were once again designated as unfit for human habitation. Whole streets and neighbourhoods were demolished as part of what was promoted as the renewal of cities like Liverpool and Manchester. The brutal reality was that the Pathfinder programme enriched the land speculators dressed up as construction companies.[18] Once again, working families tasted the fate of their displaced ancestors, enduring the depletion of the vitality of their communities.

---

16   Blundell (1994).
17   Wainwright (2011: 27).
18   Harrison (2006a: 134-136).

Leaderless World: A Prognosis

T HE cheating fostered by the Mother of Parliaments is beyond doubt. A too-close-to-home case was exposed to public gaze when the scandal of the false expense claims broke in 2009. Members of Parliament were embarrassed when the electorate realised that many MPs enriched themselves at their constituents' expense. The evidence was provided by *The Daily Telegraph*. The primary mechanism for the rip-off was the reaping of capital gains from the ownership of second homes. The mortgages for those second properties were funded by taxpayers. How can we expect politicians to institute reforms that would wreck the way they viewed the world, and who profited from the exploitation of those who voted them into power?

With the political class locked into a self-serving culture, the rest of us live in a leaderless world. If Britain is representative of the former imperial powers, we cannot be confident that the people in power will provide the leadership needed to navigate an increasingly dangerous world in the best interests of all of us. The prognosis is of a world on fire in the 21st century. For that world is constructed on the single template provided by the cheats.

In its present state, our social universe was shaped by a few colonising nations. They re-configured the consciousness of populations on other continents, to get away with appropriating their land. Societies were dismantled and realigned to divide ancient allegiances and so confuse people as to inhibit them from thinking about what was in their best interests. That process continued into the early 20th century. Britain and France – following the defeat of the Ottoman Empire – were mandated to re-contour the ethnic and bio-regional alignments of Near Eastern peoples from their offices in London and Paris. The contemporary relevance of that exercise was acknowledged by one Foreign Secretary, William Hague. Speaking in the Foreign and Commonwealth Office in Whitehall, he noted: "You think about how many lines have been drawn in this building. The world is littered with them and we should be able to explain to other countries why they were created".[19] But are Western governments capable of offering dispassionate accounts of how ancient societies were disfigured by the lines drawn on maps? Explanations make no sense unless they take into account the history of land grabs. Pain caused in the past is covered up by denial, and that leads to partial diagnosis. This is dangerous for the discourse of diplomacy. The fault-lines emerged with clarity during the Arab Spring, the ethnic divisions leading to bloodshed

---

19 Tweedie (2012).

in countries like Iraq and Syria as communities tried to adjust the imperial legacy of straight lines on maps.

Geopolitically, the West might wish to dissemble when dealing with the needs of other countries. But the need for realism was forced on Europe and America when the financial crisis broke in 2008. This crisis challenged the viability of their economic model. If analysts could not evaluate root causes, what chance was there of wise counsels prevailing on issues like the threat to the natural environment? We are not entitled to be optimistic, because the history of economics is one of persistent failure. Despite the repetitiveness of the destabilising cycles of booms and busts, politicians continued to formulate policies in ignorance of the forces that derange the economy. John Maynard Keynes recognised the existence of a profound problem as early as 1936. His diagnosis is in terms that reflect the surreal approach to politics:

> Too large a proportion of recent "mathematical" economics are mere concoctions, as imprecise as the initial assumptions they rest on, which allow the author to lose sight of the complexities and interdependences of the real world in a maze of pretentious and unhelpful symbols.[20]

The precision with which turning points in the major economic cycles can be predicted confirms that these dysfunctional events are not random. They are inscribed in the DNA of the capitalist model. So why are governments unable to apply forensic remedies? As a case study in the failure of diagnosis, and prescription, we may examine the views and actions of the economist who was charged by the British government with the duty to deliver stability in the financial markets.

Sir Mervyn King, as Governor of the Bank of England, claims that economists have long known what causes instability. And he is scathing about bankers. "For a society to base its financial system on alchemy is a poor advertisement for its rationality," he confesses. "Of all the many ways of organising banking, the worst is the one we have today." [21]

King was endowed with power and money to preside over his nation's financial system. And yet, not once during the boom years did he censure banks as unfit for purpose. But the problem, he insists, was not with economics as an intellectual discipline.

> The failure in the economic crisis was not one of intellectual imagination or economic science to understand these issues. Economists recognised

---

20 Keynes (1936: 298)
21 King (2010).

> ## Box 6:5
> ## Who Cares about the Evidence?
>
> Mervyn King and his co-author, John Kay, recalled the popular campaign at the end of the 19th century to harness land as "the principal tax base". The public, it appears, were rational in expressing their democratic will, because "the underlying intellectual argument for seeking to tax economic rent retains its force". But in Kay and King's view, it was "apparent" that economic rents were insufficient "for this to be a practical means for obtaining the resources needed to finance a modern State". They produced no statistical evidence or theoretical reasoning to support their dismissal of what they conceded was the most benign way of funding public services.
>
> Fair dealing is not the default position in economics, when issues of land and rent arise. This matters, if we accept this statement by Kay (it appeared in his column in the *Financial Times* on December 27, 2009): "You can become wealthy by creating wealth or by appropriating the wealth created by other people. When the appropriation of the wealth is illegal it is called theft or fraud. When it is legal economists call it rent-seeking".
>
> ----
>
> 1 Kay and King (1990: 179).

that distorted incentives, whether arising from implicit public subsidies, asymmetric information or a host of other imperfections, will cause a market-based outcome to be sub-optimal from the perspective of society. This idea has been at the centre of modern economics since the [1950s].[22]

King's comprehensive indictment of the financial sector includes the admission that the nation's income statistics grossly overstate the true value added by banks.

But if economic advisors to governments like Sir Mervyn really did know what was wrong with the economy, why were they and the politicians silent when banks "manufacture[d] additional assets without limit. And in the run-up to the crisis, they were aided and abetted in this endeavour by a host of vehicles and funds in the so-called shadow banking system"? Banks fabricated narratives to disclose false rates of return on their assets in both the US and UK, King conceded. He believes that this state of affairs is *natural*. Banks and crises, he says, are "natural bedfellows", and the crises will occur more frequently and on an ever larger scale.

There is no prospect of a neat solution, if we are to believe the Governor of the Bank of England. For there is no "silver bullet" remedy in the policy tool-kit

----

22 King (2010).

of governments. This pessimism is compounded if we combine King's insights with the views of his co-author, Professor John Kay.

Kay was commissioned by the British government to investigate the get-rich-quick culture of bonus-seeking financiers. He concluded: "Short-termism, or myopic behaviour, is the natural human tendency to make decisions in search of immediate gratification at the expense of future returns".[23] For Kay, as for King, there was no simple policy remedy to the failings of human nature. But nor was there any examination of the social structure within which bankers were free to pursue their short-term money-making ventures.

As I shall explain in Ch. 11, short-termism *can* be tamed. The tool for disciplining the distribution of income takes the form of one fiscal instrument. The get-rich-quick mentality would evaporate if markets were subjected to the principle to which the rest of us conform in our daily affairs: paying for the use of the services we want to use. But this policy is not allowed to intrude on the mental landscape of either Mervyn King or John Kay (Box 6:5).

Overcoming the obstacles created by the people in power will be difficult, however, because by the 1980s the get-rich-the-easy-way culture had infected the majority of people. Investment in "bricks and mortar" (no reference to land) was urged on working people as a way to acquire a "nest egg" for their retirement. Land was desired more for its profit than for the fulfilment of social and psychological purposes. People did not understand the sociological ramifications of their actions, let alone the psychological implications, but they *did* know that this was the best way to accumulate capital which they did not earn. They went in pursuit of "windfall gains", otherwise known as "unearned increments".

With Western leaders hibernating, the acquisitiveness that drives the cheating syndrome moved to its logical conclusion at the turn into the 21st century. The target was the people on very low incomes. Could they be persuaded to invest in land? The Masters of the Universe, their ambitions vaulting skywards in their towers on Wall Street and London's Canary Wharf, devised a way to turn a penny out of the penniless. They would mortgage the lives of the poor. Bankers and brokers collected their fees and paid themselves handsome bonuses for their ingenuity. Governments were complicit, as the US report into the 2008 financial crisis acknowledged:

> As a nation, we set aggressive homeownership goals with the desire to extend credit to families previously denied access to the financial markets. Yet the government failed to ensure that the philosophy of opportunity

---

23   Kay (2012: 14).

Box 6:6
The End of Capital Formation

The first Captains of Industry were born in Britain. Now, Britain is writing the epitaph for industrial entrepreneurship. The new generation is opting out: rent-yielding property is their investment of choice. The headline in the *Financial Times* (September 15, 2012) signalled the bleak future for the culture of enterprise: "Young investors put faith in buy-to-let". A property agent explained: "Many of the young landlords we see are bankers or traders who view buy-to-let as a reliable alternative to the unpredictable stock market that they work in day in, day out. They often use their annual bonus as the deposit for a buy-to-let mortgage".

Once upon a time, the first industrial nation financed the formation of capital goods out of funds that flowed into the stock market. But the new generation of money-makers have learnt their lesson. They witnessed the erosion of the value of their parents' pension funds, and have seen how the stock market has wiped billions off the value of capital assets. Acting rationally, they are opting for land-based assets. They will draw their pensions from rents. But will enough wealth creators be working to generate the rents they seek?

was being matched by the practical realities on the ground. Witness again the failure of the Federal Reserve and other regulators to rein in irresponsible lending. Home ownership peaked in the spring of 2004 and then began to decline. From that point on, the talk of opportunity was tragically at odds with the reality of a financial disaster in the making.[24]

This was the surreal end of the dream of the cheats. *The last ride on the backs of the displaced poor.* Now, all classes – from princes to patricians down to the people – were co-opted. We *all* wanted to make money from nothing. Buy a house, pay the mortgage for 25 years, and *lo and behold!* Sell the house, downsize, and pocket the capital gain!

With the Old World nations locked into a state of trauma, the vitality of the people's culture depleted by the theft of their rents, there is little reason to be optimistic about the future (Box 6:6). But we are able to produce all the material goods we need: there need be no poverty, and no living by plunder. But we cannot expect new social guidelines to come from the rent-seeking elites of the West. Might enlightened leadership emerge from the New World of the former colonial states?

---

24 Financial Crisis Inquiry Commission (2011: xxvii).

Chapter 7: The Pathway to Dystopia

T HE barbarians are not at the city gates. They are inside the city. They showed their faces to me, one warm week in May. Choreographed together, theirs was the structured depletion of what it means to be human.

It was a cold-blooded performance between three partners engaged in the cannibalisation of society. Three apparently disconnected events unfolded in a *danse macabre*.

The Plunderers: The government of the province of Buenos Aires wanted to adopt a tax on farmland. High global commodity prices had raised the value of land, but the revenue from under-assessed land had declined to a pitifully small contribution to the public purse. Provincial governor Daniel Scioli said he needed the revenue to fund investment in schools and highways. The landowners struck. They refused to sell food into the local market, and marched in protest. So ferocious was their lobbying that the government was unable to assemble a quorum. The money would not be raised to invest in the education of the children in the slums.

The Predators: His face stared out of the *Buenos Aires Herald* in the issue of May 20, 2012: the agent who protected the system at all costs. Jorge Rafael Videla, the general who led a military coup in 1976 and ordered the disappearance of 7,000 to 8,000 people. This, he told reporter Ceferino Reato, was a price to be paid to maintain the security of the nation against subversives. His first full account of the events that traumatised a nation was published in *Disposición final*. In June 2012 he was sentenced to 50 years imprisonment for directing the abduction of babies who were given to childless couples in the military.

The Prowlers: Buenos Aires is pitted with informal communities, full of scavengers at the margins of a rich city. Three of them were captured on a security camera at the reception next to the university hall where I had just lectured. The video showed three men in their early 20s, neatly dressed, fleet-fingered as they opened women's handbags to search for US dollars.

They pocketed one purse, took a satchel with a laptop, and then spotted my camera bag. Coolly, one of them placed his jacket over the bag and sat down for 90 seconds to make small talk with guests. Then he got up, threw his jacket over one arm, slipped my camera bag over his back, and walked into the night.

Three episodes. One message. Symbolising the three layers of histories of a nation that could have been one of the richest on Earth, but ended up as a failed state.

History No. 1: *what happened*. Nature's rich endowments offered prosperity for everyone, indigenous and refugee from Europe. The plunderers intervened to prevent this happening.

History No. 2: *what could have happened*. A century ago, economists claimed that Argentina had the capacity to develop as rapidly as the United States. To achieve this, the elites would have to share power with the people. The predators intervened to prevent the people from achieving their potential.

History No. 3: *what ought to have happened*. As immigrants flooded in from Spain, a resource-rich territory of almost 3m sq. km meant prosperity for everyone. This was what General Manuel Belgrano intended when he fought for independence from Spain. He brought back with him from his studies at the University of Salamanca a vision of how Argentina could flourish in freedom. The plunderers would not let it happen.

Today, Argentinians are reminded that Belgrano was the military chief who designed their national flag. Of even greater significance is what they are not taught. Belgrano brought from Spain a blueprint that could have delivered prosperity without degrading the indigenous tribes.

Belgrano was born in Buenos Aires in 1770. He travelled to Spain to complete his education. His imagination was fired by the ideas of the Age of Enlightenment. In particular, he studied the economic teachings of the French Physiocrats. They explained that the agricultural economy produced a revenue – the rent of land – which was the natural source of funding for the state. Rents should be collected by a unique tax to fund infrastructure and the services people shared in common. He translated François Quesnay's book *Maximes générales de Gouvernement Economique d'un Royaume Agricole* (*General Maxim's of the Economical Government in an Agricultural Kingdom*).

He promoted this financial policy when he returned to the Viceroyalty of the Rio de la Plata. He believed it was the best way to secure the development of the territory. His proposal was fiercely opposed by the landowners who were born in Spain and who had chosen to make their fortunes out of the rich pampas. They were known as *peninsulars*. Belgrano, who was born in Buenos Aires, was classed as a *criollo* – a notch below the *peninsulars*.

Belgrano understood that the land owners were abusing their power, but they had Spain on their side. The rejection of fiscal reform encouraged him to work for more autonomy from the colonial power. He was active in the May Revolution of 1810. He was elected a member of the Primera Junta that took power. He struck up a relationship with Bernardino Rivadavia, with whom he embarked on a diplomatic mission to Europe to seek support for the revolutionary government. Rivadavia would prove to be the politician with the vision to base the new state's revenue system on the rents of the fertile lands of the vast territory which it thought it now controlled.

The Verdict of History

Following the break from Spain, a constitution was enacted which promised land "for all men around the world who may want to dwell in it". And land there was aplenty. Today, the territory is occupied by a population of 39 million people. There was more than enough land for everyone to make a good living. And yet, the nation is blighted by misery. On December 9, 2010, the television cameras focused on thousands of families who squatted in a public park called "American Indian" in the Villa Soldati neighbourhood of Buenos Aires. The violent occupation of other locations followed, as landless people registered their desperate plight. On Christmas Eve, in the words of one observer, Dr. Héctor Sandler, a professor of law at the University of Buenos Aires, "hell broke loose in Constitution Square".[1]

Landless millions in a richly endowed land. About 85% of the population lives on less than 1% of the territory. Ninety per cent remains under-populated on what is some of the most fertile tracts in the world. James Busey (1916-2007), as professor of political science and specialist on Latin America at the University of Colorado, noted that Argentina possessed petroleum, iron, copper, uranium, tin, lead, zinc and the silver which originally attracted Spanish adventurers. Most importantly, the plains to the north, west and south of Buenos Aires – about the size of Texas – has some of the richest black soil on earth. But the problem, as Busey saw it, was that "Argentina is an almost empty country". He compared Argentina to France, which was one-fifth the size of the South American territory, in these terms:

---

1   Personal communication to the present author, December 24, 2010.

If Argentina were to have the same density of population, as it very well could given the richness of its pampa soil, it would have no less than 275m people instead of only about 34m.[2]

If the economic model had been the inclusive one advocated by Belgrano and Rivadavia, incomes could have been similar to those in the United States. Instead, by 2005, Argentina's *per capita* income was just one-third of the US's. What went wrong?

The Land of Plenty

Argentina's fate was not prescribed by natural law. We may visualise how she *might* have developed by engaging in a counterfactual exercise.

Argentina originally embarked on a trajectory of development that would have led to a radically different society to the one revealed by today's statistics. In the May Revolution of 1810, the people took their destiny into their hands when they chose not to remain locked into the European model. The key pillar of the new society was the law on property, with its analogue, the doctrine of public finance. Argentinians favoured the vision of a wholesome society. The policy that would deliver that outcome was the Law of Emphyteusis. It was enacted in 1824 by Rivadavia who, when he became president of the Argentinian provinces in 1826, founded banks, a currency system and schools. He forged commercial treaties with the UK, which became Argentina's biggest importer of beef. His key innovation, however, was fiscal.

Rivadavia's philosophy was crystallised in a single sentence which he recorded in his private papers: "No-one can make use of the land so as to prevent others to use it too." His vision was of a constitution constructed on a moral foundation. No-one would be excluded from nature's resources. Everyone would be entitled to an equal right of access to land.

The test of Rivadavia's notion of equality was a tough one: *does it protect the right of future generations to enjoy equal access to the nation's natural resources*? Busey summarised the intent of the fiscal policy which Rivadavia implemented:

He saw to enactment of a radical land reform measure designed to prevent development of the system of great estates so common in the Spanish domains. His device was to keep ownership of land in custody of the nation – i.e., the government – but to rent parcels out to individuals and companies who would use them ... occupants would be compelled to use the land

---

2 Busey (1995:50).

economically in order to pay their rents to the state, [and so that] immense,
inadequately utilized estancias *(or* haciendas*) would not emerge.*[3]

No matter how large the population grew, no matter how much of the land was
held in private use, *no-one would be disadvantaged by the claims of previous
generations.* They would all share in the public services continuously funded
out of the rents of land. No matter how few the number of land owners, they
could not monopolise the power that accrued from the control of life-sustaining
resources. That power would be democratised, by being diffused throughout
the population.

The annual fee, or rent, was called "canon". According to Dr. Sandler:
"Argentina was the first country in the modern world that attempted to secure
the equal access to land by the rule of law".[4] Land was held on 20-year leases,
with rent payable at the annual rate of 8% on the value of pasture lands and
4% on cultivated land. Rents would be revised at the end of 10 years by juries
drawn from the neighbourhood. With the land tax in place, Argentinians
would be free to develop the economy that reflected the formation of a new
social identity. The formula offered the prospect of a new kind of communal
solidarity.

At first, the economy flourished. The country became one of the richest
nations (in terms of GDP *per capita*) by the end of the 19th century.[5] And yet,
millions of immigrants – they came from practically every country in Europe –
were denied access to the good life.

Argentina had morphed into a classic case of a failed state.

Clearing the Land
The Spaniards who first colonised the hinterland around Buenos Aires in the
16th century found that the territory was not densely populated by Indian
tribes. Hunter-gatherers co-existed with those who farmed and lived in stone
villages.

With the arrival of Europeans, the clash of cultures was unavoidable. An
understanding was needed, to minimise the friction and permit the fusion of
a cultural space that would make peaceful co-existence possible. But the white
colonists did not bring such a blueprint with them. Instead, their cattle ranches
displaced the animals that were hunted by the Indians. This resulted in cattle
rustling by the tribal peoples.

---

3 Busey (1995: 51).
4 Personal communication, January 2, 2011.
5 Harrison (2008: 140-144).

With independence from Spain, work began to instil order into the process of colonisation. In 1833, the owner of the largest *hacienda*, Juan Manuel de Rosas – described by Busey as a tyrant[6] – led a successful operation to pacify the aboriginals. But it was still possible to negotiate a settlement that united all races and cultures. The key to such an outcome was the doctrine of property rights. If the Europeans honoured the philosophy of sharing the land in ways that resonated with traditional sentiments, might it not be possible to evolve a unique model of social development?

In the years which followed the enactment of the Law of Emphyteusis, land owners extended their holdings and built up their regional political strength to the point where they were able to abolish the law in 1869. Congressmen alleged that the doctrine which underpinned the sharing of nature's resources was "communist". This, even though the reciprocal of the rental payments was freedom from taxes on labour and the products of entrepreneurs! The population was unable to defend the spirit of Rivadavia's law. Many of them were to pay a terrible price.

- In 1827, over 6.5m acres had been rented to 112 corporations and individuals. Of these, 10 received more than 133,000 acres each. By 1830, 538 individuals and corporations had received 20m acres – one man holding 880,000 acres, and another, 735,000.[7]
- The land barons became "adept in dodging their obligations ... These new masters of pasture and grain field became the political and economic dictators of the nation. Their monopoly of the soil retarded settlement of European immigrants on their own farms, provoked the unhealthy growth of cities, and delayed the development of democratic institutions".[8]

Acquisitive land owners extended their estates further into the heartlands of the tribes, trampling the rights of the nomadic groups that hunted and gathered their food. Cattle stealing continued until, in 1872, a serious incursion was launched that resulted in the deaths of 300 *criollos* and the theft of 200,000 head of cattle.

In 1875, Adolfo Alsina, the Minister of War, proposed a plan to populate the desert without disturbing the Indian population. Cattle rustling continued, however, until Julio Argentina Roca became president. He believed in a final solution: exterminate or ban the Indians from the territory. He launched the Conquest of the Desert on these terms:

---

6 Busey (1995: 54).
7 Herring (1968:700).
8 Herring (1968:700)

Our self-respect as a virile people obliges us to put down as soon as possible,
by reason or by force, this handful of savages who destroy our wealth and
prevent us from definitely occupying, in the name of law, progress and our
own country, the richest and most fertile lands of the Republic.[9]

Roca achieved his ethnic cleansing with waves of attacks on aboriginal settlements
all the way to the Rio Negro. The attacks in 1879 were launched with the aid of
breech-loading Remington rifles acquired from the United States. The Mapuches
migrated to neighbouring Chile. Roca sent Col. Conrado Villegas into the field
to conquer the Neuquen Province, displacing the Indians until they surrendered
in the battle that took place on October 18, 1884. The territory was pacified
and Patagonia was colonised. By the time of the census of 1947, just 2.5% of the
population of over 16m people were of mixed European and Indian extraction.

The doctrine of land ownership embedded in the soil of Argentina was
underpinned by violence. The decades into the 20th century took their
inevitable course as the fabric of society was further degraded. The collapse
into totalitarianism began with a military coup in 1930.

In 1932, new taxes were adopted. Hector Sandler analysed the doctrine of
those taxes in these terms:

Anyone who produces, saves and consumes shall be punished. Anyone
who speculates on land shall be rewarded.

As the ranch owners grew richer, the mass of people grew poorer. Shanty towns
sprang up. Dwellings constructed from sheets of tin and cardboard were erected
alongside railway tracks, roads and vacant lots on the margins of cities. No-one
cared for the landless – the "shirtless ones" (*descamisados*), as General Juan
Peron called them. The generals were ruthless. The nation suffered the disgrace
of the "disappearances" – state-sponsored kidnapping and murder of people
who were perceived as threats to the rule of the military juntas.

By the time of the bicentenary of the May Revolution, there was no trace of
the society that might have been.

An Indicator of Trauma
System-wide social crises are most immediately registered in the financial
sector. The monetary aggregates did, indeed, expose Argentina as a failed state.
By the end of the 20th century, the economy was shattered by what became the
largest financial default in history, involving nearly $100bn of debt. In 2005,

---

9   Quoted in Roth (2002: 45).

when creditors renegotiated the terms of their contracts, they lost about 75% of their initial investments. But these numbers fail to convey the true scale of the costs inflicted by the failure to sustain Rivadavia's financial model. Another statistical index tracks one of the most traumatic responses to a failed society.

The bordellos in Buenos Aires were the interface between the displacement of the peoples in the Old World and the failure of public policy in the New World.

In a land of rich possibilities, there was no excuse for the deprivation which afflicted the migrants. That deprivation was manifest in the victimisation of women. Donna J. Guy, an American professor and specialist in Argentinian history, summarised the sociology of prostitution in these terms.

> *European prostitutes in Buenos Aires, for the most part, came from poverty-stricken families and worked out of desperation. Marginalised by the industrial revolution, driven from their homelands by hunger or by family, political, or religious persecution, they saw immigration to a new land or even a new continent as the key to survival.*[10]

But the emerging social system in Argentina was not structured to give those people a fair chance of making an honourable living. Between 1889 and 1901, 6,413 women were registered as prostitutes in Buenos Aires. Of these, almost 19% were Russian, 13% were Italian, and 9% from France. The proportion representing Argentinians (25%) rose to 43.9% in 1934. For women in the provinces who did not migrate to the capital, work in bordellos like those of Tandil was the alternative to unemployment. In the capital of Córdoba province "most Cordobese prostitutes were '*chinas*' (poor Indian or mestiza women), and their pimps were usually their Creole lovers".[11]

Contemporary entertainment is revealing. The tango is one such clue to cultural formation – or rather, its disintegration – in the bordellos frequented by the landless gauchos of the Río de la Plata. Prostitutes were the first women to dance the tango, expressing a social narrative that represented their condition in the waterfront areas of Buenos Aires and Montevideo (in Uruguay), from the 1860s to the 1930s. It took just 20 years for the raunchy displays on the dance floor to find acceptance in the salons of the middle classes. "Legs were used not only for movement, but also for the man to kick his partner in ritual fashion," writes Donna Guy.

The implicit violence between the sexes was just one manifestation of the pathologies that originated with the separation of people from the opportunities for employment. Women continued to be at the end of that chain of violence

---

10   Guy (1991: 7).
11   Guy (1991: 74).

Box 7:1
Forestalling the Cultural Commons

When people generate a stream of rents from nature's resources, they originate and deepen new layers of commons – the cultural commons. The material resources become available to fund people to leave the fields and deploy their skills in workshops and offices; buying others the time to reflect and experiment in the arts and sciences. For this to happen, however, the arts of governance have to guarantee people's access to land. No society has been able to develop a democratic financial system that is detached from a democratic tenure of land.

In Argentina, when the *latifundistas* declared themselves owners of the nation's rents, they necessarily deprived the people of the resources to create and evolve their culture. As tenants, the landless population is annexed to the lives of the land lords. As such, their culture was, at best, one that helped them to cope with their deprivation. At worst, they were, in a literal sense, no more than servile to the wishes of the land owners; just like the cattle that roamed the pampas. This was a wounding of the population with profound psychosocial, and biological, implications. Sociology, the science of society, lacks the diagnostic tools to analyse these pathologies.

despite the international treaties affirming their rights. The most visible images of their deprivation are those of fatherless families subsisting in the slums around the cities of the geographical South. The essence of their plight was articulated by a woman whose eyes filled with tears as she faced a television camera in Buenos Aires on Christmas Eve, 2010. Defiantly, she declared: "We don't want subsidies, we don't want welfare plans, all we want is a piece of land where we can take care of our children".

Millenarian Philosophies

The history of the peoples who converged on Patagonia, and who occupied the foothills of the Andes, emphasises that evolution into the modern era was accompanied with choices. They *could* have developed a social system markedly different from the one which manifested itself. But once they locked themselves into a doctrine that determined who were the owners of the benefits from land, those choices narrowed markedly. For cultural evolution is contingent on the nature of the tenure of land (Box 7:1).

A country richly endowed with minerals and fertile soil like Argentina ought to have avoided the trauma of despair and poverty. But in the 19th century, a few people ruthlessly hijacked the nation. Blight descended on the countryside, wrote James Busey, because:

Box 7:2
The Cannibalisation of Humanity

American psychiatrist Judith Herman has examined how totalitarian systems de-humanise people, even "to the extent of taking away the victim's name".[1] The Argentinian fascists led by General Videla deployed the ultimate in de-humanisation: removing 500 babies, some from their mothers' wombs. The mothers were killed, the babies handed to childless military couples. This was the ultimate form of psycho-biological terrorism to torment society and preserve the rent-seeking culture.

Videla, in an interview with the magazine *El Sur* in 2010, disclosed that he kept the Catholic hierarchy informed of his regime's policy of "disappearing" political opponents. He confirmed what was suspected by critics at the time: Catholic leaders offered advice on how to "manage" the policy. Church officials offered to inform families looking for "disappeared" relatives that they should desist, but they agreed to take this action only if they were certain the families would not use the information to denounce the junta.[2]

1 Herman (2001: 93).
2 Hennigan (2012).

a very few powerful families monopolize most of the land in enormous estancias (landed estates), and are satisfied to use it inadequately, usually for extensive livestock grazing. With but small investment per hectare, they can accumulate enormous wealth.

Imagine, in the land of the black soils, the many organically proportioned settlements that could have flourished across the country, grounded in social solidarity, defined by communal arts and personal achievements! This did not happen even though, at the beginning of the 20th century, Argentina had the material and intellectual resources to grow its economy to a level comparable to that of the United States. David Rock writes the epitaph of a shameful cultural legacy from Europe:

Until at least the First World War she was generally regarded as being capable of repeating in Latin America the phenomenal expansion of the United States. Now she is more frequently seen as just another bankrupt and stagnant, weak and exploited centre of 'South America', compelled to exist in the future, as she now has done for so long in the past, in a maelstrom of disorganisation and decay.[12]

12 Rock (1975: 1).

Will Argentina redeem herself in the 21st century? The knowledge exists to re-base the economy on foundations of the twin pillars of virtuous growth: economic efficiency and social justice. That knowledge was revived in the early 1970s

Aldo Ferrer, the Minister of Economics, commissioned a report from Fernando Skornik Gerstein, a lawyer who was working for a federation of agrarian cooperatives. Taxation, wrote Gerstein, deterred value-adding free enterprises while rewarding the under-use of land. He proposed rental charges on all land, urban and agrarian. The report aroused anxiety in the department of the Director General of Agrarian Economics. *Bases para un Régimen Impositivo sobre la renta del suelo* was published with a disclaimer: it was the private opinion of the author. This was yet another case of the fear-driven auto-censorship which pollutes the knowledge that compromises governance.

In the Argentinian case, there was good reason for fear. Rumours began to circulate about the prospect of a military coup. Gerstein was warned that he should pack his bags. In December 1975, shortly before General Videla's coup in March 1976, he relocated to Spain. Opponents of the coup were arrested, never to be seen again. The head of the Catholic Church, Cardinal Raúl Francisco Primatesta (1919-2006), refused to meet with mothers of the disappeared. He prohibited the clergy from denouncing state violence even when the death squads targeted priests who did have the courage to criticise the regime. The National Commission on the Disappearance of Persons estimated the number of victims murdered by the military at 9,000 (1976-1983). Others put the number at three times that number. Mothers continue to hold vigils for their missing children to this day (Box 7:2).

Argentina remains a society in trauma. Its policies flout its own constitution, which declares (Ch.1, Art. 16): "Equality is the basis of taxation and public burdens". That was not a principle acknowledged by the landowners of the province of Buenos Aires when they deployed extra-democratic tactics to prevent elected representatives from discussing the taxation of their land. Their actions exposed the vacuous nature of equality, when that concept is not synchronised to its fiscal pre-condition.

On May 31, 2012, the Buenos Aires Governor, Daniel Scioli, tried to overcome the opposition by signing a decree that aimed to force the re-valuation of rural land. This would pave the way for the provincial legislature to pass a Bill that would increase taxes on land. Scioli claimed that such a tax hike would strengthen the equity of the tax system. Farmers mobilised their opposition, promising strikes and roadblocks if the Bill was passed.[13] They opposed the policy even though it would increase their own incomes (Box 7:3).

---

13 Flint (2012).

Box 7:3
The Unique Tax on Land

Following the financial crisis of 2001, the Argentinian government was so desperate for revenue that it imposed a 35% tax on the export of commodities. This curbed output and reduced living standards. What would happen if that tax were abolished and replaced by a 35% levy on the rents of farmland? That question was posed by two economists at the National University of La Plata. They answered it for the province of Buenos Aires.[1]

The export tax had significantly depressed land rents. The scholars found that, by removing the tax on exports, rents would rise by 140%. In other words, the export tax was actually a levy on rent, the revenue extracted indirectly from the land owners. A 35% tax levied directly on rents would leave more money in the pockets of farmland owners. It would also encourage further production, which would create jobs for the unemployed. And yet, when the provincial government decided to reform land taxation in May 2012, the landowners went so far as to block the elected representatives from gathering a quorum to debate the proposal.

---

1 Piffano and Sturzenegger (2011).

Leaderless World: A Prognosis

I F Argentina is representative of the middle income countries of the global South, we have no reason to believe that their governing elites are better equipped to offer reasoned leadership to the world of the 21st century. They represent a culture of narcissism, which forestalls the development of their communities. Symbolic of that class is Cristina Kirchner, the President of Argentina who sought to enhance her political popularity by re-launching the dispute with Britain over the possession of the oil-rich Falkland Islands. Mrs. Kirchner was a lady with an eye for the main chance; especially one that promised a flow of rents.

Mrs. Kirchner and her late husband Nestor had amassed a fortune out of land speculation. When her husband became president in 2003, their fortune was estimated at 7m pesos ($2.35m). From then on, the family fortune soared by 900% over the course of seven years. By 2010, their assets worth $18m were made up of 27 houses, apartments, stores and hotel businesses. When complaints were laid that they had benefited from a politically-motivated hand-out of $300m in prime land, the prosecutor assigned to investigate was Nestor

Kirchner's niece.[14] In one land deal, Nestor Kirchner bought two hectares for $50,000 and flipped the land two years later, selling to a supermarket corporation for $2.4m.

The Kirchner dynasty did not originate the corruption that is a feature of life in Argentina. When Cristina succeeded her late husband as president, she may not have understood the irony behind the accusation of land grabbing that she levelled against Britain as she whipped up hysteria over the Falklands. It seems dangerous to rely on the political class for enlightened leadership. But what of the social scientists who prescribe strategies for resolving geo-political conflicts? Are their analyses objective and reliable? That is what we would expect from the work by two distinguished scholars from prestigious American universities who have developed an analytical apparatus for examining nations under stress.

Daren Acemoglu and James Robinson, professors at MIT and Harvard, sought the answers to *Why Nations Fail*. Their analysis is grounded in two significant concepts: *inclusive* and *extractive*. What they do not offer, however, are definitions of these two notions in economic language that could pinpoint the causes of stress in the structure of economies like Argentina's, so we would not expect them to formulate corresponding remedies.

Their book is a survey of history that purports (according to the sub title) to explain *The Origins of Power, Prosperity, and Poverty*. It is endorsed by five Nobel laureates and a battery of distinguished professors of history and from the social sciences. So we may assume that the analytical apparatus they offer is as good as it gets, conforming to the standards applied in the social sciences.

Their analysis runs to 500 pages. Here, surely is a tome that would empower policy-makers with the understanding of why (for example) rich nations are blighted with large numbers of impoverished citizens. Predictions and robust proposals for reforms: those are the qualities of a good theory required by statesmen who seek the well-being of their nations. Would they learn how to guide their nations in the 21st century, by reading Acemoglu and Robinson's survey of world history?

The authors admit that their theory is so abstract that there would be difficulties with their predictions. So much for their crystal ball.

What about recommendations for policies that would overcome poverty? Again, they are cautious. The "no silver bullet" card is again brought into play. Replacing extractive with inclusive institutions would be difficult because "there are no easy recipes for achieving such a transition".[15] Not much help for statesmen searching for policies to re-base their nations on new foundations.

---

14   Mount and Sherwell (2012).
15   Acemoglu and Robinson (2012: 436).

Despite their extensive survey, the social scientists offer fatuous conclusions which fail to cast beacons of light into the future. *Why Nations Fail* fails because the authors do not incorporate into their analysis the formula for cheating that now defines world culture.

Inclusive institutions, they declare, are those embedded in today's prosperous nations. Conversely, "Nations fail economically because of extractive institutions".[16] But as we have seen, capitalism is constructed on two pillars: (i) the inclusive mechanisms of the value-adding economy, and (ii) the extractive mechanisms of the Predator Culture. By failing to grapple with this reality, Acemoglu and Robinson are unable to offer sensible insights into the plight of countries like Argentina.

They note that Argentina grew rapidly in the 50 years to 1920. GDP matched that of the United Kingdom. And yet, their verdict on that outcome is odd. Argentina was an extractive nation, they conclude, while the UK – because of its adoption of universal suffrage – was an inclusive society.

- Institutions, rather than geography, are said by Acemoglu and Robinson to be the relevant elements for determining the character of a nation. How do Argentina's riches fit into this analysis? A century ago her GDP, which matched the UK's, was due to the rich natural endowment, *not* her institutions. Maize and cattle were valuable exports during a period of high world prices.

Geography and the resource endowment of location are an inextricably vital part of the equation. But the determinant of whether the society is inclusive or extractive depends entirely on how the rents are distributed. In both Argentina and Britain, the rents were privatised for the exclusive benefit of a privileged minority. To achieve inclusive outcomes, in both cases the policy reform that was needed was the one institutionalised by Rivadavia, and promulgated in the People's Budget (1909). Acemoglu and Robinson are silent on that proposition. They settle for empty pronouncements like "The solution to the economic and political failure of nations today is to transform their extractive institutions toward inclusive ones".[17] That affords no clue to policy-makers as to what they should do. If inclusiveness is defined as universal suffrage, Argentina today qualifies as an inclusive society!

- According to Acemoglu and Robinson, the UK shifted towards inclusivity a century ago with the adoption of one-man-one-vote. Did that empower

16   Acemoglu and Robinson (2012: 398).
17   Acemoglu and Robinson (2012: 402).

the people? Not sufficiently so for the People's Budget to be implemented. The reputation of the UK as an inclusive nation was further damaged in 1934 when Phillip Snowden's tax on land was dishonoured by Parliament. Should Britain really be classed as an inclusive nation?

The inclusive/extractive model developed by two star scholars leaves policy-makers bewildered. It is supposed to point governments in the direction of policies that would equalise power, increase prosperity and reduce poverty. In fact, compliance with the model would cause rich nations to sustain the *status quo* (manufacturing poverty on an awesome scale). Low-income nations that followed the advice from Acemoglu and Robinson would adopt Western institutions which favour the legal protection of free riders (as happened in post-Soviet Russia).

Why Nations Fail turns out not to be a manual for UN diplomats seeking to redraw the maps of poverty. And how could it be otherwise? The authors fail to deconstruct the concept of property. They celebrate the private ownership of land as a pillar of prosperity and, *ipso facto*, as an inclusive institution.

As for poverty, that is a reality without a theoretical explanation. Was it too dangerous for them to dig deep? For breaking poverty down into its component parts would reveal evidence which explodes their characterisation of "inclusive" societies. Most nations in the inclusive club are rich because their institutions *excluded* large numbers of people from the opportunity to be prosperous. The Acemoglu and Robinson theory, which eulogises Western "dynamism", turns out to be a contradiction in terms. Their inclusive nations (with some exceptions) are shamed by a history of extractive behaviour, practises which continue to this day.

Broadly speaking, intellectuals locked into the academic and lobbying institutions of the West have lost the competence to understand the world as it is experienced by people on the ground. But might this gloomy prognosis be modified by the nations of the East? Some analysts interpret the collectivist paradigm as favouring the development of an inclusive society.[18] Is this what we might expect from the leadership of China as the next super-power?

---

18 Stevenson (1991: 89-105).

Chapter 8:

Perfect Storm in the Middle Kingdom

WHEN the Communist Party began to dismantle China's command economy in the 1980s, its aim was "Capitalism with Chinese characteristics". There could be no return to the capitalism that Marx and Mao had demonised.

What emerged was an economics of apartheid. The people were cheated of the post-capitalist culture which they might have evolved for themselves, if they had been free to choose.

Capitalism with communist characteristics.

That was the fate of the people. A fate that was not planned. It emerged because of the failure of governance. By default, those who were supposed to be the guardians of the people's property sanctioned the theft of the nation's social income.

In medieval Europe, peasant communities lacked the tools to fend off the rent-seekers. They did not command the means of communication. The insidious aristocracies were able to capture the rents by surreptitious strategies until – too late – people realised what had been done to them. Among the imperial nations, the people of France were alone in launching a popular uprising that tempered the loss of land.

China need not have endured this fate. Her leaders proclaimed allegiance to a doctrine which ring-fenced land as public property. There would be no scope for the rent-seeking virus to incubate in the body politic. The Party, and the individuals stationed in the Politburo, were the guardians of the inalienable property of the people. This meant that there could be no systematic appropriation of the value which the population co-operatively created, because that value was anchored in land that remained their common property. *The public purse could not be cheated, so the people of China would have the money to establish a socially responsible market economy.*

That was the theory.

Today, we can track the corruption of the public purse in real-time. This is the study of the way cheats suck the cultural life blood out of the community.

The scam originated in the shadows, behind closed doors, the initiatives of individuals who were closest to the public purse. They were called public servants. Not sword-brandishing barons and knights. Pen-pushing bureaucrats. In both cases, the key to the appropriation of rent was control inside the corridors of power. Then, in Europe, and now, in Asia, the financial outcome was the depletion of the public's revenue.

In Europe, rents were captured by first converting land into private ownership. In China, the law continued to vest ownership in the people, through the state. The rent-seekers realised that this was not an obstacle. There was nothing in the constitution which said the *rents* belonged to the nation. And so, through the internet's social media, people anywhere in the world may now track the way a nation loses the freedom to choose its future. China provides the empirical evidence that, when the 1st Law of Social Dynamics is breached, the essence of humanity is undermined. When the social revenue is misappropriated by a minority, the majority are impoverished socially, economically and psychologically.

Over the years to 2030, China will be subjected to enormous internal stresses as the dispossessed peasants – those unable to find urban employment, traumatised by yet another experiment in social engineering – withdraw their allegiance to the Party. The violent consequences will be felt globally. For in the past, the safety valve that protected the rent-seeking elites was the conquest of other people's territories. Spatial expansion delivered two benefits: (i) the flow of rents into the home territory; and (ii) space into which some of the displaced people could be expelled. This reduced tensions at home. China, now on course to be captured by the Predator Culture, will conform to that model, because it will have no choice. It will have to embark on the conquest of other people's territories, to sustain the appetites of the rent-seekers. The end-game, and its alternative, was determined in the years following the fall of the last emperor, Xuāntŏng, in 1911.

Choosing a Social Paradigm

The fall of the Qing dynasty was followed by a period of ideological turbulence. The contest for power was between the champions of two contrasting doctrines. Two leaders set the course of China's bipolar history in the first half of the 20th century.

Can a few individuals really shape the destiny of a nation? Philosopher Bertrand Russell reflected on that question and identified one of the exceptional individuals in that era:

The important men in the age that ended about 1930 are Edison, Rockefeller, Lenin, and Sun Yat-sen. With the exception of Sun Yat-sen these were men devoid of culture, contemptuous of the past, self confident, and ruthless. Traditional wisdom had no place in their thoughts and feelings; mechanism and organisation were what interested them.[1]

Sun Yat-sen (1844-1925) stood apart from this panel of capitalists and communists. He was a revolutionary who came out of a land whose past was pitted with the blood of landless peasants. So on his travels to Europe and the US he studied the philosophies that were then influential, particularly those of John Stuart Mill and Henry George.

Mill, the English liberal, prescribed a gradualist approach to the adoption of a fiscal reform which would eventually result in most of the rent of land being paid into the public purse. He preferred to leave existing rents alone, and to recover future increments for the public's benefit. Henry George was unwilling to compromise with justice. Rent was community-created, and all of it should be collected to fund public services.

Sun Yat-sen plotted with others for several decades to overthrow the Qing dynasty. He persisted, and in 1912 became the first president of the new republic. His guiding doctrine was *San Min Chu I* (The Three Principles of the People). Those principles would offer a rent-led renewal programme to empower the people to define a post-feudal society of their choosing. Sun's political support came from the Kuomintang, the party opposed by communists. The struggle for the soul of China proved to be bloody, and complicated by regional warlords. Sun died without being able to institute his economic reforms. His legacy lived on.

Following the Second World War, General Chiang Kai-chek's Kuomintang forces were defeated by the communists. They retreated to the island of Formosa, 180 kilometres off China's south-eastern coast. The victorious Chairman Mao and his Little Red Book painted the mainland red with the bloody glories of the Cultural Revolution. He presided over the deaths of 45 million or more people during the Great Leap Forward (1958-61). The fate of the people of Formosa was a textbook case of prosperity enjoyed by people who were free to choose their way of life. The Kuomintang renamed the island Taiwan. Landlords were pensioned off, the land was handed to the tillers, and Sun Yat-sen's land value tax was implemented. The first Asian Tiger was born. While millions died on the mainland, sacrificed on the altar of communist utopia. On the island off their shore, millions enjoyed the freedoms that began to turn Asia into a powerhouse of entrepreneurship.

---

1   Russell (1949:200)

- Taiwan industrialised. Her enterprises moved into the high-tech sector to convert the dreams of Silicone Valley geeks into the hardware that turned up on the desks of people's homes and offices in the West.
- China ran up the flag of defeat. The Politburo remained in political power but yielded to the logic of the market. Collective farms were converted into private plots, and some loss-making state enterprises were privatised.

How did Mao's "scientific socialism" compare to Sun Yat-sen's moral economy? Despite phenomenal rates of growth in the catch-up period (1980-2010), China's *per capita* GDP in 2011 was US$8,400. Taiwan's was $37,900. Taiwan was listed 27th in the world league table (CIA World Factbook). China was 117th. The gap in material fortunes provides one measure of the degree to which the communist model robbed people of their potential. But the ideologues of the Communist Party were entitled to a second chance. When Deng Xiaoping implemented his reform programme in 1979, the Politburo was free to adopt the tax-and-tenure arrangements that incorporated the wisdom of Sun Yat-sen.

The Communist Party passed its definitive law on property in 2010. This affirmed people's right to own the property which they created. Capital was now in the private domain. Land, however, was deemed to be unique, and was retained in public ownership. By freeing people to create private enterprises on publicly owned land, China's future could be transformed. There would be no vested interest to oppose the funding policies prescribed by philosophers from Adam Smith through to J.S. Mill. People could create, own, and trade capital. They could produce goods and services for sale on the local and global markets, and the social sector would benefit from an increased flow of rents to fund infrastructure. Social solidarity would be enhanced in a multi-layered unity: partnerships in private enterprise and respect for the cultural and environmental commons.

This did not happen because the Politburo failed to understand the economics, let alone the sociology, of land.

What unfolded was a replay of the savage destruction of people's lives through the use of techniques applied to the Bororo in the South American rain forest and the peasants of the English commons. The Chinese in the heart of their communities were displaced. The shattering of the co-operative ethos was driven by a land grab orchestrated by the agents of government. Communities were reconfigured, families brusquely dislocated from rural hamlets and farms and relocated in regimented apartment blocks. Ancient hamlets were uprooted in favour of chicken hutch lifestyles, families fragmented as parents were forced to migrate in search of work, abandoning their children to other carers.

Rent privatisation began when the Politburo, the supreme authority, ordered local governments to find ways to fund much of their social services. They financed the construction of infrastructure by selling leases to land developers. To achieve this, they displaced people from homes, farms and workshops. Resistance to change was overcome with bribes and bulldozers.

Critically, land was under-valued at the point where the deals were done with developers. This provided the margin for the speculators to oil the contracts out of the rents which they knew would flow in the future. Rent, instead of being the social revenue, was converted into the means for corrupting governance. The new property magnates then realised that, to protect their privileges, they would have to expand their influence beyond the sphere of politics, to re-shape culture in general. This was necessary, to avoid a public backlash against their rent-seeking values. They began to use their fortunes to taint other institutions, as with endowments to universities.

Real estate became the searingly hot edge of the turbo-charged economy. As the new billionaires began to buy back the dynastic heirlooms that had been transported westwards during the colonial era, the plea from the peasants remained desperately familiar: "We just want the central government to solve this problem by giving us a bit of land so we can fill our bellies," said Zhuang Songkun, a 61-year-old fisherman. He spoke during one of the village sieges that sought to resist the rampage of the out-of-control growth of the economy.[2]

The economic take-off began in the early 1990s. This synchronised the Chinese economy into what had become a global property cycle. That cycle, as I have explained elsewhere, would grind to a halt in 2010.[3] The managers of state enterprises quickly learnt how to cash-in on the emerging property bubble. With access to state funds at favourably low rates of interest, the big state-owned enterprises got into the business of land speculation. "Money flows to the state-owned enterprises in the end and they can use this to get into real estate or to provide financing for others, so asset bubbles get more and more serious," reports Zhang Jun of Fudan University in Shanghai.[4]

Central government found itself flush with cash as the export of cheap products captured the markets of other nations. But regional and central governments were financially vulnerable to the vagaries of the boom/bust property market. By 2010, despite the phenomenal rise in property prices, they were bankrupt, owing US$1.7 trillion (based on official data from late 2010).

As the economy grew in those years up to 2010, riots broke out across the country. Communities fought against the appropriation of their land by

---

2 Anderlini (2011).
3 Harrison (2005).
4 Rabinovitch (2012).

municipal governments. Beijing sought to contain the discontent by offering the population a new slogan that would help them to cope with the disruption of their communities: Harmonious Society.

Too late.

China was trapped by the culture of cheating. China's entrepreneurs made their first fortunes from the value-adding factories they established near deep-sea harbours. Some of them then repeated what happened in Britain: they turned their attention to buying land leases and making their second fortunes by investing profits in real estate. Capital gains from land speculation eclipsed the rewards derived from entrepreneurship. Huge fortunes were reaped from land that was owned by the state. Leases made no provision for re-assessing the rising value of land so that the ground rents could be re-cycled back into the community. China was not alone among the former socialist countries in failing to fulfil its role as steward of the public property (Box 8:1).

Because of the pace of growth, stress within the real estate sector eclipsed the problems faced by families in the West. The affordability of housing was one indicator. In the trans-Atlantic economies in the years leading up to the land-led bust of 2008, the housing affordability index rose to a price-to-income ratio of 5-to-1. In China it exceeded 8-to-1 in 2008.

Rents that were turning politically connected entrepreneurs into billionaires were ploughed into property in Hong Kong. In 2012, some apartments were predicted to command sale prices of US$58m.[5] Cash that could have been invested in the formation of the capital that was needed to develop the rural hinterland, which would have raised productivity and wages, ended up in the pockets of land speculators. This, in turn (as happened at the beginning of England's Industrial Revolution), corrupted the entrepreneurial spirit. The work ethic was compromised as wage-workers with the right connections borrowed money at cheap rates to build buy-to-let property portfolios. In the run-up to the burst of the property bubble of 2010, about 18% of households in Beijing owned two or more properties. According to the mayor of Kunming, a city in the south-west, "It's very common for officials with power and with money to have four or five homes".[6]

Sky-high cities were dwarfed by the stratospheric prices charged for land. In an effort to "cool" the land market, in 2010 the Politburo adopted the classic capitalist policies which had repeatedly failed in the West. The central bank was instructed to curb credit. This limited the money that could be advanced as mortgages, but it also penalised the value-adding entrepreneurs who needed credit to keep their factories operating. The regulatory approach was not the

5 Tsui and Jacob (2012).
6 Rabinovitch (2012).

Box 8:1
Cross-fertilising the Cultures

The formula for instant riches was incubated in all of the former communist countries. The new class of oligarchs hedged their risks of an ideological reaction by directing some of their money westwards, pumping up the real estate markets of Europe and North America where they bought properties in the most expensive locations.

- Ukraine's richest oligarch, Rinat Akhmetov, paid £136m for an apartment overlooking London's Hyde Park. In addition, he spent a further £60m on interior work to the penthouse.[1]

The private fortunes extracted out of socially-created rent were spectacular.

- In Vietnam, Hoang Quoc Dinh was not tempted by the $2.4m for his residential plot of land overlooking a lake in the business district of Hanoi. He wanted $3.2m, more than the average paid for luxury apartments in Hong Kong or Tokyo.[2]

---

1 Thomas and O'Murchu (2011).
2 Bland (2011).

correct solution, but it was the safe one. It rested on economic reasoning that deflected attention from the source of the problem: the Politburo's failure to protect the social revenue. *The Party's leaders were responsible for creating the financial incentives that encouraged people to "over-heat" the property market.*

Home ownership achieved a rate of 80% in urban areas. But instead of enhancing the security of families, enormous stresses were imposed as house prices and rents rose faster than the increase in wages. Rents squeezed the disposable incomes of peasants and factory workers. Over the first full property cycle (1993-2011), house prices in Beijing rose by 2,242 per cent; per capita disposable income by 828 per cent. In Shanghai, house prices rose by 2,342 per cent; per capita disposable income by 743 per cent. The incentives skewed investment away from job-creating/wage-raising capital formation. Money went disproportionately into real estate. Incentives were distorted because the property tax levied a modest carrying cost on the ownership of empty apartments and houses.

The sociological implications of this financial process were epoch-making. By selling leases short, the Politburo began to lose control of The People's Republic. Citizens were embarked on a process that transformed their status into tenants of the rent-seekers, as middle class investors built buy-to-let portfolios. Rich, without having to add value to the nation's wealth, the new land tycoons purchased luxury homes in Paris, Vancouver and San Francisco.

Funding the Growth Models

China's growth model was fatally flawed. It reproduced the traumatic crises of capitalism. The failure to adopt the correct model for funding development was exposed in the development plans published by cities like Changsha in a central province. In 2012 it announced a US$130bn plan to stimulate growth. The city fathers' strategy was faithful to the State Council's plan that emphasised high tech industries and investment in infrastructure such as airports.

The flaw in the Changsha growth plan was the absence of detail on how investments would be funded. Credit at cheap rates of interest from the state would not solve the problem, because central government had announced its determination to prevent another property bubble. Lending to real estate, therefore, would be given a lower priority. That was the theory. The reality, on the ground, was more confusing.

Broadly speaking, there are two ways to fund the formation of capital invested in highways, schools or hospitals when these are in public ownership. One is to borrow from governments or the banks that create credit out of thin air. That raises the risk of inflation and indebtedness. The alternative route is to fund capital formation out of the value that is created by the investments themselves. That funding model needs to be broken down into its two parts.

- *Private investors* recover the cost of their investments out of the profits they generate when they combine their capital with labour to produce the products sold to consumers.
- *Public investors* (governments or social agencies) cover the cost of investments out of the value of the services they create. But if individual users are charged fees for the use of public services, this tends not to cover the heavy capital costs (such as investment in a highway or railway). But infrastructure *does* deliver the revenue to cover the cost of capital investments. It does so by generating rents.

For a nation to embark on the transformation of its economy – shifting from the agrarian to the urban/industrial model – it is essential that those rents are re-cycled back into the funding of the capital invested in the public sector. That eliminates the need to tax people's earned incomes.

As we have seen in the case of Britain, the major cause of tension in capitalism stems from the failure to collect the rents to defray the cost of infrastructure. In China, cities like Changsha, with a population of 7m people, would have no difficulty generating all the rent it needed to fund its development plan. The airport, mass transit systems, all would be *self-funding*. This financial model entails no risk of inflation, or of drawing credit away from other growth centres.

Box 8:2
Bring on the Cheats, Havana-style

The date on which a new phase of cheating began can be identified with precision: November 11, 2011. That date ought to be inscribed in the notebooks of the UN agencies that monitor the health of our globalised society. On that day in Cuba, citizens of the socialist revolution were empowered to buy and sell land. Rents were capitalised into selling prices.

Fidel Castro had expelled the cheats when he overthrew the corrupt regime of the sugar planters and American casino owners in 1959. His brother Raoul presided over the re-introduction of the predator virus under the mantle of a law that the communists decided was consistent with their socialist agenda. A few people will grow very rich in Cuba when American tourists are allowed back in droves to spend their dollars.

In fact, Changsha would be a net contributor to the central government's Treasury. But that is not going to happen, because Changsha is linked by its financial arteries into the culture of cheating.

Predators are stalking the producers. This will drive China's second property cycle to its peak in 2026, with a great crash in 2028. The launch of the new land boom was signalled by the price paid for a 38,869 sq m plot of land in Beijing's Haidian residential district in July 2012. The auction achieved a record price of 2.63bn yuan (€340m, £265m). Plaintively, the central government responded with a warning to local authorities to "continue to suppress speculative investments in housing".[7] Whistling in the wind. If speculators were willing to pay high prices, local governments would not forego the revenue. Over the new property cycle, China will endure deficits in two realms.

- *The social tragedy.* Land speculation will drive urban sprawl. Over-investment in real estate will oblige local governments to over-invest money in public services for neighbourhoods on the outer fringes of cities. Scarce capital will be stretched to accommodate the avarice of developers. Lopsided development will generate social discontent to test the power of the Politburo.
- *The eco-tragedy.* Over-exploitation of the natural environment will extend encroaching deserts, pollution of the atmosphere and drain away water fit for human consumption. This, because nowhere in the manuals of the globe-trotting economic consultants and Western financial institutions like the IMF is there advice on the self-funding model.

---

7 Anderlini (2012).

Box 8:3
Glasnost and Voices in the Wilderness

Mikhail Gorbachev instigated *glasnost* as the prelude to further evolution of the Soviet socialist model. He believed that land was unique and ought to remain in the public domain. He was supported by a few voices in the Western wilderness. These included three economists who had won the Nobel Prize (Franco Modigliani, James Tobin and Robert Solow). They signed an Open Letter advocating the need to base public finances on the rents of natural resources.[1]

Among the signatories was William Vickrey, a past president of the American Economic Association. He was to be honoured with the Nobel Prize (shared with James Mirrlees) in 1996. His studies documented how everyone – including land owners – would benefit financially if mass transit systems were funded out of the rents generated by such services.[2]

1 Noyes (1991: 225-230), which includes a technical appendix explaining how to phase in rent-based charges in socialist countries that had abandoned market prices in 1917.
2 Vickrey (1999).

In the scramble for growth, the other former socialist countries will also burrow deeper into the social crises foreshadowed in Europe (Box 8:2).

The Post-Capitalist Model

The return of the culture of cheating in socialist countries was not historically inevitable. In fact, according to Marx's theory of history, institutionalised cheating would be banished forever by the dictatorship of the proletariat, as socialism evolved into the state of communism.

When Mikhail Gorbachev signalled a shift in ideology in the late 1980s, the prospects for the people of the USSR *were* good. They were free to choose a post-capitalist model of development. They had that choice, because land and natural resources were in public ownership. This meant they were able to adopt the fiscal reforms that would encourage private enterprise while retaining the commons in public ownership (Box 8:3).

This did not happen, because Western economists were invited to provide advice on how to transform the command economy into free markets. The doctrinal errors of the 1990s continued into the world of the 2010s. But the ex-socialist countries were not alone in exposing their populations to the cheats. Western governments actively acknowledged their dependence on the development of real estate to rescue their economies from depression. Their delusions were wrapped up in the utopian thinking of consultants who,

Box 8:4
The Pursuit of Rents in Utopia

If we re-built civilisation from scratch, asked the author of an article in *New Scientist*, what would the world look like? The vision he assembled, based on the expert testimony of American social scientists and environmentalists, was of an urban civilisation shorn of the influences of land speculation. In this brave new world there would be no sprawl into the countryside, no over-exploitation of the most precious resource (water), and motor cars would be replaced by public transport.

All of these outcomes would be generated by the pricing system that based the public's finances on rental payments that reflected the value of the services provided by environmental and cultural commons. But the readers of *New Scientist* were given no hint of the financial reform that would remove the incentive to re-start the boom/bust cycle in this futuristic world.[1]

---

1 Holmes (2011).

chanting phrases like "sustainable development", reassured governments that there *was* a way to escape the harsh realities (Box 8:4).

But there can be no excuse for what happened in China. It had, on its doorstep, a living model that was already on its way to become a post-capitalist society.

Hong Kong.

The colony was returned to China in 1997 when the lease that was granted to Britain in the 19th century ran out. Because the British government was the leaseholder, not owner, it could not sell freehold titles. Leases were offered on long terms that gave secure possession of land. Rents were determined at auction, and the revenue was devoted to funding public services. That fiscal model became one of the best kept secrets in the world of textbook economics. Nobody discussed how most of the rents of the colony were re-cycled back into the funding of public services; not even the last Governor, Chris Patten, whose book purported to be an assessment of the British colony's achievements.[8] Hong Kong remains acknowledged as the No. 1 free and efficient economy in the world. Western media celebrate Hong Kong's achievements without giving credit where it is due (Box 8:5).

But despite her problems, China's development appears remarkable when set against the anaemic performance of Western economies. Fears mount that the West will suffer as it is eclipsed by Chinese economic expansion.

---

8 Patten (1998).

Forecasting the future is a hazardous business, as we see from Bertrand Russell's prognosis in the 1930s. He anticipated that the falling birth rate in rich nations would lead to a terminal crisis.

> *In the long run this will lead to mutinies, and reduce Europe to the condition of Haiti. In such circumstances, it would be left to the Chinese to carry on our scientific civilisation ...* [9]

Russell was correct in anticipating a demographically unbalanced West. But for Europe to be reduced to the condition of Haiti would require utter devastation (of the carpet-bombing kind that Germany experienced in 1945). But is China destined to create a scientific civilisation? Her rent-seekers are gnawing away at the power of the Politburo, whose tenuous grip is illustrated by attempts to stabilise the property market through monetary policy. The *Financial Times* reported on March 7, 2010: "Property developers find ways around Beijing's rules". While the rent-seekers fine-tune their market schemes to prey on the population, a confused Communist Party in Guangdong province worked out how to help the people to cope with their misery. It hoped for "a successful experiment of using free elections to reduce the anger felt by farmers faced with land-grabbing by party officials".[10] China's leaders are conspiring to reshape people's minds to accommodate the emerging anti-social system in which, already, the income gap between rich and poor is wider than the gap in the West.

Managed democracy will come to the aid of the cheats, as the elites proclaim their goals in the classic statements that expose the delusions of the leaders. Such was the pronouncement by Prime Minister Wen Jiabao, who claimed that

> *We aim to promote steady and robust economic development, keep prices stable and guard against financial risks by keeping the total money and credit supply at an appropriate level, and taking a cautious and flexible approach.*[11]

Western governments had tried to deliver on that agenda since the Depression of the 1930s. They failed. Repeatedly.

---

9   Russell (1949:177).
10 Jacob and Ping (2012).
11 Branigan (2012).

Box 8:5
Ministry of Misinformation

When commentators censure Western tax regimes, they occasionally draw attention to the low tax rates in Hong Kong. TV documentary film maker Martin Durkin used this technique to explain how indebted Western governments could cut taxes to escape the financial crisis of the last land-led property boom/bust. As evidence, he flew to Hong Kong to ride on a railway system that was so good it was "to die for".[1] Durkin failed to explain that Hong Kong's low taxes were possible for one reason alone: land is leased to users, so the bulk of the rents is recycled into funding public services. The capital cost of the superb metro was funded out of rents collected from commercial premises located around new stations.[2]

The inflow of millions of refugees from Mao's mainland placed great strains on the colony's finances. Even so, the colonial government built public housing and maintained social stability, facilitating the entrepreneurship that the liberated communists brought with them. They flourished in a market economy that was the antithesis of Mao's experiment in utopia.

---

1 *Britain's Trillion Pound Horror Story*, Channel 4, November 11, 2010.
2 Harrison (2006b: 87-94).

Leaderless World: A Prognosis

I F we cannot expect wise global leadership from the West (Ch.6), or from the global South (Ch.7), why should we expect it from the East?

Our litmus test is the extent to which the commons have been captured by rent-seekers. There comes a point where the cheats have to take control of society's power structure, if they wish to preserve their privileges. China already fails that test, and the Politburo knows it. That was evident when the Politburo panicked over the case of Xi Jinping.

Xi, anointed as the country's next president, wanted the people to view him as "clean". The last thing he needed was public discussion about the fortunes made by his family. His relatives owned real estate in Hong Kong valued at $55m. Bloomberg, the TV business channel, reported that family members also owned stakes in corporations valued at hundreds of millions of dollars. Bloomberg's news website was blocked by the Party to prevent it from further disseminating such information. The *Financial Times* provided a detailed survey headed "The family fortunes of Beijing's new few" (July 11, 2012). Xi Jinping had asked his relatives not to embarrass him during the period preceding his assumption of the positions of president and general secretary of the Party. But the princelings of the people in power found it difficult to contain their avarice. The Party, after all, did not forbid anyone from cashing in on the creativity of the people.

The trend towards the rent-seeking culture has deep implications for the way in which China, and the other socialist countries, affect the rest of the world over the next few decades. The Paris-based Institute for Security Studies analysed Russia in a research project co-sponsored by the European Union, and concluded:

> *Major shocks aside (such as a sudden drop in the price of oil), the next twenty years are likely to be characterised by inertial development and tactical adjustments perceived as indispensable for the Russian elites to preserve power and pursue rent-seeking opportunities. In the event of enduring socio-economic problems, xenophobic nationalism and extremism may radicalise the country, and exacerbate tensions in the neighbourhood.[12]*

That is what we expect from China. Western analysts, however, are canvassing a more benign future. One of them, Niall Ferguson, is a professor of history at Harvard. He promotes a theory of co-evolution. There was little chance of China "becoming increasingly aggressive. Both sides have a hell of a lot to lose. My money is on continued growth, market reform and, while not democracy, more constraints on party power and greater rule of law".[13] That comforting scenario lays a trap for the West. What might be the consequences if historians, who believe that we learn from history, turn out to be wrong (again)? Dare we rely on the theories of social scientists whose models are simplified to the point where, in the past, governments were lured into fatal policy errors?

The consensus view among Western commentators – expressed in their general admiration for China's economic accomplishments – is represented by the views of Daniel Bell, a professor of political theory at two universities in China: "The reform era has seen perhaps the most impressive poverty reduction in history".[14] That record might be more appropriately viewed as a tragic indictment of the communists. They crushed the creativity of people who were not allowed to pursue the Sun Yat-sen path to post-feudal development.

China is on course to become the super-power that applies the Western model of colonialism in the 21st century. Her gunboat diplomacy over islands

---

12 ISS (2012: 118).
13 Sherwell (2012). Ferguson's TV series on China was aired on Britain's Channel 4 in March 2012.
14 Bell (2012).

in the South China Seas alarms her neighbours, reviving memories of the territorial wars in Asia a century earlier. But the appraisal of how China will advance her territorial ambitions is hampered by Western analysts who remain locked in an intellectual straightjacket. They take for granted that *property rights are not at the source of the West's problems.* So why should China's adoption of Western property rights and financial policies drive the world towards conflict?

But as well as evolving the colonial model into the future, at home China is re-creating conditions that existed in the era of feudal dynasties. Periodically, discontented peasants rose up in rebellion, sparking revolts like the Taiping Rebellion (1851-1864) which claimed the lives of at least 20 million people. Herding the population into mega-cities will not inhibit people from mobilising their collective frustration in the future. Rural revolts of the past will surface as urban uprisings in the future. And when an authoritarian state like China needs to distract its people from their economic discontent, the time-honoured solution – to embark on a military adventure against a neighbour – remains a card to be played.

The best indicator of the state of China's health is her tax-and-tenure arrangements. But Western analysts continue to misinterpret the prospects because of their doctrinal prejudices. After all, they acclaim in unison, private land ownership enabled North American settlers to achieve high rates of growth compared to the settlers who migrated to South America. That is why the US and Canada out-performed Argentina and Brazil and the other Latin countries.[15] But that was in the 19th century. The 21st century is a different world, and China is driving herself into the epicentre of a perfect global storm.

- *Environmentally,* China's economic growth rate, coupled with the continued use of coal to fuel her factories, will speed up the rate of global warming. Scientists at the University of California (Berkeley) calculate that temperatures would rise by 1.5 degrees in the next 50 years: but this timescale could be reduced to 2030 by China.[16]
- *Socially,* Western nations will endure serious schisms when their populations discover that there can be no return to business-as-usual, in terms of employment and income. With China continuing to capture global markets, stresses such as those tearing apart the European Union will lead to geo-political confrontations with potentially fatal outcomes.[17]

---

15 Engerman and Sokoloff (1994).
16 Hickman (2012).
17 The application of Nazi symbols and language to taunt Germany, by Greeks and Italians suffering the stress of economic austerity policies, is a particularly unseemly indication of deteriorating international relationships.

- *Militarily*, China will seek foreign pastures as outlets for home-grown discontent. She is buying swathes of land across Africa and South America, ostensibly to grow food. Those territories will also serve as escape hatches for unemployed workers displaced from their rural villages in China.
- *Psychologically*, Westerners have been schooled to believe that their culture is pre-eminent. That is why they advocate democracy and the rule of law, the twin pillars of their vision of the free society. When it dawns on them that they are financially indebted to China and the sovereign wealth funds of the oil sheikhs, their collective trauma will deepen.

Western prognoses are grounded in obsolete paradigms. One of these is "structural transformation".[18] This is an economic theory derived from what analysts *think* happened in Western countries. If China conforms to the West's model, her economy will shift from Agriculture → Industry → Services. And so it may, in outward appearance. But that metamorphosis conceals a dangerous transformation in the structure of power. The value-creating part of the economy diminishes in response to the intrusions from the value-extracting culture. This trend does not feature in the perceptions of Western analysts. Their forecasting models are confined to three crude variables: the growth of population, the growth of productivity, and exchange rates in the financial markets. Predictions based on those categories are radically different from the ones that flow from the model that incorporates the influence of the culture of cheating. The two trajectories lead to conclusions that are worlds apart.

The population of China is not free to develop an authentic people-centred culture, one that serves the common good. The Communist Party is fostering a lethal nationalism designed to arm it with the power to manipulate popular sentiment. Patriotism is being cultivated around a culture of animosity towards neighbouring nations. Museums, memorial halls and exhibitions have been established across China to remind people of past military defeats, such as the Opium War with Britain (1840) and territorial conflicts with Japan in the 20th century.[19] By nurturing the sense of humiliation, China's leaders are strategically equipping themselves with the power to arouse sentiments like revenge, to be invoked against a military foe in the future.

For the sake of the survival of the West, we need realistic methods for appraising the trends that will seal the fate of nations in the 21st century.

---

18 Cox (2012: 163-164).
19 Wang (2012). When US secretary of state Hillary Clinton visited Beijing in September 2012, Reuters reported
    (*Financial Times*, September 5, 2012), that China warned America not to get involved in its "core national interests".
    This drew attention to regional disputes over the ownership of islands in oil and gas-rich seas.

Part 3

Re-calibrating the Western Mind

'Give us a guide,' cry men to the philosopher. 'We would escape from these miseries in which we are entangled. A better state is ever present in our imaginations, and we yearn after it; but all our efforts to realize it are fruitless. We are weary of perpetual failures; tell us by what rule we may attain our desire.'

Herbert Spencer, *Social Statics* (1850: 3)

The earliest civilisations died because their populations failed to safeguard their social revenue. Vibrant societies succumbed through the depletion of the vitality of their cultures. If the West continues to sanction cheating as a social process, it will endure the same fate.

The remedy for the great crises of our times is known, but the pathology of rent-seeking has compromised democratic institutions, religious sentiments and business practises. The culture of cheating has co-opted the agents who speak for the moral and political establishments.

A Great Awakening is needed. The mental and material resources are available to lay the foundations for a post-civilisation society. Mobilisation of those resources depends on the integrity of people who cherish the idea of justice, and their willingness to challenge the culture of cheating.

Chapter 9: The Decline of the West

A CENTURY ago, a German historian began to draft the thesis for a book which turned into a sensation. A disturbing drama was unfolding in Europe. Oswald Spengler (1880-1936) chronicled it in *The Decline of the West*. He located his analysis in a history extending back to classical Greece. This provided the broad canvas he needed to account for the cyclical rise and fall of civilisations. He was in no doubt that European culture was locked into the down phase.

In 1911, I proposed to myself to put together some broad considerations on the political phenomena of the day and their possible developments. At that time the World-War appeared to me both as imminent and also as the inevitable outward manifestation of the historical crisis.[1]

The first edition was published in 1918. Germany had been soundly defeated, and Spengler's book seemed to capture the mood of despair of the times. Millions had died, many of them gassed and machine gunned in muddy trenches in deeds that appeared to confirm that the West was, indeed, in decline. And yet, Europe recovered to fight another day. Literally, as it happens, staging displays of awesome violence. The West was locked into a perverse dialectic of destruction.

Spengler drew on the metaphysics of philosophers Johann Wolfgang von Goethe and Friedrich Nietzsche. He carefully assessed the evidence of deterioration in the cultural achievements which he claimed to observe all around Europe.

Consider the decline of art and the failing authority of science; the grave problems arising out of the victory of the megalopolis over the countryside, such as childlessness and land-depopulation; the place in society of a fluctuating Fourth Estate; the crisis in materialism, in socialism, in parliamentary government; the position of the individual vis-à-vis the state; the problem of private property with its pendant the problem of marriage.[2]

Spengler rejected the notion that the depletion of culture could be analysed using the scientific methods that were applied to electricity or gravitation. Our

---

1 Spengler (1932: Vol 1: 46).
2 Spengler (1932: Vol. 1, 48).

world, which he called a second Cosmos, did not conform to the rules of nature. History operated according to a logic that had been overlooked by historians.

Spengler's empirical observations were compelling. His metaphysics, however, distracted him from the explanation which might identify policies capable of rescuing the West. And yet, revealingly, he highlighted evidence which bears out my contention that, supported by the correct reforms, civilisations *are* sustainable. They need not terminate in Dark Ages.

The cultural health of a society is determined by the way a population produces and disposes of its material surplus. Spengler came tantalisingly close to understanding that economic reality. He lifts out of history two personalities who he treats as metaphors for the transition from growth to decline. If he had deployed the tools of classical economics he could have decoded the significance of his observations to identify the structural changes that would give the West a new lease on life.

Spengler took his symbol "of the first importance" from Rome. Marcus Licinius Crassus (115-53 BC), described by Spengler as an "all-powerful building-site speculator", was associated with conditions in which people "lived in appalling misery in the many-storied lodging-houses of dark suburbs".[3] Crassus became the richest man in the history of the empire by extracting rents out of the people who, displaced from their farms, sought refuge in Rome. One of his business practises was to bide his time as fire claimed a block of cheek-by-jowl tenements, before moving in to negotiate and acquire the land at a low price. The old-noble families were also vulnerable to the spirit of that age. They "lost their ancestral homes through standing apart from the wild rush of speculation and were reduced to renting wretched apartments".

Personal aggrandisement through the accumulation of rent was how Spengler analysed the social process that corroded the core of a civilisation which ruled the world from the Atlantic to the eastern edge of Asia Minor.

For his second symbol, Spengler selected Cecil Rhodes (1853-1902), the British adventurer who built an empire in Africa. Rhodes was driven by the need for "territorial and financial success".

I see in Cecil Rhodes the first man of a new age. He stands for the political style of a far-ranging, Western, Teutonic and especially German future, and his phrase 'expansion is everything' is the Napoleonic reassertion of the in-dwelling tendency of every Civilisation that has fully ripened – Roman, Arab or Chinese. It is not a matter of choice – it is not the conscious will of individuals, or even that of whole classes or peoples that

---

3 Spengler (1932: Vol. 1: 34).

decides. The expansive tendency is a doom, something daemonic and immense, which grips, forces into service, and uses up the late mankind of the world-city stage, willy-nilly, aware or unaware.[4]

Spengler was convinced that Germany was on the verge of becoming a territorial empire. The nation which was the leading centre of cultural innovation during the 19th century would swap the instruments of artists for the weapons of a nation that had the will to power. It would acquire new territories. "The modern Germans are a conspicuous example of a people that has become expansive without knowing it or willing it."[5]

Strip away the metaphysics, and we are left staring at the culture of the rent-seekers.

Germany's rich culture *was* being debased. She *did* try to build an empire. The 20th century *was* an unmitigated disaster for the people. But if we agree with Spengler that the people did not *will* this outcome, to whom, or what, may we assign responsibility? For if humans are free to choose, someone – or something that was willed by someone – must be responsible.

In an exquisite footnote in the second volume of his book, Spengler summarised an example of the way in which the cheats protected their interests. Referring to the popular demand for extension of the franchise in Britain, he wrote:

Afterwards – from 1832 – the English nobility itself, through a series of prudent measures, drew the bourgeoisie into co-operation with it, but under its continued guidance and, above all, in the framework of tradition, within which consequently the young talent grew up. Democracy thus actualised itself here so that the Government remained strictly "in form" – the old aristocratic form – while the individual was free to practise politics according to his bent. This transition, in a peasantless society dominated by business interests, was the most remarkable achievement of inner politics in the 19th century.[6]

The overriding mission of the English aristocracy was to capture political power to control taxation. With the extension of the franchise, for survival's sake that class *had* to deploy defensive measures against those who did not own land. The landlords who dominated the cultural life of Britain skilfully co-opted the landless into a state of acquiescence. The property-less would conform to "time-honoured" practises (those that originated with the new landowners).

---

4 Spengler (1932: Vol.1: 37).
5 Spengler (1932: Vol. 1: 37, n.1).
6 Spengler (1932: Vol. 2, 412). Emphasis in original.

Spengler understood this. If he had developed his anecdotal insights, he might have delineated a theory of the rise and fall of civilisations that would have offered practical guidance to statesmen who wanted to prevent the eclipse of European civilisation.

Tipping into Disaster

In my judgement, Western civilisation has reached the tipping point. The tools to rescue the West are available, but they are not discussed by those who are supposed to be the guardians of the public's welfare. The trauma that afflicts their societies embraces them as victims, distracting them from the root cause of crises (Box 9:1).

As an analytical starting point, the crisis of the West may be reduced to a simple arithmetical ratio. There are too few Producers to support the Predators. The production of value is not sufficient to satisfy the expectations of those who aspire to live off rents. In the 20th century, the aristocracy and gentry were joined by middle-class home-owners who relish every upward move in house prices. They had to find a way to monetise the capital gains that accrued to them while they lived in their homes. They solved the problem by converting the capital gains into debt: borrowing from banks, and offering their homes as collateral. This "leveraging" helped to crush the Western economy when house prices stalled in 2007, but it was a glorious party while it lasted!

To fathom the existential implications of this Producer/Predator ratio, however, we need to track the way the de-socialisation of rent corrupts culture.

The vitality of public life is a function of rent. When rent is privatised, the commons – of both nature and society – are depleted. *Humanity is hollowed out with every incremental shift in the reach of those who live off rents. Societies implode under the stresses caused by the shortfall in resources to sustain them.*

Humanity's achievements are reversed.

Growth is the natural momentum in both nature and society. In both the natural and social universes, communities are constituted by the interaction of participating life-forms. Bio-regions are communities of animals and vegetables, all engaged in the exchange of nature's energy to enable the bees to pollinate the plants to feed the foraging animals that … and so on. Similarly with networks of human settlements. People, working locally and trading globally, add value through their labour, which they exchange through negotiation in the markets. In the realms of both nature and society, we see the propulsion upwards, outwards, more intensively inwards – a process of increasing complexity as each organism enriches itself, the process fuelled by energy. All life forms consume and restore energy in a process of exchange that *adds value to all participants.*

> ### Box 9:1
> ### Capitalism and the Archbishop
>
> Archbishop Desmond Tutu led the spiritual crusade against apartheid in South Africa. In retirement, the "arch" continues to cast a wary eye over the moral state of the world. When he was asked whether it was possible to be both spiritual and rich – from the profits of private enterprise – he wrote: "Capitalism *per se* is not at fault. The most appealing thing about capitalism theory is the freedom for the individual. But as Milton Friedman wrote, while we are free to choose, we should not be free to deprive others of freedom".[1]
>
> But capitalism *does* deprive people of freedom. Capitalism rests on the economics of apartheid – at least, that part of it which privatises, monopolises and abuses the "commons". Friedman, a founder of the Chicago School of Economics, implicitly acknowledged this when he conceded that the rent-based revenue system was the "least bad" way for governments to raise income.[2] But he did not develop that insight in his economic discourses, so the archbishop could not know that Friedman's model of private property rights prescribed a fatally flawed idea of personal freedom.
>
> ---
> 1 Tutu and Gronblom (2012).
> 2 Harrison (1983: 299).

The reverse process should be visible in a civilisation that is exhausting itself. The sociogenic condition is one of atrophy. Personal skills, social systems and moral status systematically degraded. This is the *general* state confronting babies born in Europe and North America today. The legacy bequeathed to the next generation is inferior to the one inherited by previous generations.

Compounding the depletion of culture is the depletion of natural habitats. Prognoses rest on trends authenticated by traditionally cautious organisations like the International Energy Agency (IEA). Its warning of a clear and present danger was set out in the *World Energy Outlook* (2011). The rate at which carbon dioxide is being emitted is dangerously eroding the safety margins. Immediate defensive action is needed. For the non-nuclear energy plants now being constructed will tip the world beyond the increase of 2^0C into the global warming that will cause havoc with weather patterns. Nature and society would be at war.

Voices warn that the end is nigh (Box 9:2). Would the vested interests of the polluters prevail over the welfare of humanity? The strength of the opposition to a shift away from the use of fossil fuels may be gauged by the subsidies awarded to the rent-seeking energy industries: $409bn a year. This compares to the $66bn for renewable energy in 2010.[7] The world's governments failed the political test which came at the Rio+20 Conference in June 2012. The need for action was

---
7   IEA (2011: Fig. 14:13).

closed off by their earlier failure to prevent the land-led property boom. The crash in house prices created havoc in the Western economy and caused governments to narrow the remedial policies they were willing (or financially able) to employ.

The attention focused on weather patterns, however, helped to distract politicians from the systemic risks for which they were responsible. Have they – like the people who gained the vote in England in 1832 – been co-opted by the cheating culture? To determine the extent to which the West's culture has been corroded, we need a forensic examination which digs deep into the foundations of the human condition.

- *Morality*: is there a growing incidence of corruption? As the pursuit of debt-driven lifestyles is extended, are people tempted to abuse norms of good behaviour?
- *Aesthetics*: under the stresses of distorted labour markets, people enjoy less leisure time. Does this blunt their sense of civilised ways of behaving?
- *Spirituality*: as scepticism about worldly affairs corrodes attitudes, is the religious life undermined by secular cynicism, creating the space for false prophets?

Intuitively, based on everyday observations monitored by the media, people might agree that they are witnessing the systematic degradation of the fabric of society. They see politicians bending laws in the pursuit of power. They see alienated youth indulging in anti-social behaviour in the streets. They see corporations employing strategies to circumvent laws.

The theories advanced to account for these trends range from money as the root of all evil,[8] the quest for immortality,[9] over-population,[10] materialism/consumerism (the psychological failure of individuals) to fossil-fuel hungry machines (the failure of technology) ... the list is a long one. And yet, if we follow the money trail, we discover that the causal influences originate with the disruption of the commons.

Single cause theses (such as mine) need to be viewed with caution, and thoroughly challenged. At the same time, we need to wonder whether social scientists are trying to hide something when they trot out their favourite mantra: "There is no simple solution – no silver bullet".

The Dynamics of Civilisations
We need more than a catalogue of catastrophes to understand the forces that

8   Eisenstein (2011).
9   Cave (2012) argues that the rise and fall of civilisations is driven by the human desire for immortality.
10 Sachs (2008).

Box 9:2
Forecasts of Armageddon

Scientists, who are not in the business of proclaiming Armageddon in the style of old-time prophets, do sound like biblical characters. Two examples exemplify the mounting anxieties of scientists.

- Humans will be extinct within 100 years, warns Frank Fenner, emeritus professor of microbiology at the Australian National University. "We're going to become extinct. Whatever we do now is too late." Global warming and "unbridled consumption" are among the explanations, says the man who helped to extinguish one species in Australia: the variola virus that causes smallpox.[1]

- Nicholas Boyle offered his prediction – a Doomsday event will take place as early as 2014 – as a professor at the University of Cambridge and President of Magdalene College. His credentials were affirmed when he was elected Fellow of the prestigious British Academy. The world, he says, will suffer a calamitous event that will determine the course of the 21st century.[2]

---

1 Jones (2010).
2 Boyle (2010).

erode the vitality of civilisation.

Fig. 9:1 schematically represents the phases of growth and collapse of civilisations. This idealised picture summarises the trends of civilisations for which we have sufficient information to be confident about the turning points in their formation, corruption and collapse. The key to this process is economic rent. We trace the trends by identifying how people produce that flow of income, how rent is distributed, and how it is consumed or invested. If the circulation of rent is diverted from its role as the social revenue of the community, pathological conditions arise which restrict the capacity to reproduce the cultural commons.

I divide the history of civilisation into seven phases.

A Subsistence *The phase of socialisation* Humans spent nearly 200,000 years living lives based on subsistence: hunting and gathering sufficient resources to reproduce their families. As they extended their networks through clans and tribes they developed the skills and resources (these include intellectual and moral as well as material resources) to produce high-order culture. The breakthrough to more complex forms of social organisation was contingent on the ability to nurture additional resources out of both nature *and* themselves.

B Agricultural Surplus *The phase of innovation* Learning how to

Fig. 9:1
Schedule of the Rise & Fall of Civilisations

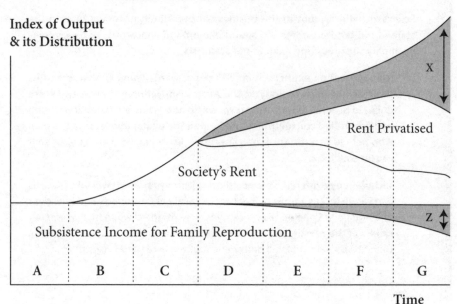

work with nature to produce food additional to the immediate needs of the household made it possible to accumulate resources in the form of capital. This capital could be used to increase output even further, while reducing the risks associated with the vagaries of the weather. This provided the time for reflection, enabling agriculturalists to diversify the household economy, specialising in new skills, developing "cottage industries". Agriculture also made it possible for co-operating communities to pool some of the surpluses to fund larger-scale enterprises that served everyone's needs.

C   Infrastructure Formation   *The phase of urbanisation*   As rents are accumulated, people invest in ever larger settlements. These require amenities (like roads, waste disposal and water supplies) which require specialists in the provision of social infrastructure. This phase is one of intense creativity and complex organisation. Rural communities pool resources so that urban centres might flourish. Rents are treated as social, even sacred, revenue. During this phase, a population is able to double the value of its output. The share retained by households may remain constant, but living standards double because of access to an ever-richer culture.

The contrary view is that civilisation was based on rents extracted from rural communities under duress. Civilisation was characterised by internal conflicts. As one survey of those theories put it,

> *The word civilisation need not connote a change for the better. Civilisations differ from primitive societies in several critical ways. Generally speaking, civilisations are not egalitarian. They contain elites or 'classes' of one sort or another who can extract and consume surpluses and their economies are re-distributive rather than reciprocal.*[11]

And yet, as that author acknowledged, "how the first civilisations actually arose … is unclear". In keeping with the fashion of academic thinking it is generally assumed that the social forces that converged on embryonic civilisations were characterised by class conflict, not co-operation. But urban theorists like Lewis Mumford base their accounts on written and archaeological evidence that survived from the later stages of extinct civilisations, by which time they *had* been corrupted (Box 9:3). It was only subsequent to the formative stages that princes intruded to distort life in cities. Once this occurred, culture was refashioned to serve the private interests of elites that grew increasingly distant from the people who produced the surplus.

In my view, *the freedom to pool resources was the pre-condition for the extension of urban settlements into civilisations.* I cannot prove this statement, which appears to be shared by some scholars.[12] The archaeological record of pre-literate societies does not provide the evidence of what people had in mind when they relinquished control over the surplus they generated out of the soil. Nonetheless, it is the most plausible account of what happened: what Cambridge cosmologist Stephen Hawking calls effective theory. This is a way of viewing the world that provides the best explanation, even when it is not possible to solve all the necessary equations that would provide a full account of observed behaviour.[13]

D   Rent appropriation   *The phase of privatisation*   Some people (strategically located to control the levers of power at the junction boxes of social organisation) begin to covet the rents for personal gratification. Some individuals exploit their religious or civil positions to grab land occupied by others. They become landlords. This reversal of social evolution is accompanied by a moral crisis. The de-socialisation of rent detaches that flow of income from its moral moorings. The whole financial system is tainted. Money is no longer compliant with codes of self-discipline (one code being: *you may consume up*

---

11   Sack (1986: 66).
12   Schneider (1974: 249), Sahlins (1965: 41)
13   Hawking & Mlodinow (2010: 46-47).

to the limit of what you produce). Thus, with a major stream of the community's income cut loose, and apparently up for grabs, activities which offend ethical practise are rewarded. In trade relations, for example, paying bribes to secure advantages in the marketplace. This phase marks a generalised deterioration in social behaviour.

E   State Taxation   *The phase of exploitation*   As rents are secularised, the power structure hardens its centralised controls. People are subjected to authoritarian forms of coercion. Because the nation-state is receiving a diminishing share of the rents, it has to fund the renewal of urban infrastructure out of taxes levied on household incomes. The process of compressing people's material lives begins in earnest. Schisms appear. In place of the co-operative spirit, adversarial techniques are deployed to "solve" problems. The solutions are necessarily second-best, and are overturned with the transfer of power to new factions. Society is rendered unstable.

F   Institutional Decadence   *The phase of corruption*   With the need to enforce ever harsher techniques for extracting revenue out of the population, the state presides over the depletion of the economy's potential. The accumulated knowledge and technologies abolish the shortage of resources: every working person's basic needs can be met. But the maldistribution of income, consolidated by abusive state taxation, renders large numbers of people unemployed or living on breadline wages. In response to social tensions, the state attempts to mitigate hardship with regulatory devices: these aggravate existing distortions to the economy, imposing new layers of tension on society.

G   Collapse   *The phase of implosion*   No amount of coercion can protect the power structure from its enemies. Leaders have lost the power to act for the common good, and are motivated by the psychology of "every man for himself". Desperately, the state plays the debt card: borrowing to fund deficits. When lenders fear that the state may default, they impose penal rates of interest. The state embarks on a final round of cultural cannibalisation: stripping the community of its heritage assets to pay creditors. Austerity is the guiding principle of statecraft. Philosophically impoverished statesmen try to keep the system afloat by degrading the living standards of the population.

In Fig 9:1, the top line represents the evolutionary trajectory. It tracks the value of cultural production that is possible if rent is retained as social revenue.

- Funding the innovative spirit increases as the synergy of a contented and integrated population fructifies in increased output. That output is composed

Box 9:3
Civilisation's Missing Records

Lewis Mumford (1895-1990) was an American historian, sociologist and influential social critic. For him, the two poles of civilisation were "mechanically organized work and mechanically organized destruction and extermination". Kingship coerced people to produce the agricultural surplus on which civilisation depended. The transition to urban living was facilitated by human sacrifices, and war became a necessary extension of that ritual. "Sated with leisure, war gave them 'something to do' and by its incidental hardships, responsibilities, and mortal risks, provided the equivalent of honorable labour." The booty brought back from war was the "easy money" which "must often have undermined the victor's economy", a poor substitute "for a permanent income tax derived annually from a thriving economic organization".[1]

The problem with Mumford's thesis about the origins of civilisation is that the evidence for the formative stages does not exist in the archaeological record. He admits that he relied on guesswork.[2]

1 Mumford (1967: 221).
2 Mumford (1967: 191, 219-220).

not just of material goods. It includes artistic and spiritual pursuits.

- Diversion of rent into narcissistic forms of consumption erodes the freedoms of the population. This translates into the loss of the powers of creativity. Production is measured in terms of base material consumption.

Fragmentation into classes generates internal conflicts that divert an ever increasing share of rents into negative uses. Social discontent has to be policed. The footloose spoils become attractive to external predators, so investment has to be increased in territorial defence. The gap shown in Fig 9:1 as X grows larger with time. This measures the loss of what it means to be human.

The most intense period of production of culture in all its forms coincides with the periods of maximum personal freedom within healthy communities. This state of affairs is represented by the capacity of a population to maximise the investment of its rents in social activities that yield the greatest fulfilment for every person in the community. The whole population engages in the creative activities that yield material, aesthetic and psychological satisfaction. But as the material basis of that creativity is privatised, the power to produce larger quantums of culture haemorrhages away. As the people in power struggle to maintain funding at levels which preserve culture at existing levels, the negative burdens on the population intensify. People endure a loss of welfare (implied by Z in Figure 9:1). The shortfall in the production of wealth arises as states intensify the burden of taxation on wages.[14]

A civilisation at risk, which wishes to renew itself, must assemble all the information needed to expose how and why it is vulnerable. It needs a Cheating Index.

The Cheating Index

The United Nations and non-government agencies compile indices which provide insights into aspects of the quality of life in every nation. One index measures corruption.[15] Another is the Body Mass Index.[16] The Cheating Index would appraise the general quality of life of a community. Its reference points would be the standards applied in a society that qualified as conforming to the norms of natural justice. The index would build a comprehensive archive of information based on tracking activities in all the realms that constitute the public life of a nation.

Weights would be used to measure behaviour which was either directly, or indirectly, disturbed by the intrusion of the rent-seeking culture. This throws up the first problem: identifying the flow of economic rent, which reflects the value of the commons of nature and society. Linking economic rent directly to specific actions would not be possible in all cases. But we may start by examining a case in which the connections are transparent.

In sport, individuals who try to cheat their way to victory are soon spotted by spectators. What happens to fair play when cheating of the lawful kind is allowed to come into play? Take, for example, a football team whose proprietor is an oligarch who reaped his fabulous fortune from the natural resources located in his East European country. If those resource rents were used to buy the best players in the world, would that be fair play? What chance does a home-grown team (whose finances depend on what the fans can pay out of their wages) stand against such a team?

The state of play in the English football Premier League illustrates the problem. The *Daily Telegraph* analysed the cash and on-field performance of teams for the 2010/11 season. Chelsea FC paid the most to its players (£189.5m). Second was Manchester City (£174m). Chelsea players were the beneficiaries of the resource rents from Russia, courtesy of the oligarch Roman Abramovich.

---

14 The technical term employed by economists is "excess burden". This delivers "deadweight losses". Economists confine their assessments of those losses (when they take the trouble to give the matter any consideration at all) to the material consequences. They do not factor into their calculations the losses in terms of psycho-social welfare.

15 In 1995, Transparency International launched the Corruption Perception Index. Every year, countries are ranked "by their perceived levels of corruption, as determined by expert assessments and opinion surveys".

16 The Body Mass Index is calculated on the basis of height and weight, and is the best proxy for the percentage of fat in a body. It is most appropriately used to assess a whole population, rather than for the prognosis of an individual person's health. Clinicians can infer the general condition of a population from this one numerical result. It indicates, for example, the proneness of a population to sedentary behaviour, and the scale of the health risks associated with obesity.

Manchester City players were the beneficiaries of the petroleum rents extracted out of the desert sands of the Gulf, courtesy of their youthful owner, Sheikh Mansour. The lowest paid team was Blackpool Football Club (£13.6m).[17]

Chelsea won the double (Premier League and FA Cup) in the 2009/10 season. In 2011/12, the glory was shared between Chelsea (FA Cup) and Manchester City (Premier League), with Chelsea becoming the first London club to win the UEFA Champions League in that year. Fair play? Manchester City came from nowhere to triumph because the oil rents (not a value produced by the labour of the sheikh himself) enabled the club to spend £930m to turn itself into title contenders. Meanwhile, in Blackpool, the fans who dip into their wage packets to support their team endure one of the shortest life-spans in Britain. As we saw in Ch. 6 (p.55), male babies born in Blackpool can expect to live 11 fewer years than male babies born in Chelsea.

UEFA, the body that governs European football, administers Financial Fair Play regulations. But the source of the money that is used to hire players like Manchester City's Yaya Touré (the Ivorian midfielder on a reputed weekly wage of £200,000) is not part of their calculation of fair play.

Accomplished athletes are role models for young people. If individual sportsmen are allowed to cheat, that sends signals to impressionable minds that they, too, can bend the rules to achieve success. There was despair when sprinter Dwain Chambers, who had been banned from athletics and barred from representing Britain at the 2012 Olympics, was reinstated by the Court of Arbitration for Sport on the grounds that the ban was not enforceable. This, wrote Sir Steve Redgrave, an Olympic Gold Medallist, "marks a dispiriting victory for the drugs cheats".[18] That was a reasonable assessment. But what about the institutional cheating in sport in which some teams buy their way to victory because their proprietors have access to rents which they did not earn by their labour?

General standards of good behaviour cannot be sustained if the moral code is debased. I emphasise that the cheating which concerns us is not of the idiosyncratic kind, except when such cases illuminate a law or institution that has been compromised. An example of a case of personal failing is the German banker who confessed to taking bribes from Bernie Ecclestone, the Formula 1 motor racing mogul. In June 2012 the banker was sentenced to eight years in prison for a transaction involving $44m (£28m), which he said was a bribe. This case does not contribute to our understanding of cheating as a systemic process, unless the money came from rent, or was calculated to create a rent-seeking benefit.

17 Scott (2012).
18 Redgrave (2012). Chambers did end up on the athletic field in the London Olympics, but failed to win a medal.

Box 9:4
"Progressively" Taxing the Rich?

A 2009 study by the Washington-based Institute on Taxation & Economic Policy calculated the relative tax burden on Americans. *Who Pays? A Distributional Analysis of the Tax Systems in All 50 States* confirmed that middle- and low-income families pay higher shares of their income to government than the very well-off.[1]

- The average state and local tax rate on the richest 1% of families in the USA was 6.4% before accounting for the tax savings from federal itemized deductions. After the federal offset, their effective tax rate was 5.2%.

- The average tax rate on families in the middle 20% of the income spectrum was 9.7% before the federal offset and 9.4% after – almost twice the effective rate paid by the richest people.

- The average tax rate on the poorest 20% of families was 10.9%, more than double the effective rate on the very wealthy.

The injustice of this fiscal discrimination is similar to what happens in the UK. [2]

---

1 Davis *et al* (2009).
2 Harrison (2006a: 28-30).

Deviant behaviour by individuals acquires its social significance when it is contextualised within a process that encourages it. Politicians, for example, through the taxes that they employ, *induce* people to invest time and money in trying to dodge their social responsibilities. This was understood in the 1820s by J.R. McCulloch (1789-1864), the first professor of political economy at University College London. He warned of the consequences that would flow from the income tax introduced by William Pitt in 1799. It would nurture tax evasion and avoidance. In an article he wrote for the 7th edition of *Encyclopaedia Britannica* in 1830, he explained:

> *The tax would fall with its full weight upon men of integrity, while the millionaire of "easy virtue" would well nigh escape it altogether. It would, in fact, be a tax on honesty, and a bounty on perjury and fraud; and, if carried to any considerable height – to such a height as to render it a prominent source of income – it would undoubtedly generate the most barefaced prostitution of principle, and would do much to obliterate that nice sense of honour which is the very foundation of national probity and virtue.*

In June 2012 the British tax authorities revealed that they were investigating the

> ### Box 9:5
> ### Bunging the Political Parties
>
> When the Conservative Party failed to achieve a majority in Britain's 2010 election, it formed a Coalition with the Liberal Democrats. The government decided to relax planning laws to encourage "sustainable development" on greenfield sites. Conservation trusts howled at the prospect of urban sprawl. Their protests fell on deaf ears. As the Tories crafted their planning legislation, the land owning and development industry donated £500,000 to the party, according to the Electoral Commission.
>
> David Cameron's planning minister successfully urged the land developers to lobby the prime minister in favour of relaxing the planning regulations. Sir Simon Jenkins, chairman of the National Trust, told a House of Commons committee that the development industry had its "fingerprints" all over the legislation.[1]
>
> ---
>
> 1 Hope (2012).

corporate tax affairs of more than 4,000 companies.[19]

 ## Politics

Governments promulgate laws that affect the lives of citizens. They justify their taxes by invoking the fairness test. Their policies are based on the principle of "progressivity". How would the democratic institution fare if the cheating test was applied? The facts appear to discredit the claims of politicians (Box 9:4).

One of the conduits through which influence is peddled is the money donated as campaign contributions. Where does that money come from? Is Britain's democratically elected Parliament still hostage to the landlords' culture, if its political parties receive money from land speculators (Box 9:5)?

 ## Media

Open channels of communication are a pre-condition for a healthy democracy. When those channels are polluted, people are denied access to honest information. Cynicism corrodes citizens' relationships with their leaders, some of whom may seek to get away with self-serving behaviour.

When journalists employ unethical techniques to obtain information, people are entitled to suspect that either the information itself is suspect, or

---

19 Pickard (2012).

the media outlet is not to be trusted. Could such cases be tracked back to the secondary effects of a cheating society? The question arose when the extent of illegal hacking of people's telephones by London-based employees of News International was exposed by the government's Inquiry into the Culture, Practice & Ethics of the Press (chairman: Lord Justice Leveson) in 2012. A House of Commons Select Committee branded that company's boss, global media mogul Rupert Murdoch, as "unfit" to administer a news corporation.

✋ Police

An open-ended interrogation of the moral fibre of a community is warranted when it turns out that senior police officers receive "gifts" for services rendered to journalists. The law enforcement system itself fell into disrepute when it was discovered that some Scotland Yard officers had developed inappropriate relationships with journalists from News International publications. Was this a case of the extension of cheating that could be tracked back to the breakdown in moral standards arising from the way society's incomes are maltreated by the law of the land?

✋ Bureaucracy

Complex societies need civil servants who act impartially. Taxpayers, for example, rely on the integrity of tax collectors who enforce the law. In Britain, the head of HM Revenue & Customs is not expected to have a close relationship with large companies which are then found to be paying a lot less than might have been expected. When such a controversial association was found to exist between Mike Clasper, chairman of Britain's tax collecting service, and a number of major corporations, there was public disquiet (he resigned).[20]

If bureaucrats are perceived to be taking advantage of their positions at the centre of government, that behaviour may encourage emulation by businessmen. And so, it was dispiriting for taxpayers to read that more than 2,000 of Britain's civil servants may have avoided tax by receiving pay through private companies. This "off payroll" arrangement allowed them to avoid certain tax liabilities.[21] This was not illegal, but it was widely perceived to be cheating the public purse by those whose taxes were deducted at source.

Tax avoidance in Britain is a social problem. Around 550 people who earn more than £1m a year pay less than the 20p basic rate of tax.[22] If the super-rich are suspected of dodging their social obligations, why should

20 Quinn (2012).
21 Stacey (2012).
22 Aldrick (2012b).

wage earners respect the citizen's obligation to comply with the tax code? Can all of these deviations from "fair play" be traced back to institutionally-sanctioned cheating of the public purse?

Education

A dynamic society relies on the integrity of its educational system to ensure that children are given an equal chance to realise their potential and to enrich society over their lifetime. Cheating the children with forms of instruction that do not serve their best interests would downgrade a nation's standing. So when it was revealed that exams in Britain had been dumbed down to make it easier for students to acquire high grades – in response to political pressure – we may conclude that those young people have been deprived of the care to which they were entitled.[23]

Should the cheating test be applied to ideas, and to the institutions of higher learning? In universities, scholars are supposed to approach their research and teaching dispassionately. One benefit is that this learning would lead to honest assessments of social problems (say, on the performance of political leaders). An example of an apparent failing of scholarship relates to the economic crisis that followed the credit crunch in 2008. Four years elapsed without what the *Financial Times* called a "proper holding to account for the crisis". The academic community had failed on the single most urgent issue: understanding the origins and nature of the economic crisis that had rendered tens of millions of people without employment.

Should we be surprised by this failure? The *Financial Times* editorial appeared on the same page, on April 12, 2012, as a letter from Dr. Hugh Goodacre, an economist at University College, London. He explained that economic departments in British universities were compromising their selection of candidates for employment and promotion on the basis of an individual's ability to specialise in "abstruse" economics. Such work was favoured by peer-reviewed US academic journals. This was "an utterly crucial factor in all aspects of the depletion of the intellectual life of UK economics departments". In Dr. Goodacre's view, this failing was at the expense of the community. Whose interests were served by these failings?

Commerce

When firms collude to raise prices above competitive levels, consumers are

---

23 Ofqual, the regulator of examination standards, confirmed that exams had been made easier over recent years in subjects like chemistry, biology, mathematics and critical thinking (Hurst 2012). This was the result of the setting of targets by government to increase the trend in academic accomplishments which many observers concluded was not associated with improvement in the educational attainment of the examination candidates.

cheated of money. Living standards are reduced to raise profit margins by methods that offend the notion of competition. To what extent is the notion of equal opportunity compromised by property rights and the way the distribution of income is sanctioned by the fiscal regime? Many low- and middle-income countries, whose laws echo the preferences of their former colonial masters, are unable to achieve parity in global markets when competing with Western multi-national corporations. Pfizer, the medical conglomerate, was fined $60m for bribery of doctors and government officials in eastern Europe, Asia and the Middle East over the decade up to 2006. Its activities contravened the US Foreign Corrupt Practices Act. Pfizer admitted bribes of $2m that generated sales of $7m.[24] To what extent was this behaviour influenced by a degraded financial system? Did the footloose money syndrome pollute the ethics of business practise?

Nature

The abuse of nature injures species in ways which prevent their self-renewal. Do tax policies encourage the exploitation of nature? Two hundred years ago, did the absence of a rental charge on the disposal of waste into the atmosphere and rivers bias inventors in favour of "dirty" technologies? Is this bias alive and kicking – killing – today?

The list of issues that requires exploration, for the purpose of compiling a Cheating Index, goes on. The arts, for example, need to be examined to determine whether natural instincts have been blunted by contemporary culture. The capacity to express ideas in artistic form is ingrained in every one of us. But to develop one's aesthetic sensibilities requires leisure time and peace of mind. Today, relatively few people engage in artistic pursuits.

Denis Dutton, a professor of the philosophy of art at the University of Canterbury (New Zealand), affirms that art is an inherited instinct. His book is subtitled *Beauty, Pleasure, and Human Evolution.* But his account of art is curiously incongruent. Artistic objects and performances, he writes, "are typically among the most opulent, extravagant, glittering, and profligate creations of the human mind. The arts squander brain power, physical effort, time, and precious resources". This he contrasts with Darwinian natural selection, which "is economical and abstemious: it weeds out inefficiency and waste".[25]

In formulating a measure for judging whether a population is being cheated of its artistic propensities, we need an idea of what the arts would look like if people were not subjected to the constraints of modern life. Dutton's

24 Jack (2012).
25 Dutton (2009: 136).

description of art fits a society in which artists feel obliged to bend their creations to accommodate the narcissistic needs of the rent-seekers. The aristocracy commandeered the material means required to liberate the minds of the peoples of the commons. But in a free society, the devotion of mental energy to artistic pursuits cannot "squander brain power". Such activities are stimulating, liberating, a way to expand brain power and aesthetic sensibilities. But to engage in such pursuits requires leisure time. If these are not at the disposal of people in general, it is not surprising that art has become a commodity for the rich. They lock some of their money in assets that have little to do with aesthetics and everything to do with hoarding wealth.

Rogues or Rotten System?

Rent-seekers will object to the compilation of a Cheating Index. One line of defence is the claim that deviant behaviour is no more than evidence of human frailty, for which the laws of the land cannot be held responsible.

We see this idea embedded in popular culture. Hollywood movies rely on it for resolving cases of cheating which make for exciting visual drama, but which – if scrutinised too closely – would also disturb the community. So, whether the narrative is built around 19th century cowboys, 20th century Cold War spies or 21st century virtual time travellers, the Bad Guys are always shot dead. The social system is cathartically cleansed. Audiences return home content that the Good Guys represent the prevailing norms of society.

The technique of exonerating the system by singling out a Bad Guy was employed by New York State's financial watchdog, the Department of Financial Services (DFS), when it threatened to revoke the license of a British bank. Standard Chartered was branded a "rogue institution", accused of hiding $250bn of transactions with Iran and leaving "the US financial system vulnerable to terrorists, weapons dealers, drug kingpins and corrupt regimes". DFS alleged that financial transactions generated "hundreds of millions of dollars" in fees for the bank. Standard Chartered robustly denied it had breached US economic sanctions against Iran. But its chief, Peter Sands, admitted that "mistakes were made" for which he was "very sorry" (Box 9:6).[26]

Was there a cultural component to this episode, one that encouraged rule-bending in financial institutions? Frank Partnoy, professor of law and finance at the University of San Diego, suggests there was. In his view,

As recent debacles at Barclays, HSBC and now Standard Chartered demonstrate, employees of big global banks increasingly lack a moral

---

26 Braithwaite and Goff (2012); Armistead (2012).

Box 9:6
Kinds of Cheating: I

Standard Chartered had weathered the financial crisis of 2008 with a clean sheet, and it denied the allegation that it had breached US money-laundering laws. So what could be behind the "rogue institution" allegation by Benjamin Lawsky, superintendent of the DFS, who painted the British bank as a conscious corporate villain? *The Financial Times* offered a theory (August 8, 2012):

"Standard Chartered fits well into an emerging American narrative which sees irresponsible finance, even by US groups, as something that happens in the City of London. It may be convenient for US politicians to deflect blame beyond its borders; it is nonetheless a gross simplification."

Standard Chartered agreed to pay $340m (£217m) to head off a public enquiry into the allegations by Lawsky. Analysts suggested that, before this episode was closed, StanChart would end up paying money to other US financial agencies, taking the total to a possible $700m.

compass. Some general counsels and compliance officers do provide ethical guidance. But many are facilitators or loophole instructors, there to show employees the best way to avoid the law. Not even mafia lawyers go that far.[27]

Were the dodgy financial deals really exceptional, or were they symptomatic of a money-making culture incubated by the culture of cheating? Anecdotal evidence is not sufficient to answer that question. The US financial regulators have alleged financial misbehaviour by firms like JPMorgan Chase and HSBC, but do these tell us anything about the general culture within which banks operate?

In fairness to those who are accused of cheating, a forensic examination of the health of society is required that correlates rent to culture. What, for example, do we make of the case of top managers and traders in the employ of Barclays Bank who, scattered across three continents, sought to rig two global benchmark interest rates? Barclays paid a fine of £290m for behaviour which affected millions of people by raising the cost of mortgages. Were the champagne-swilling bankers conforming to a culture of corruption?[28] Was the entrapment of low-income people in mortgages they could not afford a case of a corrupt culture or the failings of a few financiers (Box 9:7)?

27   Partnoy (2012).
28   Wilson (2012).

> **Box 9:7**
> **Kinds of Cheating: II**
>
> WHAT elevates idiosyncratic cheating into the systemic kind? Is it the number of cases, or the scale of the deeds, or the extent of the pain that is inflicted on the public? How do we classify the behaviour of Wells Fargo, America's biggest mortgage lender, which sold sub-prime mortgages to people who could not afford them? In 2011, the bank paid $85m in a settlement with the US Federal Reserve over allegations that perhaps more than 10,000 of its borrowers were inappropriately steered into more expensive sub-prime mortgages or who had their loan documents falsified by bank staff.
>
> In 2012, Wells Fargo agreed to pay at least $175m to settle allegations by the Department of Justice that it discriminated against African-American and Hispanic borrowers by steering them into high-cost mortgages. Wells Fargo claimed to be innocent of the allegations.[1] Many families had homes repossessed in African-American neighbourhoods in cities like Baltimore.
>
> ---
> 1 Braithwaite et al (2012).

The Disposition towards Amnesia

In the past, civilisations were unable to recover from their final phase of imperialism. There is no inevitable reason why the West should suffer a similar fate. Ours can now evolve, if we retrieve and deploy ancient and modern (sacred and secular) wisdoms.

The suppression of knowledge to protect rent-seeking is a continuous process. Beneficiaries have a vested interest in the cover up. But, in addition, victims conspire, enabling them to cope with the trauma of land loss. The secondary shocks, inflicted on each new generation, are transmitted through brutal taxes and by institutions that safeguard the doctrine of rent appropriation. Psychotherapists have documented cases in which painful knowledge was suppressed in realms such as research into "hysteria" in women at the end of the 19th century, and "shell shock" endured by war veterans in the 20th century. These terminated in "episodic amnesia" for reasons given by Judith Herman: "To study psychological trauma means bearing witness to horrible events … Repression, dissociation, and denial are phenomena of social as well as individual consciousness".[29]

To combat the suppression of knowledge about land loss, the support of a political movement is needed. Otherwise, the systematic abuses of rent-seeking will continue. We, The People, will decide what now happens to the West. Either by decision, or by default.

---
29 Herman (2001: 7,9).

Chapter 10: The Algorithm of Life

H E is one of Her Majesty's peers. Bedecked in ermine, parading in the ancient rituals of the Palace of Westminster, Baron Sugar of Clapton is famous worldwide for his television show, *The Apprentice*, in which budding entrepreneurs compete to be hired by his lordship.

Alan Sugar epitomises everything that is good, and everything that is bad, about capitalism. The duality of the social system is mirrored in the split personality of Sugar's business biography. He began as an East End jack-the-lad. He turned raw wit into profit by dealing in goods from the back of his car. He started with electrical goods and ended up in the Big Time, making and selling the first generation of personal computers to people (like me) who earned their living by pounding the keys of typewriters.

His plain-speaking lordship does not mince his words. The title of one of the chapters in his autobiography declares: "I don't like Liars, Bull-shitters, Cheats and Schmoozers". But he was, in fact, a cheat. Not by choice: the law does not outlaw making money out of nothing. But that is what he did when he combined Adam Smith's entrepreneurial archetype with the *live-off-the-fat-of-the-land* aristocrat rolled into one.

From barrow boy to baron: capitalism's success story. And our society's tragedy.

Sugar made his first fortune by building a business that created jobs and satisfied its customers. Diligently, he cut costs to avoid waste. He scoured the world for partners who could supply the electronic components that laid the foundations for a business empire. He added value. I appreciated his work and became one of his customers. And the nation was the wealthier for it.

And then he made his second fortune out of land.

The best testimony is provided by Lord Sugar himself. His autobiography *What You See is What You Get* is a frank confession. He made money out of property without having to comply with the standards of entrepreneurship laid out in Adam Smith's textbook.

His first deal was in 1968. He bought a house for £4,700. Three years later – without lifting a finger – he sold it for £15,700. Then he bought a new house for £27,000. Cash, no mortgage. Sold it 10 years later for £100,000. The hustler in the world of electronics had discovered that, when dealing in land, the profit came out of nowhere, costless.

As a manufacturer, Alan Sugar was not content with 10%. He wanted a 33% return on his capital. To achieve that result, he had to work for it – "think of a product that is sought after and that no one else has, and then ensure that you beat down the cost price to achieve a great retail price. A no-brainer, right?"[1]

Right!

To achieve this margin, he toured Asia's factories to find the quality manufacturers who could deliver the goods at the right price and on time to keep his customers happy. He went through Japan and Hong Kong to Taiwan. Alan Sugar turned himself into a fully-fledged globe-trotting tycoon.

Then he sold his value-adding business and made his second fortune from property. His company, Amsprop, was not his first love. Why should it be? He admits that, in the early days, "I hadn't fully concentrated on the property side of the things". That was not surprising because, as he observed: "I'd always viewed it as an investment, but boring". Making money out of nothing was no challenge for the entrepreneur. He had been lured into land by values that had nothing to do with *adding* value, everything to do with location. That was why he bought a building in Old Park Lane in London's West End – "which I wanted simply because it was in such a prime location".[2]

Lord Sugar is contemptuous of hustlers in the property business. They gave him bad advice on the costs of refurbishing his Mayfair building and on the price he might get for the apartments. One "idiot agent" put forward offers for the apartments of £3m to £3.5m each, which "I summarily rejected ... along came a couple ... They paid £5.5m for the second floor – just like that, without blinking. I think a picture now emerges of what total tossers some of these estate agents are ... this was just one of *many* experiences I've had with these people".[3] He sold the penthouse apartment for £7.25m to an Indian steel billionaire. So he recovered his outlay on that building from the sale of two of the apartments, leaving him with pure profit from the sale of the remaining apartments. *Location value.*

What could Lord Sugar expect of people engaged in real estate? Adam Smith had shredded the reputations of the people who lived by pocketing society's rents. Money that comes without labour does not encourage the diligent application to the detail of investing capital to create goods for sale in the marketplace. This was no secret to Baron Sugar.

---

1 Sugar (2010: 329).
2 Sugar (2010: 543-544).
3 Sugar (2010: 547).

I've concluded over the years that there is no science to the real estate market – it just tracks the general economy. If retailers are doing well and business is booming, premises will be taken and high rents will be paid. I've sat through a few peaks and troughs of booms and recessions and seen the value of buildings rise and fall like a yo-yo … Eventually, through one of the cycles of boom and bust, you will have the opportunity to sell at the top of the market or buy at the bottom.[4]

His lordship openly admits that he is not an expert on real estate. "As I've said, I find it a bit boring." Boring, because making money out of land is no test of the skills of a self-respecting entrepreneur. For, as he confessed: "If it is played correctly, it's a safe place to be". Little risk, high returns: a combination that undermines the spirit of the creativity that goes into a good, honest deal in the marketplace.

We cannot censure Alan Sugar for taking his piece out of the Community Chest. It is, after all, an activity sanctioned by the rule of law. In fact, it would not make sense for players in the game of Monopoly not to go for the highest stakes. Those stakes (in the case of London) are located in Mayfair, which his lordship favoured for the location values. The conversion of East End lad into West End baron was prescribed by the capitalist order, which is predicated on the incentives afforded by the tax regime. Those incentives *automatically* push entrepreneurs into the boring business of making money out of nothing.

There are no evil men in smoke-filled rooms plotting to lure good people like Alan Sugar into the ranks of the rent-seekers. There is no need for a conspiracy theory, because the process is embedded in the DNA of capitalism. Rational people are attracted by the algorithm which reveals how to make money out of nothing.

The logic of that algorithm was forced on Lord Sugar when he married and needed a home for his family. It's called "getting on the housing ladder". In the commercial sector, it is more complicated. The investor has to spend money and time to upgrade buildings to meet the needs of buyers or tenants. Paying attention to the improvements on top of a piece of land is necessary, to unlock the residual value that is anchored in the location. Sugar's commitment to that activity illuminates the psychosis in the system. The owner of a building *does* add value, and for that he is entitled to a return on his labour and capital. But as for the rest, it is pure unearned income. Capital gains.

But where did that pure profit come from? As far as the bored Alan Sugar was concerned, it might just as well have been transported to Earth as a gift to

---

4 Sugar (2010: 548).

him from a philanthropic alien on another planet. All he had to do was ride the business cycle, and *Hey Presto!* the capital was his for the pocketing.

In the real world, however, others have to work to create the value that appears to come from out of the ground. When we drill down, we discover that it is a value that comes from three sources: nature, society and every working individual in the community. All play a part in its creation. They are the agents of the algorithm of life. That synthesis of the life forces from nature and society converge on a pricing mechanism that early humans invented to make possible the self-conscious lives we enjoy today.

Convergence of Pricing Mechanisms

First, there was nature's pricing mechanism. Living entities – animal and vegetable – trade in units of energy. This is a reciprocal exchange. Outputs are balanced with equivalent inputs. The units of energy change their appearance, but the deal is successfully clinched by ensuring that the books are balanced. Nature's pricing mechanism enabled animals and vegetables to allocate energy between competing possibilities in the evolution of life. We call those units of energy *joules* (after the British physicist James Prescott Joule [1818-1889]). Scientists codify the universal laws that harmonise the flow of energy between nature's three factors of production: animal, vegetable and mineral.

The notion of *production*, when related to nature, may seem incongruous, but it is the reality. Once upon a time, Earth was barren. By conforming to the laws of physics – exchanging energy to achieve optimum outcomes – the most primitive single cells turned energy into the most glorious concatenation of life forms. Nature, by conforming to the laws which it evolved, produced itself. Minerals were on planet Earth in abundance. But there were no animals or vegetables. By trading units of energy through evolutionary timescales, the planet was transformed into the haven in which micro-bugs became lions and elephants. Charles Darwin and Alfred Russel Wallace described the process of evolution as a continuous process of expansion in the diversity and volume of life. This was possible because nature's accounting system ensured conservation in the use of energy. Nature abhors waste. The costs of consumption were *at least* offset with equivalent benefits. The principle of reciprocity was applied in the natural world long before humans articulated the benefits that were derived from co-operation.

In the social universe, the early, healthy societies were self-funding. They paid their way. Natural resources were shared, social transactions executed by generating equal value in benefits to the users of services. Small bands merged into larger units to derive additional benefits. The enlargement from kinship groups to tribes to confederations would not have been possible if people had not been willing to pay their way, and to fund the costs of cultural aggregation. To transform from hunting groups into the villages that grew into towns, communities had to evolve the organic pricing mechanism that made everyone richer, materially, psychologically and spiritually. By developing that pricing mechanism, early humans were able to take their first steps out of nature.

Over the past 10,000 years, Neolithic people accelerated developments that increased the complexity of the social universe. To make this happen, they needed a new kind of currency. This currency had to combine the distinctive energies that were generated in both the natural and social universes. The emerging creativity of people had to be melded with the power of nature in a partnership that would yield a unique way of life on Earth. The new currency had to harmonise the three factors of production that made the social universe possible. Land, Labour and Capital.

Classical economists defined the concept of land to represent not just the living space we occupy for residential and employment purposes. It includes everything in the world of animals, vegetables and minerals. To create the value that underpinned the new currency, land was combined with labour, and with the tools (capital) which humans employed to ease the burden of work (conservation of energy). Land, Labour and Capital. In their correct combinations, the outcome would be the flourishing of urban civilisations that could metaphorically (the ziggurats) and then literally (space ships to the moon) reach for the stars. This creation of humans was achieved by respecting, and conforming to the laws of nature. Nature abhors inefficiency (Box 10:1).

A major step forward in the evolution of the human sense of comparative values emerged through cross-border barter. People exchanged the products of their labour (say, the moulding of crockery out of clay) for implements hammered out of flint stone. Participants engaged in this embryonic market arrived at a mutual understanding of the relative worth of the inputs of Land, Labour and Capital to execute The Transaction. This process evolved organically, naturally, as humans became aware that the exchange of goods would make them all better off in life's journey through time and space. So they developed rules for engaging in trade by isolating the relative value of the three inputs. The basic function was to stay alive. The biological imperative was fulfilled by securing enough energy to allow the reproduction of families (wages). The next step was to ease the amount of labour that had to be committed to fulfilling the biological necessities. This was achieved by inventing tools for capturing and herding animals and, subsequently, farming additional energy out of the soil (capital). Once they had cracked the formula, a universe of their own, apart from the lives of other species, was theirs for the making.

Box 10:1
Evolutionary Efficiency

Humans cannot operate as a parallel universe to the natural world by contradicting the laws of nature. Efficiency is an evolutionary principle. People adhered to it as they sought to satisfy their desires with the least possible exertion. Why go on a round-about route from A to B if the direct route saves time and energy? This behaviour conforms to the law of the conservation of energy. In the natural world, we find no case of living entities that sustain themselves without exertion, or cases where they expend (say) twice as much energy as necessary to accomplish the tasks of everyday living.

Capitalism is supposed to be the efficient way to produce and distribute wealth. The value-adding component of that culture does conform to the principle. The Predator Culture within it, however, imposes burdens that oblige people to act inefficiently. The ensuing depletion of energy within the social universe is matched by the destruction of energy (as measured by the loss of species and their habitats) in the natural universe. Biologically speaking, this is anti-evolutionary. Morally speaking, it is offensive to the spirit of humanity.

The universe visualised by *Homo sapiens* was not possible without the investment of energy that was dedicated to releasing a creative power that included the aesthetic and spiritual sensibilities. Through Co-operation+Competition, humans added a value that was beyond the accomplishment of isolated individuals. This process was described by Peter Corning, who directs the Institute for the Study of Complex Systems in Palo Alto, California. Each individual, he notes,

> had a stake in the viability and well-being of the group as a survival unit. The 'public interest,' as it were, was rooted in the group and its potential for collective synergy. It provided an incentive for collective measures to contain conflict and enhance co-operation. For instance, a larger group was more likely – all other things being equal – to benefit from synergies of scale in confrontations with other groups of predators or competitors (not to mention potential prey). The same principle of collective synergy undergirds human societies today.[5]

Aboriginal communities devised cultures to replicate nature's propensity to maintain eco-systems in balance (*homeostasis*). Social organisations were sustained over tens of thousands of years. This bought humans the time necessary for the brain to expand its capacity to the point where they could

---

5 Corning (2003: 211).

invent skills to nurture an added value out of nature. This was a mutually beneficial outcome. Nature gained when humans learnt not just to live off, but also to enrich, their habitats. The terracing of hillsides, for example, enabled nature to provide yet more resources for other species that co-habited with the human communities that nestled in the valleys below.

The added value could be created by refining the rules that governed The Transaction. Part of the output had to be reserved to fund the extension of social life. That added value was called *economic rent*. If organically defined finance remained faithful to the principles of nature's pricing mechanism, the limits to people's lives would only be bounded by their imagination.

The Morality of Money

Modern humans worked out that money had to be combined with morality, if this social tool was to facilitate the dense social arrangements associated with urban lifestyles. Without morality – and money – people could not have produced the working capital and the cultural tools which made civilisation possible.

Whether money took the form of clay tablets or bits of mineral or slips of paper, it is what it represented that mattered. Money was needed to do more than just measure units of labour inputs into the production process. It also had to facilitate ethical sensibilities and the needs of the community. This was achieved by combining money with the social functions of the market. This made it possible to divide the total product of labour between the portion which needed to be retained for private consumption (wages), and the portion which needed to be set aside to fund the services which people shared in common. Through the production and exchange of goods and services, part of the ensuing value was *externalised*. Part of the value that people produced was separated from the reward for their investment of labour and capital. That additional value was cast out, as it were, free from the claims of any one individual. Thus isolated, it could be collected and used to fund the innovations that were necessary for rural settlements to evolve into complex urban organisms.

In the Near East, arid regions beyond the reach of the two great rivers of Mesopotamia limited the possibilities of life. Nature's constraint, however, could be overcome. Water could be transported by canals. Constructing those irrigation networks was beyond the capacity of individual farmers. Investment in the infrastructure was made possible when farmers pooled (externalised) part of their product to enable their community leaders to organise the construction of the channels and to maintain the canals in working order.

And so we arrive at an enigma. Today, money is popularly believed to be the root of all evil. How did this come about?

If the morality associated with organic finance is honoured, money is the instrument for the good of the individual and society – and nature.

The morality of money can only be sustained, however, if society enforces the golden rule in the financial sector: all costs of production must be *internalised*. This is a technical way of stating the obvious (because we think we apply this rule every day, in all our transactions): those who create costs must bear the burden; and those who create benefits must reap the rewards. When consistently applied within the market economy, this allows no scope for cheating.

The cheating begins and ends with the fate of that value which is *necessarily* externalised out of the labour and capital markets, and into its own dedicated market. This is traditionally called the land market, but that is a misnomer. Much more is entailed than the contribution from nature. It would be more accurate to call it the community (or location) market. Why? Because that stream of income – rent – is the measure of the contribution from both nature and society. Rent is not a value unanchored, footloose, cast out into the ether, unclaimed and up for grabs by the Toughest Man in Town. *Nature and society have the same right as individuals to claim their portion of the total product.*

- If a community creates a cost, it must bear the burden. At the same time, if it contributes to aggregate value, it is entitled to claim its share of the output.
- For practical purposes, the community must act as proxy for nature. The two are elegantly intertwined, and it is only through society that nature's well-being can be protected from the misbehaviour of individuals.

Thus, for money to retain its moral content, rent must be ring-fenced to fund public goods and services. The collection system is the public pricing mechanism. This is administered by government or other agencies that may be authorised to fulfil that function on behalf of the community. It *complements* – is not in conflict with – the pricing mechanism in private markets, *when the golden rule is enforced in the financial sector.* By this means, morality-based money is the conduit through which natural justice is upheld between the individual and government, and between communities and their habitats.

Money loses its moral status when the social function of rent is corrupted. That is when pathological problems arise. The moral foundations and biological functions of the economy are undermined as the community loses the resources needed to fund the production of culture. The greater the haemorrhage of rent, the deeper the cultural crisis. The consequences were described by Raphael Lemkin in his treatise on genocide:

> *The destruction of the foundations of the economic existence of a national group necessarily brings about a crippling of its development, even a retrogression. The lowering of the standards of living creates difficulties in fulfilling cultural-spiritual requirements. Furthermore, a daily fight literally for bread and for physical survival may handicap thinking in both general and national terms.*[6]

Some fundamental environmentalists oppose the putting of a cash price on natural resources for the purpose of conserving nature's services. But in pricing nature, we are conforming to nature's own rules: exchanging units of energy, contributing back *at least* as much as we extract. The genius of the "land" (community) market is that we are able to perform this valuation in a routine way, without the arbitrary intervention of rent-seekers who gain by rigging market outcomes.

Think about the sun. The warm stretches of beaches along the Mediterranean coastline are a favourite retirement and vacation destination for Europeans. They occupy the coastline villas and hotels. If, through climate change, the sun stopped shining on those beaches, what would happen to property values? They would plummet. Fewer people would take their vacations in Spain or southern France. Northerners from colder climes would no longer buy retirement homes in southern Italy. The drop in the price of land would be the measure hitherto placed on the services of the sun.

If the community did not charge for the service of the sun, would the sun be any better off?

What about the value of hotels and holiday chalets in the Alps? If nature stopped cascading snow on the mountains, skiers would no longer take their vacations in Switzerland. The drop in property prices would be the measure of the value placed on snow. Snow (the natural kind) costs nothing, so the value of its service is a pure economic rent. It is the same with rain. If the clouds stopped bursting, farmland values would suffer.

If the community did not charge for the service of the snow or rain, would the rents go unclaimed? Or would they be pocketed by those who occupied the locations through which the rents are measured?

The rents of nature's services amount to vast sums. That unique value is continuously increasing in line with human ingenuity and nature's generosity.

---

6 Lemkin (1944: 85).

Think of the value of the sea lanes used by cargo ships to transport goods around the world. Some locations offer short cuts between continents. They are congested. Thanks to those short cuts the reduction in the costs of transportation are reflected in the rents that could be charged for the use of the sea lanes, just as motorists are charged for using the fast lanes on congested highways. Governments do not charge rents for those sea lanes. That does not mean that the economic rent of those locations does not exist. By failing to extend the pricing mechanism to the high seas, the rents are captured by the multi-national corporations that use the sea lanes.

There is no such thing as a free lunch in nature. Biological systems, from micro-organisms to bio-regions, have operating costs and capital costs. We offend the rules of both nature and of morality by permitting some people to enjoy a free ride on the backs of nature, and on the backs of others within our social universe. That is a problem of governance. We should not blame money for the negative consequences of that failure.

Who's the Whore?

Karl Marx, in *Economic and Philosophical Manuscripts* (1844), branded money as "the universal whore, the universal pimp of men and peoples". Colourful, harsh, but a fair assessment of the way money as a social institution had been manipulated against people's private and social interests.

Money has been hijacked to serve a function which, instead of empowering people to add value, undermines their liberties. The nation-state, for example, is supposed to provide the protection and stability that builds the confidence that makes possible the production and exchange of goods and services. Trust is necessary to assure people that tokens of money will be redeemed at a future time and place for products and services of equivalent value. But when the state betrays its primary function – providing security and stability – people lose faith. Anti-social behaviour comes to the fore to corrode trust. This is clear in the malfunctioning financial sector. It is only when rent is deemed to be footloose, unanchored, up for grabs by the Toughest Man in Town, that financiers can play fast and loose with money. All market-based discipline is gone. This then corrodes society.

In commerce, when rent becomes undifferentiated from money from other sources, two things happen. First, money is made to conceal the nature of the transaction between land owner and the working population. The land owner becomes a free rider. Second, the moral content of money is eviscerated. This yields the toxic alchemy by which money is polluted by the values of free riders, and becomes a means for making money out of money. Money loses its primary function as the measure of transactions between producers and consumers. It becomes the tool for making money: which is another way of saying that it is now the channel for capturing the rents produced by others.

In politics, the corruption of the morality of money enables the governing elites to work against the grain of people's interests. When cheating is sanctioned by law, the disciplines of public service are compromised. One consequence is that the guardians of the public's finances (who have proved to be derelict in their duty) may spend money that is not in the public's purse: the resort to debt financing transfers the cost of today's consumption onto future generations.

Society is disabled, the population traumatised by the million-and-one ways in which dysfunctional behaviour adds to the stresses of everyday living.

Participants in the process of cheating are not consciously aware of what they are doing. Lord Sugar, in admonishing his would-be apprentices, is sincere in preaching the need to combine profit-seeking with delivering value for money. His conscience is not disturbed by making money from Mayfair locations. But if we wish to restore health to our societies, we need to remind ourselves that appropriating the value created by others degrades the commons of both nature and society. This process continued through to the 20th century, and it continues to compromise our lives today (Box 10.2).

Restoring Morality to Money

Rebalancing the economy relies on the willingness of people to challenge the conventional wisdoms about taxation.

Ideologists peddle the notion that tax policies are "progressive". If they were, after 60 years of what were supposed to be re-distributive taxes under the aegis of the Welfare State, poverty and the gap between the rich and the poor would have diminished. Instead, those taxes camouflaged some of the damage caused by the pricing mechanism that was constructed by the cheats of old. Large numbers of people remain permanently locked into the state of dependency, forced to endure the indignity of living off others rather than on the products of their own labour.

The progressive tax doctrine endures because politicians persist in claiming that their taxes are grounded in an ethical code. That claim does not stand up to the test of fairness.

Fig. 10:1 represents, for fiscal purposes, people's incomes along two dimensions. On the horizontal axis we measure ability to pay. A person is located on this scale according to the size of income. The richest are located at the right hand end of the scale. According to conventional political philosophy, those with the highest incomes should pay more than those on the lowest incomes. That is as deep as the discussion goes. No consideration is devoted to

Box 10:2
Hoodwinking the Hikers

In Britain, Parliament continued to sanction the grabbing of the commons into the 20th century. An example of the tactics employed against the people of the commons was the deceit deployed to appropriate the commons by the River Thames between Richmond and Kingston, in Surrey. That case is interesting for the way the Lord of the Manor (the Earl of Dysart) manipulated language to overcome democratic opposition.

Ham Fields was a choice leisure location. Walking through the fields besides the Thames was a favourite pastime. It gave town dwellers the experience of living in the countryside. Local residents mounted strong opposition to his lordship's plan to enclose 200 acres. So the earl re-worded his Act of Parliament. Standing reality on its head, he called his law the *Richmond Hill (Preservation of View) Bill*. Residents would not be able to walk through the land, but they could stand on Richmond Hill and look at the view! The Bill sailed through Parliament, and his lordship pocketed a £10m profit (in today's values) by developing the field.

how a person became rich (did he earn his income?), or why he is living on a low income (is this a lifestyle choice?), to determine tax liability.

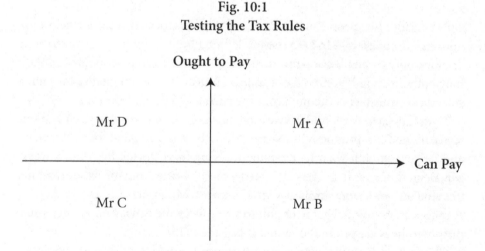

Fig. 10:1
Testing the Tax Rules

The vertical scale measures the basis on which people *ought* to pay based on the source of income. This is value judgment made explicit. In my terms, someone who works for his income should be at the bottom of the scale – paying no tax.[7] Someone receiving unearned income, however, is a legitimate

---

7   In a longer treatment of this issue, we would refine this assertion to note that some taxes on earned incomes may be justified, for public health reasons.

target for the fiscal authorities. The issue that ought to concern us is *how* the income was acquired.

Take two entrepreneurs, each receiving an identical, high income. Mr. A is located in the top right hand quadrant, while Mr. B is placed in the bottom right quadrant. Mr. A pockets his money from the rents of land and nature's resources. He has a legal right to do so, but he does not add a single penny to the wealth of the nation. Mr. B's £1m is the result of creative activity in the production of goods or services which are purchased by consumers. Why is it fair to tax Mr. B at the same rate as Mr. A? The two relevant issues are these.

- Mr. A has no cost of production. The value he captures is produced by others. On moral grounds, why should he be allowed to retain a red cent of rent? Mr. B does incur costs of production. Should he not be allowed to keep his profits without impediment from the tax authorities?
- According to the advocates of progressive taxation, Mr. B should be required to pay his share of the costs of public services. But why are those services unfunded? They create rents that are at least equal to the costs of providing the services to the public. If the rents are not collected by government on behalf of the community, why should Mr. B be penalised for this dereliction of public service?

Now consider two people on low incomes. Mr. C is located at the corner of the bottom left quadrant, Mr. D at the top left quadrant. Why the discrimination? They are both on an identical low income. According to conventional tax policy, they both ought to be relieved of taxation. Indeed, they both qualify for public subsidies – transfers of income from the rich. Let's take a closer look.

Mr. C goes to work for his low income. He is classed as a marginal worker: few skills and low productivity. Nonetheless, there is a demand for his services, and he gets by with what he earns by working from 9-to-5, five days a week. Mr. D, on the other hand, has inherited a piece of land from his parents, which he rents out for a sum similar to Mr. C's wages. Mr. D sits at home all day. He manages an occasional game of golf to while away the time. And yet, for fiscal purposes, he is classed in the same tax bracket as Mr. C.

Morally, there is no equivalence between the two low-income people, or the two rich people. And yet, governments fail to distinguish between them. They apply invasive tax policies because "it's fair that the rich should pay more than the poor, and that the rich should subsidise the poor".[8] The injustice of that doctrine has allowed the divergence of incomes to the point where, in

---

8 The low-income Mr. C might be worthy of a public subsidy; but why subsidise Mr. D, who has opted for his low-income lifestyle?

the US, 23% of all national income is appropriated by 1% of Americans. What drove that yawning gap between rich and poor? Not a supernatural force. According to economist James Galbraith, a professor at the University of Texas (Austin), almost all of the rising gap between rich and poor up to 2008 was the result of activity in the financial sector.[9] The economy expanded since the early 1980s on the back of the growth of credit. Under the prevailing monetary system, this placed bankers in the economic driving seat – not the people who produced the value that was traded in the markets. And so, following the reasoning of conventional economics, bankers were held responsible for the "market failures" that delivered unequal outcomes. But these outcomes were only possible because of the failure of governance in the realm of public finance.

The theory of progressive taxation helps to camouflage the deeply troubling issues. Why was the finance industry free to ride roughshod over the economy? Why did the economy lose its value-adding capacity? Why should this state of affairs result in inequality of outcomes? The capitalist economy obviously operates on an unsustainable basis. But in politics, critics of tax policy focus their attention on *how much* a government raises, and not on *how* it raises its revenue. The outcome is an economy, and society, in chaos.

---

9 Galbraith (2012).

Chapter 11: Society's Automatic Stabiliser

CAPITALISM is programmed to fail. The cyclical character of economic activity exposes the in-built propensity to distort economic activity. Capitalism is a crippled formation that needs an automatic stabiliser. We cannot specify the components of that stabiliser until we identify the flaw. That leads to an obvious question: why, despite more than 200 years of economic data, are economists still unable to offer a coherent explanation for the regularity of disturbing booms and economic busts?

To single out one theorist as derelict in his duty to provide an account that could lead to a steady-state market economy may seem invidious. But Robert J. Shiller invited scrutiny when he published a book in the middle of a depression with the title *Finance and the Good Society*.

Shiller is Professor of Economics at an Ivy League university. He is also a household name in America. His name appears on the Cave-Shiller Index which monitors house price trends in 20 cities. This closely watched barometer of the housing market suggests that Shiller must be an expert on the dynamics of the market economy. So when he links High Finance to a vision of the Good Society, we must assume that what he writes is as good as it gets, from the perspective of economic theory.

Shiller published his book in the year when unemployment among school leavers and university graduates in some Western countries was over 50%. Could that grotesque deprivation have been avoided if a century's worth of theorising had realistically focused on why the capitalist economy savages people's lives? But the aspiration of a stable economy, according to Shiller, was spurious.

We ultimately cannot completely prevent major economic fluctuations with monetary or fiscal policy, but we can still lessen the impact of those fluctuations on individuals by setting up appropriate financial institutions. These are known as automatic stabilisers.[1]

---

1 Shiller (2012: 116).

So far, there is no evidence that economists have been able to specify the elements of automatic stabilisers. But the post-classical economists have an explanation for that failure. Recessions, says Shiller, are unpredictable because they stem from the psychology of individuals. Psychotherapists need to be consulted for remedies. This has created a new sub-discipline. Economists have ventured into matters of the mind to try and unravel what Shiller calls *irrational exuberance*,[2] and *animal spirits*. The study of the economy, apparently, is beyond the methods of science.

> *One cannot do controlled experiments with national economies to learn their dynamics.*[3]

Shiller recounts the optimistic pronouncements offered by the West's central bankers in 2006. From the Open Market Committee of the US Federal Reserve to the European Central Bank and the IMF – they all consulted their crystal balls and saw continuous growth, and they were all wrong. This sad performance was in line with the best of intelligence available from around the world, as gathered by America's security agencies. Understanding global trends is one of the functions of well-endowed institutions like the CIA. The American superpower needs to know where – and when – instability might surface, to deploy diplomatic and military resources in defence of its interest. And so, the CIA reassured its paymasters in Washington that all would be stable in the global economy up to 2015. There would be accelerated growth of the Chinese Trojan. Nevertheless, the US would remain buoyant, along with its NATO partners. According to the CIA's Long-Term Growth Model, published in 2000, there was no prospect of a sclerotic seizure of the financial arteries (Figure 11:1). Although I lacked the CIA's resources and global spy network, I had already warned, *three years before the CIA ran its model*, that growth would stall in 2007 as the prelude to depression in the 2010s.[4]

The problem with the erroneous forecasts was not with the computers that generated the predictions. There is a well known adage: garbage in, garbage out. The models devised by forecasters rest on assumptions that could deliver one result only: continuous growth. This growth was celebrated as the New Economy by Alan Greenspan, the then Chairman of the US Federal Reserve. It was a foolish critic who dared to challenge the collective wisdom of Western intelligence agencies, distinguished professors and consultants who drew fat fees for advice to clients on Wall Street and in the City of London.

---

2   Shiller (2000), which offers references in the index to the income of Labour and Capital, but is silent on the rewards to the owners of Land.
3   Shiller (2012: 117).
4   Harrison (1997: 27).

Figure 11:1
Forecasting with Intelligence?

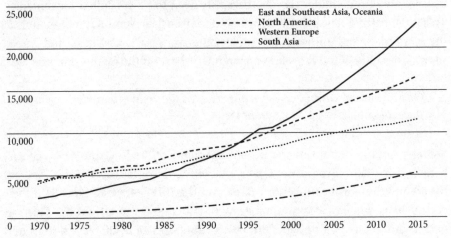

Billions of 1998 US$ (purchasing power parity)

———— East and Southeast Asia, Oceania
- - - - - North America
·············· Western Europe
—·—·— South Asia

Source: CIA Long-Term Growth Model, cited in National Intelligence Council (2000: 35).

When I published my forecast in 1997, I was subjecting theory to as close as one can get to a controlled experiment. The economy was my laboratory. I predicted the trends and the outcomes (p.90 above). There was nothing special about the analytical tools at my disposal. The library at Yale could provide Professor Shiller with the same materials. But the economics profession was found wanting because, as a discipline, it has been reduced to mumbo-jumbo. "Bubbles," claims Professor Shiller, "are a phenomenon that may be compared to a social mental illness ... We need something like the diagnostic criteria that the American Psychiatric Association has provided."[5] Unfortunately, there is little point in such explorations of the mind to account for business cycles, not least because the predictions would be no more reliable than the ones which were offered in the past. As Shiller notes:

We have to rely on modern neuro-science as well in understanding bubbles. The co-ordination of all the different agents that make up the brain is imperfect, for the evolutionary processes that shaped the human brain have not made it into a perfect machine. In our evolution the mammalian brain was built "on top of" the reptilian brain, and there is a degree of duplication and contradiction within our brains.[6]

5   Shiller (2012: 179).
6   Shiller (2012: 180).

And so, if you rely on economists like Shiller for advice on how to invest the assets in your pension fund, you should know that people like him "use their intuitive judgment, as well as formal models". Unfortunately, that kind of psycho-neuro-scientific forecasting will not warn you that the next major global depression will begin in 2028, preceded by the mid-cycle crisis in 2019. My forecast rests exclusively on how income is distributed under the current rules, by understanding how tax policies reward land speculation, and how rent-seeking incentives distort the value-adding side of the economy.

The *homeostatic* Pricing Mechanism

The capitalist economy needs the services of an automatic stabiliser, but what would it look like?

Pre-literate peoples evolved customs and practises that were the internal mechanisms in their communities which maintained a balanced relationship with nature. Folklore transmitted wisdom through the generations to achieve *homeostasis*, the sustainable way of living. The cultural signals secured adjustments in the behaviour of individuals to preclude deviant activities that would jeopardise the well-being of others. These communities acted as if they had a scientific understanding of the laws which, in a later age, would be re-constructed in laboratories.

Organic finance, as I explained it in Ch. 10, replicates within the social universe nature's principle of *homeostasis*. Society's automatic stabiliser is the pricing mechanism based on rent. The necessity for that financial arrangement was recognised by the philosophers of the Scottish Enlightenment. Adam Smith was notable for merging the moral and material considerations into his account of public finance to achieve harmony in competitive markets. In treating rent as public revenue, incentives in the labour and capital markets are not distorted.

> *Both ground-rents and the ordinary rent of land are a species of revenue which the owner, in many cases, enjoys without any care or attention of his own. Though a part of this revenue should be taken from him in order to defray the expenses of the state, no discouragement will thereby be given to any sort of industry.*[7]

Smith understood that taxes on wages and profits diminished the output of wealth. Not so with the Land Tax. He noted:

---

7   Smith (1776, Bk. V, Ch. II, Pt. II, Art. I).

The annual product of the land and labour of the society, the real wealth and revenue of the great body of the people, might be the same after such a tax as before. Ground-rents, and the ordinary rent of land, are, therefore, perhaps, the species of revenue which can best bear to have a peculiar tax imposed upon them.

Smith understood the need to exempt from taxation the buildings and other improvements invested in and on the land. In adopting this tax arrangement, government was rendered neutral in relation to the choices people made about how they worked or invested their money. He was emphatic about the ethics that distinguished rent from other forms of revenue.

Nothing can be more reasonable than that a fund which owes its existence to the good government of the state, should be taxed peculiarly, or should contribute something more than the greater part of other funds, towards the support of that government.

Smith's ethical sensibilities enabled him to analyse the way in which taxes could ricochet around the economy. He condemned taxes like those on windows "as they must frequently fall much heavier upon the poor than upon the rich". Taxes on wages harmed labourers. But a public charge on rent could not be passed on in the form of higher prices to tenants. The levy would remain upon the landlord. Smith was describing the operation of feedback loops which, in the late 20th century, would feature in a new discipline: cybernetics. A modern re-statement of Smith's Land Tax was offered by Joseph Stiglitz and his co-author, Professor (now Sir) Anthony Atkinson of Nuffield College, Oxford. In their lectures they explain that "the land tax [is] non-distortionary, but also it is the 'single tax' required to finance the public good".[8]

When governments fail to recycle rents into the funding of public services, that income is turned into a compound that corrodes culture. It is forced to become the incentive for activity that ruptures production and employment. By recovering it for the public purse, it is converted back into society's primary automatic stabiliser. As productivity increases, so rents increase even faster as a proportion of national income (because, unlike labour and capital, "land" – for short- to medium term practical purposes – is in fixed supply). *Good news*, if that flow of income is invested for the common good. *Bad news*, if rents are capitalised into the pockets of speculators.

---

8   Atkinson and Stiglitz (1980: 525).

Figure 11:2
Automatic Stabilisation of the Value-adding Economy

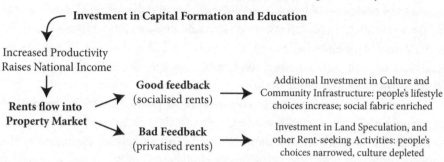

The choices faced by society are traced in Fig. 11:2. As people improve their skills and invest in the formation of more capital, they increase their productivity. Part of the additional income ends up in asset markets. The assets in fixed supply (land, and especially the choicest urban locations) command the greatest bargaining power, so they extract a larger proportion of the additional national income as rent. The impact of this varies according to the quality of governance.

- *Good governance* Rents are determined through competition in the market and recycled to fund public goods. This increases the production of culture in general, by engaging the creative talents of everyone. This is the efficient feedback mechanism in action, stabilising activity around an equilibrium that is anchored in the moral values of the community.
- *Bad governance* If rents are privatised, social revenue is diverted into self-serving activities that are necessarily contrary to the public's interests. This triggers an endless sequence of feedbacks that destabilise the community at all levels until the economy collapses, along with the deterioration in the infrastructure of culture in all its forms.

In the schizophrenic condition that is capitalism, the feedback loops are engaged in an unequal dual with the welfare of humanity. The collision of cultures between value-adders and value-extractors squashes personalities and undermines human creativity.

Fear the Looming Mega-trends
Our civilisation has mislaid the wisdom of ancient peoples and the knowledge of the classical philosophers. If we wish to restore balance to society, the immediate task is to recover that knowledge. The sociogenic approach mobilises and synthesises old methodologies (from history, archaeology, anthropology) with

new disciplines (epigenetics and evolutionary psychology). The objective is to refresh our minds and elevate the discourse on which our futures depend. We would then be equipped to contextualise the cheating that resulted, for example, in the financial *débacle* of 2008. And we could answer difficult questions, like: why do we tolerate the behaviour of those who inflict damage on nature and who then offload their personal responsibilities with the collective noun "we" when it comes to attributing blame?

The penalties for failure will be awesome, a prospect stressed by the US Government's National Intelligence Council (NIC). It recognises that global trends are becoming ever more unpredictable. The threats are identified by the concept of *mega-trends*. The NIC uses "globalisation" to illustrate the power of mega-trends. These are defined as:

> *a force so ubiquitous that it will substantially shape all of the other major trends in the world of 2020.*[9]

Consider three categories of trends – Ecological, Social and Economic – as trains running on parallel tracks. The carriages are wobbling because their locomotives are unstable. If one train comes off its track, it will trigger a chain reaction. The collapsing carriages strike the adjacent carriages, which then strike the third train. They all collapse. For so long as the three trains continue to run on their own tracks, there is hope of being able to apply the brakes. Time, however, is running out. A junction is just ahead, where two of the tracks merge. At that point, two trains *will* collide. That collision *will* topple the third train. Most passengers may not survive.

America's intelligence community has evaluated the looming collision between poverty and politics.

> *If the growing problem of abject poverty and bad governance in troubled states in Sub-Saharan Africa, Eurasia, the Middle East, and Latin America persists, these areas will become more fertile grounds for terrorism, organised crime, and pandemic disease. Forced migration also is likely to be an important dimension of any downward spiral.*[10]

Poverty is an endemic feature of the capitalist economy, a destabilising mechanism that threatens the welfare of everyone. As such, there is little prospect of defusing the threats that emanate from mass poverty, unless we install robust mechanisms for stabilising what has become a globalised civilisation. The most

---

9   National Intelligence Council (2004: 27).
10 NIC (2004: 34).

Box 11:1
Combining the Feedback Loop Effects

Positive feedbacks are *amplifications* of a trend (which can be dangerous, de-stabilising). Negative feedback mechanisms (such as a thermostat in a heating system) yield *constancy* of values (a problem, when growth is wanted). In capitalism, as productivity grows, so rents rise faster than wages and profits. This becomes dangerous as rents are capitalised into the trading prices of land which, in turn, encourages speculation, rocketing prices and reckless credit-creating behaviour. We need to combine growth without violent swings (boom/busts).

When rents are collected to fund public services, the community is free to exercise choices. Instead of opting for interminable growth of material goods, it can increase the share that is funnelled into non-economic activities - arts and recreation – that require increased amounts of leisure time. No matter how productive it becomes, an economy's amplitudes would not get out of control. For choices made by people in the markets would smooth out the production of material goods as they reduced working time in favour of leisure. The financial incentives that reward reckless land speculation would be absent.

effective automatic stabiliser is the public pricing mechanism that treats rent as society's revenue (Box 11:1).

Poverty & the Gold Paradox

The first industrial society manufactured poverty alongside the products it marketed to the rest of the world. We may name this process The Gold Paradox after Alfred Russel Wallace (1823-1913), the co-inventor of the theory of evolution.

Gold, wrote Wallace, was "*not* wealth; it is neither a necessary nor a luxury of life, in the true sense of the word". Gold served two purposes. It was a token (like cowry shells of an earlier age) that facilitated the exchange of commodities. And in the arts, it was mainly an ornament or an *indication* of wealth.[11] But our deluded society pursued gold as if it were real wealth. This contributed to the process of impoverishment. Put in terms of the language of the theory of evolution, the population under-achieved its natural potential by failing to adapt to the realities of the social universe. This is how Wallace put the apparent paradox.

The larger the proportion of the population of a country that devotes itself to gold-production, the smaller the numbers left to produce real wealth – food, clothing, houses, fuel, roads, machinery, and all the innumerable

---

11 Wallace (1901: 370).

conveniences, comforts, and wholesome luxuries of life. Hence, whatever appearances may indicate, gold-production makes a country poor, and by furnishing new means of investment and speculation helps to keep it poor.[12]

Wallace was angered by the "wretchedness, starvation, and crime which, as we have seen, has gone on increasing to the very end of our century". But this was not a paradox for Wallace. He had travelled to Asia to collect the evidence which provided him with the insights that led him to formulate the theory of evolution. In February 1858, while living in the islands known as the Moluccas, he crafted the article which he sent "by the next post to Mr. Darwin".[13] Darwin went on to popularise the biological theory of evolution. He did not match the insights into social systems that Wallace offered in the works he wrote on his return to England. Most importantly, Wallace recognised that the anti-evolutionary trends within European society were grounded in the property rights of land ownership. These nurtured two forms of pathological behaviour.

First, there was no paradox about the co-existence of prosperity with poverty. Henry George had got it right in *Progress and Poverty*, Wallace noted.[14] The creative potential of the mass of working people was suppressed by landlords. People laboured to produce wealth, but the cream was siphoned off for the benefit of the few. This gave a perverse twist to the notion of the "struggle for life". In nature, a biologically related population worked both competitively and in partnership to adapt to its environment. It conformed to the territorial imperatives of the natural universe. But in Europe, the elites had rejected the 1st Law of Social Dynamics. They actively deprived people of access to the natural resources they needed if they were to achieve the potential that was inscribed in their DNA. Abject poverty and its premature deaths served no natural or social purpose.

The second manifestation of pathological behaviour was the mal-treatment of the natural world. In a chapter entitled The Plunder of the Earth, Wallace chronicled "a reckless destruction of the stored-up products of nature".[15] In a description that anticipated the work of late 20th century ecologists, Wallace condemned the consequences of deforestation, the depletion of finite fossil fuels, the degradation of the soil by hydraulic mining and the erasure of the fertility of land "wholly in the interest of landlords and capitalists". Armed with his evolutionary perspective, he was able to trace the way this ecocide was reprised in the corruption of people's moral and physical characteristics.

---

12 Wallace (1901: 370).
13 Wallace (1901: 139).
14 Wallace (1901: 364).
15 Wallace (1901: 367).

Wallace wrote from personal experience when he noted how, in Ceylon, "virgin forests were entirely removed, producing unnatural conditions, and the growth of the young trees was stimulated by manure. Soon there came disease and insect enemies … the rich soil, the product of thousands of years of slow decomposition of the rock, fertilised by the humus formed from decaying forest trees, being no longer protected by the covering of dense vegetation, was quickly washed away by the tropical rains, leaving great areas of bare rock or furrowed clay, absolutely sterile, and which will probably not re-gain its former fertility for hundreds, perhaps thousands, of years". [16]

Wallace was not an economist. He was, however, able to tie his observations into the theory of rent when he condemned the way in which Britain exploited peasants in India. He had no doubt that "our greatest mistakes of all are, the collection of revenue in money, at fixed times, from the very poorest cultivators of the soil; and the strict enforcement of our laws relating to landed property, to loans, mortgages, and foreclosures, which are utterly unsuited to the people, and have led to the most cruel oppression, and the transfer of numbers of small farms from the ryots [cultivators] to the money-lenders. Hence, the peasants become poorer and poorer; thousands have been made tenants instead of owners of their farms; and an immense number are in the clutches of the money-lenders, and always in the most extreme poverty".[17] This exploitation fits the description of what happened in the USA and UK in the 21st century that led to the sub-prime mortgage crisis. India, today, has more poverty-stricken people than in the whole of Sub-Saharan Africa. And it all traces back to the destabilisation of society through the misaligned distribution of rent.

Coming Home: the Sociology of Vertical Integration

The core remedy for the instabilities in modern society is the policy that leads a population to reoccupy its homeland on terms that restored the rights of everyone.

The tenure-and-tax doctrine of the aristocracy relied on a flat earth, or horizontal, form of development. This caused the extensive displacement of people and their creative power, undermining social evolution by dissipating energy. The progressive future of humanity is conditional on the coming home of the dispossessed. By this, I mean the repossession of people's equal rights of access to the commons within their societies. This would automatically release their talents through the optimum use of creative energy. This results in the "vertical" growth of communities; meaning, compact cities and depth of development of culture and personal lives. This is schematically illustrated in Figure 11:3.

---

16 Wallace (1901: 371).
17 Wallace (1901: 374).

Figure 11:3
The Spatial Dynamics of Tenure and Taxation

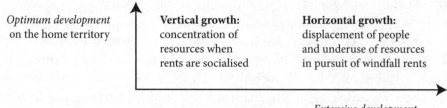

Optimum development
on the home territory

Vertical growth:
concentration of
resources when
rents are socialised

Horizontal growth:
displacement of people
and underuse of resources
in pursuit of windfall rents

Extensive development
on other people's territory

Progress is not possible without understanding the feedback linkages between the natural and social universes. A back-to-basics approach to politics and economics is required; which, ultimately, means the re-education of the political classes (Box 11:2).

On occasion, the truth does put politicians on the spot. This happened with the publication of a report by a distinguished panel of academics and economic advisors led by Nobel laureate Sir James Mirrlees.[18] Publicly, the blue ribbon report was well received by David Cameron's Coalition government. The *Review of the Tax System* restated the principles of land taxation, and concluded:

> *The taxation of property in the UK is currently something of a mess. As we have seen when considering the practicalities involved in implementing an ideal system, up to a point this is understandable. But **it remains both desirable and feasible to clear up much of the mess**. Our conclusions can be summarized thus: There is a strong case for introducing a land value tax. The priority should be to use it to replace the economically damaging business rates system.[19]*

Mirrlees and his associates employ non-scholastic language to leave their readers in no doubt about their view on the state of the tax regime. They want a direct charge on land. But the severe limits to their ambitions are revealed in their concluding paragraph (page 39).

> *This is a radical set of proposals, and the changes would need to be phased in carefully. But this is also an area where the **current practise** is a long*

---

18 James Mirrlees (Cambridge University and the Chinese University of Hong Kong), Stuart Adam (Institute for Fiscal Studies), Tim Besley (Bank of England and the London School of Economics), Richard Blundell (University College London), Stephen Bond (Oxford University), Robert Chote (IFS Director until October 2010), Malcolm Gammie QC (One Essex Court and the IFS Tax Law Review Committee), Paul Johnson (Frontier Economics), Gareth Myles (Exeter University), and James Poterba (US National Bureau of Economic Research and the National Tax Association).
19 Mirrlees, (2011: 36) Emphasis added.

Box 11:2
The Glazed-eye Look

Sir Samuel Brittan is the doyen of columnists on London's *Financial Times*. Over the years his call for fiscal reform has fallen on deaf political ears. There was no problem with the theory: "The case for a land tax is one of the oldest and least disputed propositions in economic thought". But when the case is put before finance ministers, their eyes "glaze over if you as much as mention the subject".[1]

Spurious reasons are deployed. One is the alleged difficulty of identifying the value of land. Brittan: "The difficulty is exaggerated. Property developers within a mile of the Financial Times building tell me they have no worries on the issue. After all if two buildings with very similar characteristics sell at very different prices, the difference can be reasonably attributed to land values". And: "If politicians really want to think about the unthinkable, as they sometimes claim, here is the place to start".

---

1 Brittan (2012).

way from an economically rational and efficient system. Stamp duty and business rates defy the most basic of economic principles by taxing transactions and produced inputs respectively. Income tax and capital gains tax create a significant bias against the rental market in favour of owner-occupation. Meanwhile, council tax is indefensibly regressive and, thanks to **spineless government** *refusal to undertake a revaluation, we find ourselves in the absurd position that tax bills are still based on relative property prices in 1991. Over time, this arrangement will come to be seen as more and more untenable. At some point, some government will have to grasp the challenge of making the case for intelligent reform.*

I have added the emphases.

Why, then, does this panel of experts confine the direct charge on land to raising a tiny fraction of the budgetary requirements of the state? Alongside their affirmation of the correctness of the theory of charges on rents, they advocate the taxation of consumption. This can only be explained in terms of ideological prejudice. It certainly did not make sense in terms of the needs of the depressed economy, which was locked in the trough of the severest downturn since the 1930s. To climb out of the depths of recession, it was vital that consumers should spend more in the shops. So why impose taxes on the price of goods?

ATCOR: All Taxes Come Out of Rent

Economists claim that rent is a small fraction of a nation's income. If this is correct, how can it serve as the economy's automatic stabiliser? It could not, if economists were correct in their claim that rent is no more than 1% to 4% of national income. Paul Krugman, a Princeton professor of economics and 2008 Nobel Prize winner, teaches students that rent is just 1% of GDP.[20]

Mason Gaffney, a professor at the University of California (Riverside), searched the archives to discover the reason why neo-classical economists would make rent disappear. They were under the influence of robber baron philanthropists who endowed American universities and think-tanks with their rents.[21]

Rent is at least 33% of a modern nation's annual revenue, in my opinion. As such, it is sufficient to cover fiscal needs of nations that are not saddled with the costs of carrying millions of unemployed people. This is sufficient to meet fiscal needs, as Gaffney has explained.[22] Joseph Stiglitz argues that rents ought to be collected at a tax rate of 100% (Box 11:3).

But if government statisticians and Nobel Prize economists can trace barely any evidence of land rent in an economy like America's, why do I claim that this flow of revenue represents something like one-third of national income? The clue was first provided by John Locke more than 300 years ago. A nation's income that has been distorted by pathological taxes is not what it seems. The starting point for disentangling the financial mess is Locke's warning in a letter to Parliament, dated 1691, and published as *Some Considerations of the Lowering of Interest and the Raising the Value of Money*, in which he examined the influences on the rent of land. On the impact of taxes, he wrote:

> *It is in vain in a country whose great fund is land to hope to lay the public charge of the government on anything else; there at least it will terminate. The merchant (do what you can) will not bear it, the labourer cannot, and therefore the landholder must: and whether he were best do it by laying it directly where it will at last settle, or by letting it come to him by the sinking of his rents, which when they are fallen, every one knows they are not easily raised again, let him consider.*

To raise revenue by levying a tax on wages was delusional. To defend their living standards, people would pass on a tax to their landlords. If they could not pay, they would not pay, all other things being equal. If wage earners are taxed, they have less left over to pay as rent. So the land owner, indirectly, bears the tax burden in the end. It is possible to quibble about the detail, and point

---

20 The 1% figure appears in a pie chart in Krugman and Wells (2006: 283). The figure drops to a barely measurable 0.079% (1992 data) in Case and Fair (1994: 559).
21 Gaffney (1994).
22 Gaffney (1998: 221-233).

> **Box 11:3**
> **The Henry George Principle**
>
> Joseph Stiglitz, the former chairman of the US President's Council of Economic Advisors, former chief economist at the World Bank and winner of the Nobel Prize for economics in 2001, declared in a speech in Washington, DC, in December 2010:
>
> > *In the area of taxes, there's a long standing principle, called "the Henry George principle," which is that you ought to tax factors which are in "inelastic supply" because they don't respond, the supply doesn't respond. Henry George focused on land, but really, the real source of – the major source – of income of inelastic revenues are natural resources. Taxing natural resources, the natural resources don't disappear. You have to make sure there are incentives maybe to extract them, but the rents associated with natural resources should be taxed, and our goal should be a tax of 100%, or close to 100%, of the "rents" associated with those natural resources.*
>
> In this speech Stiglitz elaborated the economics of what he called The Generalised Henry George Principle.

to exceptions. But the thrust of Locke's point was correct then, and it remains so now.

The landlords in the era of what historians now call bastard feudalism were not interested in Locke's clinical analysis. They wanted to reduce the Land Tax, and transfer the costs of the affairs of state onto the peasants. So they initiated a process of taxation which, by the 19th century, culminated in the phenomenon which can only be disentangled by working with the theory which Mason Gaffney calls ATCOR: All Taxes Come Out of Rent. Today, 30% or more of national income is collected by governments as tax. If the taxes were abolished, in a tax-free economy most of that revenue would quickly reassert itself as the rent of land and nature's resources.

If government is collecting the rents anyway, albeit indirectly, why reform the tax structure to collect the revenue with a direct charge on rent? *Because the collection costs and the million-and-one distortions arising from the indirect approach impose enormous burdens on the population.* Just how damaging are existing taxes may be illustrated by an example of ATCOR in action.

Consider, for example, what happens when a government *reduces* taxes that ostensibly fall on wages or the profits of capital. Who, ultimately, benefits? *Landlords!* This is what happened when the UK decided to support the worthy work of charities, by reducing their tax liability.

To meet the needs of low-income families, and to raise revenue for their causes, many charities have turned themselves into retail chains. They operate shops in the high streets of every town in Britain. Second-hand goods are donated by well-wishers, and the proceeds are used to help the blind, Romanian orphans, cancer research, and (through OXFAM) drought victims in Africa. The government decided that charities need only pay 20% of the property tax for the premises that they occupied. A humane policy? That is what electorates believe, because they are not schooled in the economics of John Locke.

Walk down the high street and observe the signs of change: the exodus of businesses that once gave the central locations their vitality. The British government was so alarmed at the loss of small and family-run enterprises from town centres that it created a commission to investigate what might be done to rehabilitate the high streets. Out-of-town supermarkets were blamed for drawing customers away from town centres. The civil servants in the Treasury did not advise the policy-makers that, by granting tax relief to charities, government would be adding to the pressures on the high street.

The realities did not escape the attention of the citizens of Welshpool, a small town in mid-Wales.[23] They analysed the impact on their high street retailers, and found that the property tax relief was distorting the market. They documented the process in a one-page report in 2011. What they found was this.

- When a shop fell vacant, a charity outbid a local entrepreneur for the lease. It did so by offering more than the going rate as rent for the lease. How could the charity afford to do this? By offering an additional sum equivalent to 80% of the property tax – the sum that the local tradesman could not offer, because he had to pay that sum as property tax. By this means, local firms lost out in the bid to secure premises in the high street.
- The charities, however, were no better off after all. They paid the tax relief as higher rents to the landlord. The winner was the owner of the location. The land owner, through the competitive market process, pocketed the money that would otherwise have gone into the public coffers.

The crisis in the high street was not confined to this first round of distortions to competition, however.

- Existing businesses come under extraordinary pressure from their landlords. When rent reviews were undertaken, firms whose leases were running out were informed that adjacent properties (occupied by charities) were paying much higher levels of rents. That evidence was used to force up

---

23 Welshpool (2011).

the rents of existing tenants to levels that some could not afford. They were forced to quit their premises, leaving shops empty in the high street.

What was presented as an altruistic initiative by government – a reduced tax liability on charities – crushed enterprises, killed jobs and hollowed out the high street. Some shops survived the rent review, but that was not the end of the problem for some of them.

- Some of the charity chains also sell new goods at lower prices than nearby commercial competitors. How could they afford to do so? Their retail assistants give their labour without charge, to support the worthy causes. Their running costs are lower, so they can afford to under-cut competitors … some of whom are forced out of business.

In Britain, new charity shops pushed the total to 10,000 by the end of 2012, even as commercial retailers shut shop. Government tax policy escaped censure, because economists did not explain that reduced tax rates causes rents to rise. Conversely, an increase in the tax rate causes rents to decline. These are the fierce fiscal processes that reveal the reality: ATCOR. When we examine the amount that governments collect from all sources, *and* take into account that some rents remain uncollected by them, the aggregate value is, indeed, at least equal to the public expenses that a healthy society would incur to fund public services.

Governments are the chief architects of instability in the capitalist economy. The switch of taxes away from earned incomes, onto rents, would rebalance the economy and society. Phased in over a reasonable period of time, the change would install the mechanism for automatically stabilising a dynamic economy. Rebasing the public's revenue on rent would restore health to the community, but it would need to be undertaken as a therapeutic process. Communities that were traumatised by the displacement of the people from the commons do not need another dose of "shock therapy" of the kind inflicted on post-Soviet populations. The need is for careful treatment, so that communities may heal. There can be no room for revenge against rent-seekers. Most of them, today, are the middle-class homeowners whose support would be needed if the public's finances are to be democratised. Compassion and reconciliation are the keynotes of fiscal reform. By agreeing to reform the financial system, people would automatically correct the injustices inherited from the past. The quest must be a just society today, for the benefit of future generations.

Chapter 12: Between Eden and Nod

ONCE again, we are back at the existential cross-road. Humans are the chaos in the cosmos. We need to do something about this. Quickly.

Our pre-literate ancestors worked out how their existence depended on a wise deal with nature. Ownership was not possible, because that granted individuals the power of life and death. Mortals were not entitled to that power. So ownership was assigned to the deities.

Now, we must renegotiate our place on the planet, irrespective of whether our civilisation's existence is at stake. What is beyond doubt is that we are inflicting mortal damage to life on Earth. There *is* something terribly wrong with our civilisation, because some of us have assumed the right of the gods. The right to determine life and death over other people. Previous civilisations ceased to be viable once their leaders arrogated that power to themselves. Slowly, but surely, they drained the vitality out of their communities until these ceased to exist.

If we wish to avoid their fate, we must refresh the covenant. Whether that covenant is an act of faith in God, or secular promulgation on parchment, is a matter for agreement. But a consensus will not arise unless we reshape the way that we perceive the world. We have to reconfigure our minds: our collective consciousness. Is that possible? It was done in the past. Why not again today?

The first step in the formation of the Western mind was taken by people who were slaves in the Egypt of the Pharaohs. They escaped into the desert, landless. Here, as they wandered, they came to realise that successful re-settlement would require a new code of conduct. Their monotheistic theology linked the occupation of land to efficient governance and ethical behaviour. Theirs was a pragmatic deal with God. The next mind-wrenching step came with the Athenians. They developed a new way of thinking (philosophy) and a new way of behaving (politics). Combined, these yielded a new collective consciousness and group identity. We need to remind ourselves of how this happened.

The classical Greek mind emerged through interaction with a spatial entity: the public meeting place. Language was developed to incorporate spatial images, to enshrine new civil processes and to facilitate a quantum leap in self-awareness. This was the dynamic creation of a new layer of the commons within the social universe. Personality was deepened by association in the *agora*, where people met to resolve the issues that challenged their community. Buildings were located around that communal venue, which doubled as the market place. It was a radical departure from the model employed in Mycenae, the city located to the south-west of Athens which dominated the region in the second millennium BC. There, the community located itself around the palace and its military authority.

Under the Athenian model, obsolete belief systems were side-lined. The texture of Athenian culture was enriched as the royal citadel was replaced by the temple that was open to public worship. The sacred life was complemented by profane interactions in the *agora*, to lay the foundations for the *polis*. The people reassembled their social spirit to sustain the community and their personal welfare. The content of their minds traces the transformation. It was the interaction between minds and the spatial parameters of the city that was crucial to the formation of the new personality and the new politics. This process was inextricably bound to the recognition that the distribution of power – the power to be human – was associated with the right of access to land.[1]

Combining all that we know about the evolution of humans, we are led inexorably to this conclusion: the spatial dimension is the template for cultural evolution. *If that social space is disrupted, corrupted, people lose contact with their collective consciousness and their authentic identity.* Such a rupture is psychologically traumatic, and fatal for the associated customs and practises.

After the Greek revolution, the modern mind faced one further upheaval. The scientific revolution. This was a completely new way of thinking about the natural universe. But was it a completely new way of living? Could it provide the rules that would enable people to adjust their communities to a more complex order, one that enriched the totality of human experience?

Something vital was absent from the science-based paradigm. It explicitly rejected value judgement. It disallowed the ethical component which, in former times, was needed to tie people into a harmonious relationship with nature. Consequently, science became a tool of abuse for a culture of materialism. This occurred, however, not because there was a problem with science *per se*, but with the timing of the revolution. It occurred just as the formation of the rent-seeking culture was gathering pace. England was on the cusp of these events. Religion was cynically exploited, starting with the antics of the lascivious Henry VIII. He wanted to remain loyal to Catholicism, but he had placed himself in an awkward position. In the 1530s he manipulated the laws of the land. He wanted

---

1   Vernant (1982: 39, 46).

to steal the sacred acres of the monasteries while remaining on the right side of the law. He had no choice but to develop a new kind of statecraft.

Henry, his courtiers and their successors required a model of property rights which separated land from God. Because of the violence – nearly all of the monasteries and abbeys were demolished, so there was no going back to the old way of life – it was necessary to make sure that the new owners would not be accountable to God. If nature was to lose its revered status, the religion which embodied the God of the Landless would have to be silenced. Henry's solution was the tactic employed by the tyrants of previous civilisations. He anointed himself head of a new church. In the Church of England there would be no talk about the theology of land, or about the plight of the landless. Not from the pulpit, anyway.

Science was developed within a godless world.

At the time, was it possible (in principle) to combine science with reverence for nature? Could this have been achieved while preserving people's traditional rights of access to the commons? I believe so, if the people of the commons were able to generate additional material resources. Those resources would be needed to fund the evolution of a socially responsible science that did not jeopardise respectful co-existence with other forms of life.

The common people of England rose to this challenge in magnificent style. They combined work in the fields with cottage industries to produce an increased stream of rents. Those material resources could have endowed new skills and new halls of learning in the villages and county towns, to combine all that was good in humanity with the new knowledge that promised to further enrich the totality of life on planet Earth. In such a community, we might have observed the emergence of new Servant Leaders who could provide new directions to the political life of the people of the commons (Box 12:1).

That additional revenue was produced, but it was hijacked, withdrawn from the reach of the public domain.

> Rent records show a rise of 600 to 1,000 percent in rent levels from the 1540s to the 1640s. Yet this increase in gentry income remained beyond the reach of royal taxation.[2]

The secularisation of science and the de-socialisation of rent, combined with the new statecraft, proved to be a lethal combination. It increased the killing power of the nation-states of Europe. If we wish to reverse that history, we need to agree on the terms of a new covenant.

---

2 Goldstone (1991: 97).

Box 12:1
The Role of Servant Leaders

The concept of the Servant Leader was developed by Walter Wink, Professor of Biblical Interpretation at Auburn Theological Seminary in New York City. He writes we must recognise that

> to liberate from, without liberating to, has created new separatisms and even genocide. Liberation from, alone, is an idol. Full liberation involves exorcism of the internalized values and presuppositions of the Domination System, and healing from the wounds inflicted by the crushing of self. Liberation also requires becoming part of a sustaining community that welcomes even the former enemy. We are liberated in order to liberate. The ultimate service, then, is to give one's life for others.[1]

Ideally, this is the role that every one of us ought now to assume, to a greater or less degree. That is a matter for each of us to resolve. But what is not beyond every one of us is the acceptance of the goals. If we cannot accept them, we deny our humanity.

---

1 Wink (2002: 93).

New Covenant: I

The world's crises cannot be resolved from within the existing social paradigm, which is a confused *mélange* of the secular and the spiritual. The 20th century was one long attempt at reaching new settlements within capitalism or its reactionary opposite (communism). It failed. The crises not only persist; they are expanding on an ever-increasing scale. Re-negotiation of the covenant could be undertaken by reviving the theology of land, but that would place a responsibility on the great religions. None of them, today, addresses the issue that gives the Old Testament its social significance.

New Covenant: II

Humanists maintain that science can deliver the solutions we need. But secular society has so far failed to repeat what was achieved by pre-scientific communities. Our ancestors invented deities to serve a vital purpose: they were the independent source of authority over the natural universe. By this means, it was possible to avoid internecine disputes over ownership rights. The individual's right to use land was contingent on the respectful use of the riches in their habitats; and respect for the equal rights of others. This relationship with the supernatural was the first attempt at philosophy. What began as a discourse on nature became an introspection on the nature of humanity. If the scientific society wishes to exclude God from the reckoning, it must deliver a constitution of land rights which fulfils the needs of both nature and humanity. Humanists maintain that this is the function of the rule of law.

The Rule of Law

Heinrich Rommen (1897-1967) was a German lawyer who reflected deeply on the relationship between the laws of nature and the laws of men. He did so under the pressure of events in the early 1930s. As he witnessed the rise of the Nazis, and monitored the way they used the rule of law to impose totalitarian rule, he wrote *The Natural Law* (1936). He subsequently fled to America where he became a lecturer at Georgetown University.

Rommen argued that natural law had to be revived when the laws of men (positive law) were bent to the cause of the unjust.

[T]he natural law reappears whenever the positive law is transformed into objective injustice through the evolution and play of vital forces and the functional changes of communities.[3]

Rommen noted that Hitler "aimed not [at] a revolution, but at a legal grasp of power according to the formal democratic processes".[4] Advocates of the rule of law would describe this outcome as unintended. But as we documented for England and the evolution of parliamentary democracy (Ch. 6), the legacy which was endured in the 1930s, and which we endure today – the laws of the land – *was* intended. Hitler was a footnote in that pathological history.

Now, as in the 1930s, the rule of law continues to be preached by the agents of democracy to preserve a culture which cheats people of their natural freedoms. This is achieved by manipulating minds. That manipulation begins with the fashioning of language in small and subtle ways. Take, as an example, the definition of the word "bedrock" as taught to people who consult the *American Heritage Dictionary of the English Language* on the internet. It explains: "Bedrock: The Very basis; the foundation: *Ownership of land is the bedrock of democracy*" (emphasis in original). And so it is, in the landlords' version of democracy, conforming to their rule of law. By such means are minds coloured and behaviour controlled.

Is it possible to enshrine the justice that is embedded in natural law in a constitution that can replicate the achievements of pre-literate communities without recourse to theology? What would it take to initiate an open-minded review of the law of the land? Open access to the means of communication is a pre-condition for the democratic consensus to emerge. Is this achievable, today?

---

3 Rommen (1988: 230).
4 Rommen (1988: xi).

If the penetration of the culture of cheating has been so absolute, we would expect attempts at such a debate to crash against barriers erected to protect rent-seeking. Do such obstacles exist? Athens, as the cradle of democracy and a formative influence on the Western mind, may provide the answer. Can the Greeks, today, lead the debate on action to abolish the rent-seeking that caused the financial crisis of 2008 and displaced millions of Europeans from their homes and jobs?

Antonis Perris had earned a good living in Athens as a musician. None of his neighbours knew what he had on his mind when he and his elderly mother climbed the stairs to the roof of their apartment building one day in May 2012. He had circulated a note in an online forum revealing that he had run out of money to buy food. "I have no solution in front of me," he wrote. Antonis Perris and his mother leapt to their death. Why, his neighbours wondered, did he not come out into the square, to the coffee shop, to talk to them and ask for help?[5]

Greece is a shattered nation. Riot-torn Athens in the 2010s was at the epicentre of the financial implosion of the European Union's *no-more-world-wars* project. Politicians lost control over the destiny of their populations. Rising levels of suicide registered the despair felt by people who lost their jobs and lost their faith in the institutions that were supposed to protect them. The trend began in 2008, and jumped by 40% in the first six months of 2011. How could this happen in the cradle of democracy? Were the people inhibited from talking through their problems, obstructed from identifying remedies that would restore vitality to the nation of the first Olympians?

At the heart of the Greek tragedy was the failure of policies associated with the public's finances. The Greeks failed to develop benign home-grown solutions: the price of the IMF/European Union bail-out was severe cuts in public spending. This deepened the distress. Had the Greeks explored all the policy options, or was that debate ham-strung?

Clarity of thought depends on a healthy public space that facilitates full and frank debate. That was the model developed by the classical Athenians in the *agora*. Why was that intellectual arena apparently not available to modern Greeks like Antonis Perris and his mother? Pavlos Eleftheriadis, a Fellow in Law at Oxford University, provided the answer.

Public discourse in Athens had been transformed from the personal contact in the public squares of antiquity to communications through the airwaves of television. One of nature's exotic resources, the electro-magnetic spectrum, had been harnessed by scientists to create a new public space that could extend and deepen debate. The technology of the digital age had made possible a system of

---

5 Cha (2012).

communication that could reach millions. Greece was not benefitting from this accomplishment.

In the 1990s, public property – the spectrum through which TV programmes were broadcast – was hijacked. Without securing legal rights to do so, businessmen created broadcasting corporations that used the public airwaves.

> *They were effectively stealing the frequencies. The government of the day did not react. Eight stations were given 'temporary licences' in 1993, which were renewed in 2007 ... Politicians have been afraid to rock the boat. How does this tawdry episode mark the demise of the press? The TV stations absorb the print media. Most do not respect rules for objectivity or moderation. Owner interference is rampant and blatantly self-serving. The heated rhetoric of the politicians is reproduced and enhanced by TV journalists. There is little room for reflection of consensus.[6]*

The corruption of the collective consciousness was sponsored by a few individuals who appropriated the rents of a publicly owned asset. This gave them the financial power to buy the newspapers. That, in turn, gave them monopoly power over the terms of public debate. Would those rent-seekers want an informed, measured debate about the nation's finances? Reason would prescribe the need to re-base government revenue on rents. This would yield a raft of benefits: alleviate the fiscal burden on wage earners, increase employment prospects, raise national income and prevent tax-dodging (land cannot be concealed in a Swiss bank account). Why did such a debate not take place in Athens?

> *Greek politics has been privatised. Unscrupulous politicians, cynical trade unions and media oligarchs have hijacked our public life. They cared little about the [national] debt, and even less about reform ... Given their extravagant gains, the internal distribution of resources is far more important to them than the overall size of the pie.[7]*

The danger posed by an orderly debate is that it might have led to the media barons paying rents into the public purse for using the radio spectrum. That would have eroded their grip on media outlets, leading to the debates about policies that might have avoided the financial bail-out that brought the devastation of IMF-imposed austerity to Greece.

---

6 Eleftheriadis (2012).
7 Eleftheriadis (2012).

Antonis Perris and his mother might still be alive today.

From the depths of their despair, can the people of Greece, the land that gave us Socrates and Plato, wrest control of the public space from the monopolists? To do so, they would have to decide who owns the commons.

Wild Law

The anthropocentric treatment of nature is vulnerable to the interventions of humans with the power to discriminate and destroy.

If we do not assign property rights to a supernatural proprietor, we would need to treat nature as existing in its own right, *with its own rights*, with ourselves as stewards of its welfare. Such a cosmology would need to be based on Wild Law. London lawyers Ian Mason and Begonia Filgueira explain that Earth jurisprudence is

> 'the philosophy of law and regulation that gives formal recognition to the reciprocal relationship between humans and the rest of nature'. The argument is that nature itself can enhance human freedom and well-being if the reciprocal nature of the relationship is fully recognised and allowed to be effective.[8]

This redefinition of nature's status entails a respect that obliges us to modify our language. The word "resource", for example, implies that we value the earth for its economic value alone. The stewardship function entails a new kind of responsibility on all of us to intervene on behalf of nature. Lawyers need the power to intercede in cases where people (corporate or personal) abuse nature. Scottish lawyer Polly Higgins argues that, in cases of ecocide, her colleagues should have the power to prosecute offenders and exact restitution.[9]

Reformulating the law is a major challenge, for "there appears to be no legal culture in the world today, with the possible exception of Ecuador that seriously considers nature herself as having rights which need to be spoken for and represented in human legal systems".[10] The culture of cheating will not readily yield to the proposal to transform the legal status of nature. But the necessity for a new jurisprudence flows naturally from the doctrine of organic finance. Property rights need to be configured with the rights and responsibilities that express our natural moral sensibilities. The need for a new relationship with nature directs us back to a new understanding of ourselves and of our communities.

---

8   Mason and Filgueira (2009: 260).
9   Higgins (2010).
10   Mason and Filgueira (2009: 268).

This is the dynamic interaction driven by adherence to the principles of organic finance. Justice is achieved by liberating people so that – in partnership with each other, and with nature – they may add value to the wealth of their communities. This process is restorative: it rehabilitates both human behaviour and the planet.

The Social Commons

The covenant with God was a land deal based on the premise that God created nature. But humanity was made possible by the fact that *commons were also created by human ingenuity.* These cultural commons did not pre-exist on Earth. Their creation was made possible by the co-operative pooling of resources that have since been privatised. To recover the social commons, we need a covenant with ourselves. We need to re-establish, and defend, the boundaries between the private and public spaces. Whether we choose the route of science or the supernatural, either way, we need to negotiate a social contract that commands general respect. When based on justice, we would all want to defend the contract through eternal vigilance against attempts to subvert it.

This becomes part of the process of recovering our humanity, by healing our minds. The sociogenic approach is the study of what Alastair McIntosh, the Scottish social activist, pastor and scholar, calls human ecology. Given the dangerous state of the world today, confining the re-exploration of our minds to the scientific method and its value-free ethic may prove to be self-defeating. We may have to interrogate God, once again, if that is what it takes to understand ourselves.[11] The metaphysical approach worked in the past. Can we make it work for us again?

We cannot retreat to the state of nature: the gates of the Garden of Eden have been closed. But nor should we accept the life of wandering in the Land of Nod, to which Cain was banished for murdering his brother. We need to create a new way of living in the space between Eden and Nod. Ours is the most privileged generation ever to have lived, because we can articulate the existential challenge with the benefit of knowing what happened to previous civilisations. We can become the architects of a post-civilisation. There is no need to endure the lurking Dark Age. To rise to this challenge, however, we have to accept that rights of access to the commons are necessarily aligned to corresponding duties.

The agents of the cheating culture claim that they are working earnestly to restore order to a world in chaos. But they refuse to engage in discussion on the role of organic finance in the new order.

---

11   McIntosh (2012: 44).

Box 12: 2
Truth, but where's the Reconciliation?

South Africa's post-apartheid ANC Government believes it champions the rights of the indigenous people whose land was appropriated a century ago. And yet that government destroyed the best locally-administered property tax (rates) in the world. The rates on South Africa's urban properties were levied on the value of land alone. This was changed by Act of Parliament in 2004. Now, local authority rates fall on the value of improvements (buildings) as well as on the land. The reverse ought to have happened: the levy on the rental value of land should have been raised. This would have refreshed the faltering land reform programme.

Youths in the shanty towns of Johannesburg and Cape Town, unemployed and in despair, are trying to recover some of the practises of their ancestors. To raise their spirits, they are reviving the ancient art of *intonga* (stick fighting). This was practised among rural herders as a method for settling disputes which did not end in fatalities. For such initiatives to achieve more than novelty value among a few, the fragmented communities need the glue of organic finance.

The future depends on people taking back their power, the power of democracy, and renewing themselves and re-booting their communities.

Trauma Treatment

The act of seeking honest solutions is in itself the therapy of healing. Approaches that have been tried thus far, such as South Africa's Truth and Reconciliation Commission, have fallen short of their promise. In all cases, it was the inability to heal the trauma caused by separating people from their land that led to failure (Box 12:2).

Many techniques exist to assist the recovery process. One would be the compilation of a register of all natural resources. Absent from existing national databases (Japan is a notable exception) is systematic information about current market values of locations and natural resources. The compilation of that inventory would contribute towards the re-education of our selves, especially if it was a community-led exercise. Until recently in Denmark, the location value of urban sites was assessed by panels of local residents.[12] Such experiences remind people that they contribute to the formation of the added value, which therefore ought to belong to them, not the rent-seekers.

---

12 The switch from land valuation by local residents to computer-assisted valuations saved money (Müller and Mørch-Lassen [1989:175]), but at the cost of disconnecting people from democratic involvement in what was once an exemplary property tax (Lefmann and Larsen [2000]).

Four examples of the failure of conventional approaches to conflict resolution highlight the need for a paradigm shift in the focus of such initiatives. The restoration of rents would have the cathartic effect of healing and enriching while excluding none.

Catharsis I: Ulster & the Peace Dividend

The Good Friday peace accord was signed in 1998, signalling the official end to "knee-capping", car bombings and assassinations in the United Kingdom. The IRA (which wants the six counties of Ulster to be integrated into the Republic of Ireland) handed in their weapons.

The 30 years of The Troubles were represented as a religious conflict. Catholics *versus* Protestants. Poverty was somewhere in the mix, but few recalled the trauma of the displacement of Celts from their tribal lands. In the early 17th century, what became known as the Plantation resulted in the confiscation of about 500,000 acres from the Celtic tribes. They were supplanted by migrants from Scotland and wealthy land owners from England. The pain of that displacement is relived every year, conveyed intergenerationally, through the parades that remind everyone of the original injustice. If their leaders had been wise, and the people willing, the peace accord could have resolved the ancient territorial dispute by deploying the fiscal solution. This would have provided the money to fund the psycho-social renewal of the divided population.

There *was* a peace dividend. People invested their savings in the province, which increased the region's income. Under the current fiscal regime, the money representing that net gain was mopped up in the land market. If we take house prices as the proxy for the price of land, we can see what happened from Fig. 12:1. House prices shot up, overtaking the rate of increase in the rest of the UK and in the Republic of Ireland. As I had forecast in 1997 in *The Chaos Makers*, the peak in prices would be in 2007, followed by a steep crash into the ravine.

The peace accord could do no more than buy breathing space for the combatants. With the onset of hard times, following the crash in property prices, the shootings and bombings resumed at an increased pace (Fig. 12:2). Peter Sheridan, chief executive of Co-Operation Ireland, a charity which works with young people in deprived communities in towns like Londonderry, warned that the depression of the 2010s was the recruiting sergeant for paramilitary gangs. Furthermore: "The growth in violent extremism has the potential to be a longer-term threat to the economy than the current recession. The dissidents are growing in strength and capability". Richard Ramsey, an economist at Ulster Bank, explained: "The big picture is that we had a housing boom and bust like no other part of the UK. Almost all our problems can be traced back to

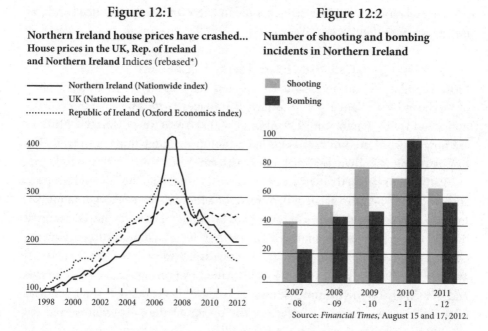

Figure 12:1

Northern Ireland house prices have crashed...
House prices in the UK, Rep. of Ireland
and Northern Ireland Indices (rebased*)

——————— Northern Ireland (Nationwide index)
- - - - - - UK (Nationwide index)
·············· Republic of Ireland (Oxford Economics index)

Figure 12:2

**Number of shooting and bombing
incidents in Northern Ireland**

▨ Shooting
■ Bombing

Source: *Financial Times*, August 15 and 17, 2012.

that".[13] Economists ought to have predicted this outcome. *The net gains of any significant improvement in the welfare of a community are captured through the rents of land.*

Would unification with the Republic have made a difference? The Republic had to be bailed-out by the EU following its land boom.

What would have happened if Ulster had adopted the organic finance model to restore justice? Catholics would have experienced the relief of the acknowledgement that the ancient wrongs inflicted on their ancestors were recognised. Protestants would have enjoyed the relief of knowing that they were no longer the target of car bombs. Everyone would have benefitted from the security of a stable economy. Talking through the historical wrongs and future rights would have united the communities, rendering the geo-political issues of peripheral significance. Would it matter whether the province was part of the UK or the Republic of Ireland? The determination of the people of Ulster to sign up to a new covenant would have provided the leadership which might have encouraged Britain and Ireland to traverse the same path into the future. The territorial borders, after all, had been dismantled by the European Union.

This did not happen. But it is never too late to restore justice. Ulster could rebuild itself out of the trough of the depression of 2010 by re-aligning the

---

13 Smyth (2012).

pricing mechanisms, empowering people to keep what they produced and pay for the services they received.

Catharsis II: Israel & the Palestinians

Mortal combat for the Holy Land. Israelis and Palestinians claim the same piece of territory by ancient right. The Jewish refugees from Europe achieved the upper hand with a victory in 1948. About 750,000 Arabs were displaced. Millions are now concentrated in camps, or live as refugees in far-flung countries. The dispossession is known as al-Nakba (catastrophe).

Zionism originated to serve a twin purpose. First, help the Jews of Europe to cope with anti-Semitism. Second, a creed for action: displace Palestinian Arabs to make way for Jews. The Holocaust gave Jews the right to territorial security, but did one crime justify another? The state of Israel continues to employ the classic tactics of a colonising power. Having displaced people from their farms and homes, the landscape is being transformed by erasing Arabic place names and burying settlements under forests of trees. This (a) distorts the memories of the dispossessed while comforting the minds of the perpetrators; and (b) creates the metaphysical space for new myths.

There are some who still deny the evils of Hitler. Denial is also a device employed by Israel, which challenges the nature of the Nakba. This makes it possible for state-sponsored terrorism in the streets of Haifa. Humanicide in action is reported in the media, but it elicits few protests from a largely complicit international community. To observe a population in trauma, search no further than the children concentrated in the camps of Gaza. They feel the loss of their parents' ancestral lands every day. There is no relief from a coping doctrine that can soothe the anguish of degraded lives.

Now imagine an agreement whereby the peace dividend in the Holy Land was pooled and devoted to upgrading the lives of everyone in the two communities. Land would cease to be a contested issue. It would be held on terms that afforded everyone a home and the opportunity to work. Those with the skills to generate the highest rents would hold the choice locations, and pay the rents into the Community Chest. That fund would finance the re-skilling of peasant farmers and the education of their children. New hope, new prosperity, new multi-cultural affinities.

Catharsis III: Zimbabwe

It was only a matter of time before Zimbabwe fell into anarchy. The breakdown in order was initiated by Robert Mugabe, the revolutionary leader who had fought the British to gain independence. The sequence, from cause to effect, is documented in the files of the Foreign Office in London.

Colonisation began at the end of the 19th century. British settlers appropriated the choice parts of a territory which they named in honour of Cecil Rhodes. Tribes were forcibly herded on to reservations. Then, with independence looming in 1980, Britain refused to relinquish control over the terms of a land reform to a future Zimbabwean government. White settlers retained their land. The outcome was dissatisfaction with the course of economic development. And so, the government of Prime Minister Robert Mugabe assaulted its citizens in what he claimed was a "land reform". His family and friends appropriated the white-owned farms of their choice. The population was brutalised. The colonial trauma was compounded by a home-grown trauma. Millions fled the country.

There can be no return to pastoral forms of social organisation on tribally-administered territories. But a rent-led land reform would reintegrate the population back into their eco-systems. That model was proposed by Joshua Nkomo, one of Zimbabwe's post-independence leaders. He was eliminated by Mugabe's associates.[14] The policy of sharing the rents could be recovered to lead the renewal of the nation. Such an experiment in transformation would have enormous implications for the rest of Africa. The continent continues to lack a model of leadership capable of healing the scars inflicted during the European scramble that began in the late 1880s.

Africa's peace dividend would not only empower its people; it would also relieve the stress on Europe, by creating the jobs that enabled people to remain in their homelands. Migration across the Mediterranean in search of work would decline to a trickle. That rise in living standards across the continent would also help to renew and rebalance the global economy.

Catharsis IV: First settlers & the US

Western nations like the US consider themselves champions of human rights, but their law-makers are reluctant to discuss the plight of their first settlers. James Anaya discovered that when he was commissioned by the UN to investigate the plight of Native Americans, the first such formal enquiry in the history of the US.

Anaya, a law professor at the University of Arizona, is the UN's special rapporteur on the rights of indigenous peoples. His appraisal of the condition of American Indians would test the US's endorsement of the UN declaration on the rights of indigenous peoples.[15] How does the reality on the ground square with the notion of The American Dream? Many of the first settlers are systematically excluded by the economics of apartheid. This discrimination is not sanctioned by law, but it is the logical consequence of the law of the land.

14   Harrison (2008: 101-107).
15   MacAskill (2012).

What would happen to the constitution of America if, as a result of enquiries such as Anaya's, the people moved towards a justice-based solution that worked with the grain of the free market? Americans do not like cheats. They perceive themselves as value-creators. So far, however, they have assiduously avoided the financial reform that would place all citizens on a level playing field. Land speculation is a national sport; capital gains the prize for those who are not trapped in negative equity.

By assessing minority groups in America as victims of a humanicide *that is being perpetrated today*, popular outrage might lead America to amend the Founding Fathers' dictum *Life, Liberty and the Pursuit of Happiness*. We, The People need a constitution that enshrines the equal right to *Life, Liberty and Land*. With it, the American Dream would become a reality. Organic finance would not deprive current owners of their land. Possession would be secured against the payment of rent for those services that were derived from nature and the community.

That would take America beyond capitalism. To a land that protected the personal and property rights of people who worked to enrich themselves and their communities.

In that constitution, there would be no toleration of cheating.

Money Makes the World Go Round

"Money," sang Liza Minnelli in the stage show *Cabaret*, "makes the world go round." And so it does, if money represents the tradable energy in our two universes. By restoring integrity to the monetary system, our world would go round efficiently and fairly. It does not do so now because rent-seeking is a nihilistic assault on the natural order.

Engaging in democratic debate on how to rehabilitate money has the therapeutic effect of reminding ourselves about the values that really make the world go round. In the process, local communities would automatically renew themselves. But no nation is an island. Rents are not just generated within territorial borders. They also emerge at the interface with neighbouring nations and from within the globalised community of nations. In the case of Britain and France, for example, rents are generated by the sea lanes in the channel that separates the two countries. Both countries contribute to those rents through the provision of sea ports and safe passage. But the sea lanes would have little value if the trading nations in the rest of the world did not use them. So the sharing of those rents ought to be through global institutions and devoted to priorities that serve the common good.

The process of democratising the public's finances entails the compilation of an inventory of the assets that define the commons. Those assets need to be

Box 12:3
On the Causes of Happiness

What makes people happy? Gardening tops the list. Persistent polling across the world leaves no doubt that it is not money or luxury holidays, but the pleasure of pottering in the garden at least once a week that makes people happier on average than the rest. Those who never garden are less likely to be satisfied with their life. Caring for a plant is positively related to well-being. Neuroscientist Tali Sharot points out that it is possible that gardening and happiness are correlated because they are both caused by a third factor. Having more free time may explain both well-being and the likelihood of working in one's garden.[1]

We can visualise lifestyles that are more relaxed, in which nurturing activities link us to nature and to our communities. While scientists worry about the difference between correlation and causation, the people of the commons – that's all of us – are fitted to figure out what is good for our health, wealth and welfare. But what is it that denies people the free time, and the peace of mind, to develop their preferred pursuits?

---

1 Sharot (2012:74-75).

classified according to the source of the rents: local, national or global. As this assessment progresses, an informed discussion begins on how to distribute the rents. Ethical awareness is heightened and identities sharpened as people re-acquaint themselves with their natural habitats. The capacity to use reference points located in the environment was lost with the enclosures, and need to be retrieved.

Agreement would also be needed on which taxes to reduce or cancel first. Priorities would depend on where, on the business cycle, the economy was located.

- *In recession* Abolish income taxes to increase disposable incomes, encourage employment and lay plans to rebalance the economy.
- *In boom times* Convert property taxes into charges on land rents to pre-empt the coming crash in real estate.

Our generation is the first in history to consciously understand the benefits of addressing these issues in relation to the long-term prospects for our civilisation. Re-balancing the monetary system would foster what Aristotle called *eudaimonia*.

This Greek concept is misleadingly translated as happiness. The political attraction of such a mistranslation is evident: politicians can prescribe the need for happiness without being held to account by anyone who feels deprived of that psychological state. But the Greek philosopher meant something more tangible. To have *eudaimonia* is to flourish.[16] For a person to flourish, society would have to be healthy. The component parts need to be harmoniously integrated in a balanced relationship between the individual, the population at large and the natural environment. That locates public policy at the heart of the debate that involves all of us. And it makes policy-makers accountable if they fail to deliver the shared services on which we depend for *eudaimonia*.

The elements of that matrix of relationships were elaborated by Henry George. In one page and a short footnote he specified the terms of the healthy community. Organic finance was the organising principle that yielded a synergy composed of three parts.

1. *Population evenly dispersed in the countryside*, clustered in villages to benefit from the close associations that come with density of settlements.
2. *Cities not over-populated*, with homes surrounded by gardens, providing the benefits of specialised activities that did not pollute (Box 12:3).
3. *Nature's rights respected*, with farmland not over-exploited, and human waste not dumped into rivers and flushed into the oceans.

In a few bold strokes of his pen, Henry George outlined a spatial theory that encompassed the essentials of demography, ecology and economics. This was the blueprint for the freedom within which people could flourish, all of it predicated on the termination of the land speculation that causes urban sprawl and an unbalanced economy.

> *The people of the cities would thus get more of the pure air and sunshine of the country, the people of the country more of the economies and social life of the city ... Wealth would not only be enormously increased; it would be equally distributed ... The inequalities that continued to exist would be those of nature, not the artificial inequalities produced by the denial of natural law. The non-producer would no longer roll in luxury while the producer got but the barest necessities of animal existence.*[17]

Politicians are unable to articulate that vision. For it to be recaptured, do we have to turn to artists (Box 12:4)?

The termination of state-sponsored cheating would elevate consumption and production to something more than finding the quickest route to material

---

16 Appiah (2010: xiv).
17 George (1879: 451-453).

> **Box 12:4**
> **Heaven on Earth?**
>
> Italian artist Michelangelo Pistoletto staged an exhibition in London's Hyde Park in the summer of 2011 dedicated to his vision of a Third Paradise. This represented the synthesis of the first two paradises – that of the natural world, and the universe evolved by humans. The vision is beautiful. Every individual must accept responsibility for his and her fate to unite local communities while respecting the rights of others in a global society. Art, in Pistoletto's view, is the medium through which people may come to understand the need for change and avoid the collapse of civilisation. We must scrutinise ourselves in the mirror as the step towards redefining "collective morals by modifying all those terms that contain defects and vices which can no longer be tolerated".[1]
>
> A Heaven on Earth is achievable, and Pistoletto may be correct in contending that art provides the tools for motivating people to dismantle the barriers to the Good Life. But we need to remind ourselves that there is a difference between the art patronised by the aristocratic rent-seekers, and the art of the people of the commons.
>
> ---
> 1 Pistoletto (2010: 85).

satiation. Each of us would be free to allocate more time to discovering how good we were at our preferred preoccupations in sport, art, exploring the world scientifically, engaging with our local communities, caring for others or in the joy of gardening.

Civilisation need not turn out to be humanity's burial ground. If we equalise the access to rents, the market economy and political process would automatically adjust to favour freedom. Power would be devolved. A new kind of social organisation would emerge, a society *beyond* civilisation. People's behaviour would be modified in ways which deepened their personalities and enriched their societies through new levels of engagement. This is what I mean by "coming home" and developing internally, vertically, humanely, rather than extensively, materialistically, intrusively.

We cannot know what lies at the outer boundaries of human possibility; how rich the culture, how noble the achievements, exquisite the aesthetic accomplishments, majestic the valour. There is one way only to find out.

Stop the cheating.

Share the rents.

Epilogue: The Making of World War III

WE need to prepare for World War III. Not to survive it, but to prevent it. This can be achieved if we neutralise the culture of cheating. Otherwise, in my judgement, all the objective conditions are present for a re-run of what happened in 1914 and 1939. A 21st century version of world war looms, and we need to forestall it.

A battle of one kind or another is unavoidable. The rent-seekers will have to be fought to submission. The big question is the lengths to which that culture will go to resist change. It is impervious to reason. It wilfully sacrificed the monarchical form of absolute power, in order to perpetuate itself over piles of bloody bodies. Is it willing to see the death of democracy rather than yield its grip on our lives?

Let it be the fight for life with the weapons of wisdom, not war.

Is a world war really possible? History suggests it. Rent-seeking prescribes it. My theory of cheating leaves little room for doubting it. I am aware of the responsibility associated with issuing a warning about the prospect of a world war. So I am obliged to provide compelling reasons why my forecast should be treated seriously. First, I will cite three cases of the violence which the cheating culture is willing to deploy in defence of its interests. I will then survey the conditions which point to the coming global conflagration.

Case I: The Killing of Dynasties

Once upon a time, East and West were ruled by monarchs who exercised absolute authority. They were unrelenting in defence of their interests, and would show little or no sympathy for the pain endured by their peasants. Over time, pressures in the countryside would intensify to the point where the peasants became a threat to their emperors. To secure the survival of their dynasties, self-interest ought to have encouraged the monarchs to adapt their economies to keep the peasants happy, and themselves in power. To do so, however, they would have had to alter the distribution of the rents of their nations. Equity required the sharing of those rents for the welfare of the whole population.

• **The French Revolution** As the 18th century unfolded, it became clear to Anne

Robert Turgot that discontent could lead to civil disturbance. As the minister responsible for the nation's finances and economic policy, he advised Louis XVI to sanction a tax on land values. This, explained Turgot, would remove the barriers to prosperity and keep the peasants and townsfolk happy.[1] The king demurred. He ended up losing his head to Madam Guillotine in 1793. Many others were also sacrificed in The Terror that followed.

- **The Russian Revolution** As the 19th century drew to a close it became clear to Count Leo Tolstoy that discontent in the countryside was fostering civil disturbance in the towns. He was consulted by the Tsar, Nicholas II, about what to do. Tolstoy, himself the owner of an estate, recommended the adoption of a tax on land values.[2] The Tsar demurred. He abdicated in 1917, and together with his family ended up in front of a Bolshevik firing squad. Millions died in the Soviet campaign to collectivise agricultural land.

- **The Chinese Revolution** As the 20th century dawned the Qing dynasty's spies monitored the deep-seated discontent across the vast land of the Middle Kingdom. The emperor was kept informed. One of the revolutionaries, Sun Yat-sen, was promoting a land value tax to restore harmony in the countryside. No remedial action was taken. The dynasty was toppled by the Xinhai Revolution in 1911. Sun Yat-sen was prevented from introducing fiscal reform, and millions died in Mao's Cultural Revolution (see Ch. 8).

Time and again, history could have evolved in new directions. But the agents of the rent-seeking culture would not negotiate a compromise. The emperors listened to their courtiers rather than those who counselled tax-and-tenure reforms. The dynasties collapsed. The culture of cheating survived.

Case II: The Killing of Cultures

In 1945 the allied powers determined that there should be no repeat of the atrocities of World War II. The Nuremburg trials revealed what had happened in Belsen and Dachau. The United Nations was created, and a Universal Declaration of Human Rights adopted. Raphael Lemkin worked with the committee that was established to define the crime of genocide; but, as we saw in the Prologue, he was defeated on the core issue. Cultural genocide was deleted from the definition of this crime against humanity. The pared-down version meant that "The heart had been ripped out of the Convention and a

---

1 Jupp (1999, 2005).
2 Redfearn (1992: 178-181).

major method of genocide was not criminalised" notes Anja Gauger and co-
workers at the Human Rights Consortium in the School of Advanced Study
(University of London).[3]

Lawyers and scholars were distracted down judicial by-ways. Eventually,
reviews were necessary within the UN because the law's effectiveness was
questioned. "[I]t was not being used and seemed to offer little to those groups
it was designed to protect".[4]

Some individuals have been prosecuted for genocide of the mass murder
kind. Cultural genocide continues apace, within Europe as well as in the rest
of the world. The "excess deaths" that would otherwise have been avoided now
exceed in number the deaths in World War II.

Why was cultural genocide erased from the agenda?

The raw energy that goes into creating and sustaining culture is *economic
rent*. The termination of cultural genocide entails the restoration of rent to the
people in general, so that they might develop authentic cultures of their own,
rather than live by the hand-me-downs from the aristocracies of the past.

Case III: The Killing of Nature

In 1970 the *New York Times* reported that, at a Conference on War and National
Responsibility in Washington DC, Prof. Arthur W. Galston "proposed a new
international agreement to ban 'ecocide'".[5] Galston was a botanist whose
research had identified the defoliant properties of a chemical which was
developed as Agent Orange. It was used by the US as a devastating weapon in
Vietnam. Galston realised that a war on nature could be turned into a war on
people. He began to campaign against Agent Orange in 1965.

But what of the wars on nature by corporations pursuing profits in
peacetime? Natural habitats, on which we and our co-habitants – other species
– depend for our lives, were also being annihilated. An Ecocide Convention was
drafted in 1973 by Richard A. Falk which emphasised that "man has consciously
and unconsciously inflicted irreparable damage to the environment in times of
war and peace".[6] From then on, discussions on the proposal to turn ecocide
into a punishable crime took place at the highest levels of diplomacy and the
UN. The discussions stretched through to 1995. Then, all of a sudden, ecocide
disappeared from the agenda.

Despite support from many governments, ecocide was excluded from the
draft *Code of Crimes Against the Peace and Security of Mankind* prepared by the

---

3   Gauger *et. al.* (2012: 8).
4   Gauger *et al* (2012: 8).
5   Quoted in Weisberg (1970).
6   Falk (1973).

UN's International Law Commission. The opponents were the Netherlands, the UK and the USA.

> *Despite the overwhelming support for a law to prohibit ecocide during war and peacetime ... the proposal was unilaterally removed overnight without record of why this occurred ... What is so remarkable is that the collective memory has erased this crime in just 15 years.*[7]

Corporations are punished by courts for causing environmental damage (as with oil spills); but the executives who make the decisions that wreck rainforests, pollute the seas and sky, kill species and wreck eco-systems, are not arraigned in court to be held accountable.

The outlawing of ecocide would create a crisis for rent-seekers. Nation-states would be confronted with the sovereign responsibility to eliminate the financial incentives which encourage such behaviour. There is one way only to achieve this: charging rent for the use of nature's services. In calculating the rents, some services would be deemed to be so precious that no amount of money would justify their depletion. The net effect of the institutional and fiscal reforms would be at the exclusive expense of one group: the rent-seekers. That is why the violence against nature continues unabated.

Depression & World War

To understand why economic depression leads to world war, we need to trace the internal logic that drives the rent-seeking culture.

Cheating, to preserve itself as a social process, must defend its values by being prepared to do two things: grab other people's territories, and kill those who get in the way.

1. Depression is the condition of a bankrupt economy. That is, bankrupt both financially and philosophically. To relieve the financial pressures within the sovereign territory, the nation-state must gain access to new sources of rents. The only way to achieve this – to overcome the debt problem – is to embark on a new phase of colonialism.

2. To appropriate land belonging to others, the colonising state must wilfully engage in killing people. There are two target populations.

    (i) People who are surplus to requirements at home. The demographic crisis can be alleviated through (a) premature deaths in the Kill Zones (see p.53). And (b) expelling unwanted people onto the newly acquired territories.

---

7 Gauger *et al.* (2012: 2).

(ii) Indigenous people who occupy the land being colonised. Resistance is met with violence. Where first settlers agree to be relocated on reservations, many die through cultural attrition (see p.61, Table 4:1).

If we relate this model to the size of today's global surplus population, we may infer that enormous pressures are building up on policy-makers. They are caught in a pincer movement. From above, there are the paymasters (the funders of political parties, who are active rent-seekers). From below, the armies of the unemployed (Box E:1).

How did the dynamics of the rent-seeking culture relieve the pressure of the depressions of the 1870s and 1930s?

The depression of the 1870s ought to have dissolved any remaining illusions about the viability of capitalism as a twin-track culture (value-adding Producers and value-extracting Predators). Previously, this schizophrenic culture operated by displacing part of the population from their land, rendering them unproductive, and making up for the shortfall in production by appropriating rents from other people's territories. The sovereign nations of Europe resorted to this problem-solving model when they assembled in Berlin in 1884 to co-ordinate the Scramble for Africa. Germany, as the latecomer to nationalism and colonialism, received the leftovers. The leading imperial powers acquired the choice territories into which they could dump unwanted citizens and extract the gold, timber and other rent-yielding resources to balance the sovereign and corporate books.

Germany had no intention of living with that settlement. One day there would be a reckoning. The power nexus in Europe would have to be re-structured. Germany's Dogs of War began to raise their voices. They deployed Darwin's theory of evolution to legitimise the pronouncements of Nietzsche, who claimed that the future belonged to the super heroes with the will to power.

In nature, natural selection did not entail the violent displacement of other living species. Living entities conjoined to create the habitats they occupied. Far from *supplanting* others, the emphasis was on *extending*, by deepening, the variety of life-generating opportunities. This was a partnership in life, animals and vegetables living off each other in a co-operation that multiplied the variety of life forms, automatically increasing the opportunities for latecomers. The warmongers of Europe could not accept such an interpretation of the Darwin/Wallace theory of evolution. Instead, they validated their dreams of territorial conquest by contemptuously visiting their barbaric prejudices on to nature.

In Germany, the paranoid Kaiser fuelled the growing national fear of Germany's "encirclement" by the neighbouring Great Powers. He aroused French anxiety by sending the German gunboat *Panther* to the shores of Morocco. France was colonising that corner of Africa to extract rents and into

Box E:1
Deadweight People

In June 2012 the McKinsey Global Institute published its estimate that, by 2020, the world will have a surplus of at least 90 million low-skilled workers who face long-term unemployment. Employers, on the other hand, will need 45 million more medium-skilled workers. Even if governments could satisfy that demand by raising educational attainments (they cannot do so: most of them now do not have the money), that would still leave the other half of low-skilled people without jobs.

By 2020, the US will need to create 21m jobs to achieve full employment. France will have to create 240,000 net new jobs to cut unemployment to the 5.5% EU average, a performance that is not attainable: it represents more than double the current projected rate of job creation.[1]

It is not in the interests of rent-seekers to re-skill workers. Increasingly sophisticated robots are being deployed on conveyor belts to take over blue-collar jobs. This reduces corporate wage bills. Through the marketplace, higher corporate profits translate into higher rents for those who control resources that are in fixed supply – land.

---

1 Labaye *et al.* (2012: 2).

which she displaced the people who were surplus to requirements.[8] Germany was a threat to the imperial powers. The reckoning came in 1914. Germany lost.

And so, on to the next 18-year land-led real estate cycle. This culminated in the infamous land booms in places like Florida, and the Wall Street crash came in 1929. Because capitalism was a bankrupt model, the trans-Atlantic economies could not enjoy a speedy recovery. Depression returned. It took four years for people in Europe to realise that there would be no spontaneous return to full employment. The despair was compounded, in Germany, by the reparations which she had to pay to the allies who defeated her in World War I.

Adolf Hitler had a plan. If Germany could not expand southwards, in Africa, there were territories to the east of her borders that were waiting to be plucked. Germany's unemployed workers could be relocated in the expanses of Poland and the Ukraine. First, however, he would have to clear Europeans from their homes. But this was not like supplanting American Indians or Tutsi tribes from their homelands. This was an assault on European Christians. It was an unacceptable form of colonialism. Hitler had to be stopped. He was.

This time, with the depression of the 2010s, there is one big difference. The outcomes cannot be similar to those that followed 1918 and 1945. This

---

8   Tuchman (1994); Harrison (2010a: 104-105).

time, Europe is not Top Dog, and America's superpower status is challenged by China. The scope for recovery from the forthcoming devastation no longer exists (within the existing economic paradigm).

Europe and the US took a decade to recover from World War II. By the mid-1950s they were back on pre-war trends. The swift recovery from the utter desolation was possible for two reasons. First, the manufacturing sectors could lead the way to full employment by exporting products to the rest of the world. Second, the de-colonisation process was negotiated on terms which retained Europe's right to collect global rents through the banking system. All the cards appeared to be stacked in favour of the trans-Atlantic economy.

The first 18-year post-war business cycle came to an end in the early 1970s.[9] The demand for labour and capital slackened. From then on, the real living standards of most people began to either level off, or decline. The death knell of capitalism, however, was still being postponed. There were two primary reasons. First, the Cold War. This provided the psychological glue that secured the compliance of populations which were showing a dangerous willingness to challenge authority in Europe and North America (beginning with student demonstrations in the late 1960s). Second, financially bankrupt governments could continue to fund the Welfare State by printing and borrowing money. Keynes had made "deficit financing" respectable. If consumer demand fell short of producer supply – print money, create inflation, and devalue out of the crisis.

The downturn of the early 1990s echoed the crisis of the early 1970s. But the noose was tightening. The global rules were being re-written. The USSR capitulated in 1991. With this, the discipline of the Cold War was removed and a new layer of rent-seeking (the new class of oligarchs) emerged. And Communist China re-entered world markets with a vengeance. The 18-year cycle that began in 1992 sustained itself through the dot.com bubble because the whole world was hooked on debt. The crash caused by the land boom in the early years of the 21st century had to turn into a depression unbounded. This time, the classic safety value is not available to rescue Europe.

The Depression of 2028

Those who construct futuristic scenarios on behalf of agencies like the IMF, the CIA and the EU assume that the world will somehow return to business-as-usual, with adjustments to accommodate China. In my view the next 18-year business cycle, which would ordinarily culminate in a recession in 2028, will not conform to previous trends. World War III will disrupt the cycle.

---

9 Harrison (1983: 78-79).

- The trans-Atlantic nations cannot overcome the Depression of the 2010s by capturing other people's lands or rents. China has shut down the safety valve. Floundering Europe and the US are printing hundreds of billions of euros and dollars to try to cushion the collapse of their economies.
- If poverty in Africa continues to drive the migration of footloose Africans northwards, through Greece and Italy into Western Europe, racial conflict is a high probability. Political leaders in Germany, France and the UK have served notice that "multi-culturalism" has not worked in their countries.[10]
- In the US, the massacre of six Sikh worshippers by a neo-Nazi gunman in August 2012 drew attention to the growth of militia cells. These had multiplied from 50 to more than 260 in the four years of depression that began in 2008,[11] while politics in Washington remained gridlocked in the discredited nostrums of the past.

Anecdotal evidence of social stress points are numerous. They gain their global significance through the mega-trend effect (see p.178), which triggers the escalation of crises. The US intelligence community, examining the implications of rising food prices, explained the risks in these terms:

> Food and water also are intertwined with climate change, energy, and demography ... A switch from use of arable land for food to fuel crops provides a limited solution and could exacerbate both the energy and food situations. Climatically, rainfall anomalies and constricted seasonal flows of snow and glacial melts are aggravating water scarcities, harming agriculture in many parts of the globe. Energy and climate dynamics also combine to amplify a number of other ills such as health problems, agricultural losses to pests, and storm damage. The greatest danger may arise from the convergence and interaction of many stresses simultaneously. **Such a complex and unprecedented syndrome of problems could overload decision-makers, making it difficult for them to take actions in time to enhance good outcomes or avoid bad ones.**[12]

I have emphasised the last sentence. Governments are *already* unable to influence the outcomes of the trends which threaten the future. Poverty stems solely from the fact that policy-makers, and their advisers, exclude from

---

10 Mass migration out of North Africa, following the rebellion against autocratic rulers in the spring of 2011, caused political tensions within the European Union. The migrants landed in Italy. Italy's foreign minister, Franco Frattini, voiced dismay at the lack of offers from neighbours to re-settle refugees in their countries (Kington [2011]). In August 2012 the Greek Public Order Minister, Nikos Dendias, noted the "unprecedented invasion" of illegal immigrants, and declared: "Our social fabric is at risk of unravelling".

11 Halperin (2012).

12 NIC (2004: 41).

consideration the root cause of the mega-trends. That helplessness is wilful, because the knowledge that is needed to construct the stabilising mechanisms *is* available. The sterility of political imagination and purpose renders all of us vulnerable to life-threatening risks.[13] When a civilisation ceases to be viable, the major outward manifestation is a struggle to death.

Economic depressions are testimonies to the unbearable weight of the load carried by the producers of a nation's wealth. The contours of the crisis are clear for all to see. A productive economy relies on the flow of resources into the public sector to provide the services and infrastructure that make commerce possible. When the rents which fund those services are prevented from circulating within the public sector, the aggregate energy infused into the system is insufficient to sustain it. A deficit accumulates to the point where the foundations buckle. In the past, the West avoided reform by resorting to violence against others. Capturing other peoples' land added a new flow of rents into Europe, helping to restart the economy. That violence also helped by depleting unemployed people as casualties of war.

As in the 1930s, so now.

Profound social and economic stresses tempt people to brush aside the norms of natural law in favour of authoritarianism. Then, in 1930s America, the outcome was the New Deal. In Europe, it was Adolph Hitler.

Now?

Counterfactual History

Historians have imagined how Europe might have evolved if small details were changed.[14] Exercises in "what if" enrich our awareness of the present and challenge our moral sensibilities. If we can visualise how the past might have been different, we might resolve to change course into the future.

Neither of the two world wars need have happened. If one of the imperial nations had demonstrated the viable alternative to the rest of Europe, the demonstration effect would have been explosive, providing hope to others that they, too, could enjoy sustained prosperity alongside peace.

Britain was the world's super power at the end of the 19th century. As noted in Ch. 6 (p.97), at the turn into the 20th century the people granted a democratic mandate to the Liberal Party to change the tax regime. Lloyd George's 1909 budget enshrined the principle of a special fiscal levy on land and natural resources. Winston Churchill was at pains to explain that this would re-align the distribution

---

13 According to a scientific assessment of the social impact of El Niño – a natural phenomenon –changes in climate
   double the risk of civil war. Fifty of the 250 conflicts between 1950 and 2004 were triggered by the El Niño cycle
   (Schiermeier, 2011). How much worse would those civil disturbances be if compounded by man-made climate changes?
14 Ferguson (1997).

Box E:2
"Why we must halt the land cycle"

The reason why the financial sector seized up in 2008 was identified by *Financial Times* chief economic writer Martin Wolf in his comments on my book *2010: The Inquest*. He wrote: "The people of the US, UK, Spain and Ireland became feverish speculators in Land. Today, the toxic waste poisons the entire world economy".

Wolf identified the solution: "I have long been persuaded that resource rents should be socialised, not accrued to individual owners. Yet, as Mr. Harrison tellingly remarks, 'as a community we socialise our privately earned incomes (wages and salaries), while our social income (from land) is privatised.' Yet, whatever one thinks of the justice of this arrangement, the practical consequences have become calamitous".

Wolf, a member of the UK government's Independent Commission on Banking, believed that politicians would not wear the 100% capture of land rents. But, he suggested, perhaps they could restore the economy on the back of a John Stuart Mill-like reform: "Socialising any gain from here on".[1]

---

1 Wolf (2010).

of power. The initiative would secure full employment, the equalisation of economic opportunities and the dismantling of the class structure. The landlords refused to allow the budget to be implemented. The budget's innovative provisions were stillborn. What might have happened within the UK, and for the geo-politics of Europe, if Parliament had implemented the democratic will?

It could be objected that events were too far gone by 1909 for Europe to embark on a different course. So, think again. In 1931, a Labour Chancellor of the Exchequer, Philip Snowden, introduced a carefully crafted Bill into the House of Commons which provided for the taxation of land values. Britain, Europe, and North America were in the early stages of a depression. What if Britain had triggered a quick recovery on the back of this financial model?

- Consumption would have been boosted by cuts to the taxes that penalised people who worked, saved and invested.
- Cutting the cost of hiring people (by untaxing their wages) would have reduced the dole queues and raised the spirits of the people.
- Cash-rich entrepreneurs would have drawn down their reserves to create capital goods to take advantage of the new opportunities.

By preventing a depression, Britain would have demonstrated to the rest of Europe that prosperity was the handmaiden of peaceful social relationships. Why would the people of Germany have listened to Hitler if they could see a

Box E:3
Reparations as the Spoils of Victory

Territorial conflicts create the conditions that contribute to the next confrontation. Under the peace terms enforced in 1871, which brought an end to the Franco-German conflict, France surrendered Alsace-Lorraine and was ordered to pay an indemnity of 5bn francs, a heavy price to bear during the depression of that decade. France secured her revenge in 1918, recovering her land and imposing reparations on Germany ... a payment to the allies that rankled with Adolf Hitler, a corporal who fought in the First World War. He swore an oath of revenge. The depression of the 1930s was the perfect moment for his intervention in history.

Germany lost the war for supremacy in Europe, but won the peace. With the onset of the depression in 2008, reparations were exacted from the losers, the southern states in the euro-zone. Germany insisted on the austerity policies that cost the jobs of millions of people from Athens to Madrid, some of whom characterised Germany in terms of Hitler's Nazi regime.

viable alternative route to social security playing out in the British Isles? But, again, Snowden's Act was not implemented by Parliament. Britain was still in thrall to the agents who were required to protect the rent-seeking interests. The law was deleted from the statute book in 1934.

Today, at the time of writing (August 2012), advocacy of the kind offered by Turgot/Tolstoy/Sun, and by Lloyd George/Winston Churchill, is confined to a few isolated voices (Box E:2).

Pundits who cannot wrap their minds around the horrors of rent-seeking, advocate coping strategies. We are told that the inequality that afflicts trans-Atlantic societies must be reversed if there is to be recovery in the economy.[15] But the prognosis is for an even deeper inequality as a result of the austerity policies implemented in an effort to cut sovereign debts. This austerity echoes the conditions of the inter-war years. But this time, Germany is the nation seeking reparations (see Box E:3).

No serious political attempt was made to explain to the public that the solution lay in the application of a new kind of public finance. A low-grade property tax was proposed for Ireland, Italy, Greece and Spain. These were impositions on the improvements on the land, and they were not offset by reductions in other taxes. Many Irish home owners refused to pay the tax. In Italy the Northern League encouraged municipal governments to refuse to collect the new property tax.[16]

Once again, we are back to the poverty of philosophy of the kind that afflicted the 1930s. Between 1929 and 1933, in the US, the finest brains failed to

---

15   Lansley (2012).
16   Dinmore & Segreti (2012).

Box E:4
Is the West History?

Niall Ferguson is a popular conduit of conservative ideology through his televised treatments of epic events. He claims that the game is not up for capitalism. As evidence, he argues that the right to own land distinguished the emerging Anglo-American settler civilisation in the North from the mixed-race colonies of South America. The latter were constructed on Spanish-owned plantations in which settlers were excluded from a share of the spoils. The willingness to diffuse private property rights in land is one of Ferguson's "killer apps" reasons for the rise of the American empire.[1]

But what about the traumatised African-American population? Ferguson concedes that slavery spoilt his narrative of the "Land of the Free". By 1820, about 4m souls were shipped as slaves across the Atlantic. The culture of the United States is disfigured by a social violence that is inextricably connected to differential rights to property in land. For Africans, then as now, the killer application is literally that: many more die from the social conditions prevailing in America, than would be the case in a justice-based society.

---

1 Ferguson (2011).

serve up a recipe for reconstructing the devastated economy. And so it is today, with Democrats and Republicans trading meaningless *clichés*. With the passage of time, the options for recovery narrow. Public spending cuts and increases in taxes will protract the crisis. In Europe, savage austerity measures brought yet more people on to the streets to protest against the failures of governance.

Governments of the Left which might have celebrated the opportunity to accelerate the collapse of capitalism strained themselves to inject trillions of euros and pounds into salvaging the system. Governments of the Right conspired with their ideological enemies to sustain the bankrupt system, all the time talking about the need to protect "hard working middle class homeowners". They diligently remained silent about the predators that had leached the life out of the system.[17]

Misdiagnosis feeds delusions. Social scientists from all schools of thought had their uninformed say. One suggestion: the bias towards optimism "was a root cause for the financial meltdown of 2008".[18] Being optimistic may be a good way to cope with difficult situations, but when it becomes an excuse for sloppy thinking it turns into a threat with grievous implications.

Nowhere in the analyses was there a trace of understanding about the cheating that had co-opted the middle classes into the process that weakened

---

17 Architects of the financial pyramid that collapsed in the US, economists like Lawrence Summers (Treasury Secretary in the Presidency of Bill Clinton, who was subsequently appointed Professor of Economics at Harvard University), pontificated in ways that treated symptoms rather than causes. Summers (2012) censured European policy-makers without offering the slightest hint of a fresh insight into how to re-boot the economy.
18 Sharot (2012: 200).

society and wrecked the natural environment. Does this consign the West to history? Have no fear, the West can be saved. Six "killer apps", as Harvard historian Niall Ferguson calls them, would come to the aid of Western civilisation (Box E:4). His views on the exemplary contribution to Western prosperity are shared by others, like Chicago professors of finance Raghuram Rajan and Luigi Zingales. They affirm that the private ownership of land is the route to virtuous growth.[19] The link between land distribution and responsive government was not a coincidence, they assert. The sub-title of their book is *Unleashing the Power of Financial Markets to Create Wealth and Spread Opportunity*. Their celebration of the financial system was published in 2003, just as the bankers of Wall Street were concocting their toxic packages of sub-prime mortgages that would wreck the Western banking system. The delusions that disgrace the social science community are unbounded.

Policy failures of the past were not out of ignorance. The viable alternative was available to those who postured as custodians of the welfare of their societies. If the cheating culture was powerful enough to cause the downfall of the emperors, will it now consign the democracies to history?

Last Gasp of the Cheating Culture?

The bankrupt capitalist model is now driving the last stake into what remains of the value-adding sectors of the economy. This is happening under the guise of stimulating the depressed economies back to life. Governments assume that pouring money they do not have into vast infrastructure projects will kick-start moribund markets. But as these projects are completed over the next decade, they will increase the stream of rents. This will deepen the barriers to businessmen who want to start enterprises.

The financial logic for the public sector strategy can be inferred from the balance sheets of cash-rich corporations. As the global economy slumped, they hoarded their money. From the macro-economic point of view, those firms ought to have invested in capital formation to increase productivity, reduce costs and stimulate employment. They opted to sit on their piles of money. Why? By doing so, they maintained operations at levels which generated greater profits in the short-term. That translated into higher bonuses for executives. *If those firms had invested for long-term growth, the rate of return would have been lower. This would have meant smaller bonuses.* As Adam Smith long ago noted, rent-seeking prescribes those decisions that reward idleness.

So, to compensate for the corruption of the entrepreneurial spirit, governments had to step in with Keynesian pump-priming, debt-funded

---

19 Rajan and Zingales (2003: 10-12).

investment in mega projects like building roads and railways. This, in turn, diverted scarce capital resources away from the small to medium-sized businesses (SMEs) that would have maximised the creation of jobs. Mason Gaffney has drawn attention to these distortions in the capital markets.[20]

This strategy does not just compound the misalignment of capital. Over the course of the business cycle, the new infrastructure rewards land hoarding, which contributes to above-trend rises in rents. This embeds distortions deeper into the labour and capital markets. Under these conditions, good governance recedes under the stress of domestic economic policy.

The Flash Points

We cannot predict the event that will trigger the next world war. It was impossible to anticipate the assassination of an archduke as the excuse for World War I. The trigger next time could come from any of the theatres of conflict that are now in the making.

The Asian Theatre How the Communist Party's high command evolves its domestic politics in China will shape the geo-politics of this region. A clue was provided by the scandal involving Bo Xilai, who was expected to join the Politburo in 2012. He became embroiled in financial scandals, and his wife murdered a British businessman over a land deal. The Politburo was desperate to smother public awareness of the extent to which members of the highest ranks in the party had corruptly acquired fortunes. In Bo's case, his family had accumulated a portfolio of properties including two London flats worth more than £2m.[21] The Politburo was aligned to the values of rent-seekers, so its outlook on the world will be coloured by the tactics employed by the Predator Culture.

Regional stresses over maritime access to disputed territories echo events of a century ago. Japanese vessels now shadow Chinese patrol ships near the disputed Senkaku Islands. As the US shifts its military focus away from Europe and towards the South China Seas, a majority of American citizens declare their wish for a tougher stance against China. America's superpower status is challenged. China's currency is in the ascendancy and her economy may eclipse America's (measured in purchasing power parity) by the early 2020s.

In Vietnam, mass demonstrations in Hanoi register anger at China's interest in vast deposits of oil and gas in disputed areas of the South China Sea. All countries in the region are growing concerned over the control of shipping routes and fishing rights, with sovereign control over waters disputed. It is difficult to assess China's diplomatic plans over the next 20 years in any terms other than that of rent-seeking territorial aggrandisement. As the aspirations

---

20 Gaffney (2009).
21 Gainsbury (2012).

of China's rural population are thwarted, will the Politburo look northwards to the empty lands of Mongolia with its newly-discovered mineral deposits? Will China covet the steppes on which to re-deploy her malcontents? Will China's acquisition of Africa's resources be challenged by the US?

India's control over the Himalayan waters heightens the risk of war with a nuclear neighbour (Box E:5). Energy blackouts across the nation have exposed the fragility of the economy, while land-poor communities in the north-east are an ever-present threat to political stability. While investing in space projects, India cannot diminish the growing poverty that is creating rural landlessness. Author Ramachandra Guha, a reliable observer of the corrupt political establishment, warns that "in the current, fragmented, political scenario, short-term rent-seeking will take precedence over long-term policy-making".[22] India's official auditor has accused the government of losing revenue by privatising rent-generating assets at less than their market value. These include the loss of $33bn in coal rents, and the loss of $39bn in rent revenue from the misallocation of second-generation mobile telephone licences.[23]

The Arctic Spoils States surrounding the ice cap covet the oil and gas and other resources beneath the ocean bed. Fears grow of ensuing environmental damage and pollution, with negative climatic effects.

The Middle East Cauldron The legacy of the Arab Spring is a region in which authoritarian rule has been replaced by populist anarchy. The post-colonial settlement, as an extension of the European legacy of cheating, is not being negotiated in an orderly way: the factions contesting for power have no agenda to unite all the ethnic and religious groups. Al Qaeda is re-building its strength and failed states are armed to the teeth.

The Eurozone Débâcle From 1929, it took just four years for the fascists to realise that their time had come. From 2008, it took just four years for the comparable despair to permeate the populations of southern Europe, among whom the attractions of fascism once again emerged as an organised force. Civil conflict over urban spaces (gated communities fending off the spread of popular discontent) may lead to new coalitions of nations to dismantle the original ethos of the European Union. The North/South divide has been established by the euro crisis. This will be amplified as employment creeps back to northern countries, while increased numbers of young people in the South remain marooned in unemployment. The exodus of skilled workers and innovative entrepreneurs will deplete the South, turning them into backwaters and providing the fertile ground for extremist ideologues.

---

22 Guha (2012).
23 Mallet and Crabtree (2012).

Box E:5
Bombed Out, but with The Bomb

Pakistan is not so much a nation-state as a buffer zone at the hot edges of all the regional conflicts. The military retains the power of veto, and it is guided by the values of land speculation. It holds vast tracts of farmland, and real estate in choice locations in the big cities like Karachi. The profits from land speculation enrich the officer class, which is ever-ready to launch a coup in defence of its interests.

Armed with nuclear weapons, Pakistan will prove to be a dangerous enemy when the water wars break out over the coming 20 years. Pakistan relies heavily on water to irrigate the farms owned by the military elites. America's controlling influence over Pakistan is deteriorating. Nearly 70% of Pakistanis say they regard America as an enemy.

The list of potential flashpoints could be extended. They all need to be monitored, but *understood* for their geo-political ramifications.

We should not expect the next world war to be a replay of the 20th century versions, of foot soldiers dying in trenches. We have entered a leaderless age in which the former imperial powers no longer wield influence through the G7 or the expanded G20 group of nations. Anarchy will be resolved either through violent attrition or a covenant in which all nations will derive a peace dividend. If we assume that the latter option is not realistic, the prudent strategy is to assume the onset of a world war. That conflict will bear the features of the digital age, with America leading the way in technology. Her new generation of bomber drones will be piloted from the safety of bunkers in the middle of an American desert.

The geo-political stesses will surface in forms like:

- *Currency wars* (China flooding markets with surplus dollars to destabilise America and give her an edge in global markets) ...
- *water wars* ...
- *cyberspace wars* (Western companies are already registering losses from state-sponsored cyber attacks against their computer systems: damage can be inflicted without launching missiles) ...
- *resource nationalism* (nations in the global South are leading a trend to nationalise European-owned corporations that control their resources) ...
- *economic depressions* (Western governments preside over policy failure for what will become two Lost Decades) ...

Any combination of these could trigger the conflict in the making. A metaphor for the eerie echoes from the military past was the crisis that blew up in September 2012. Violent demonstrations broke out across China when Japan's government purchased the Senkaku islands. Threats were published aimed at

- attacking Japan's financial system (China is Japan's biggest creditor), and
- cutting off the supply of rare earth metals (without that mineral, Japan's high-tech industry would seize up).

On the day Premier Wen Jiabao berated the European Union for refusing to lift its arms embargo on Beijing, the *Financial Times* (September 21, 2012) interviewed a peasant whose land had been stolen and sold to a developer in the village of Wukan. Beijing would have to deal with widespread anger over its mishandling of the land issue, he said, or find a way to "shift attention by fighting a war in the South China Sea". In reaction, will Japan rearm herself? Hermes Fund Managers, a £25bn UK investment house, encouraged clients to price in the risk of war. CEO Saker Nusseibeh (in *Political Risk: The impact on investors*), warned: "The idea of war between developed nations in modern times may seem absurd, yet it is not that far-fetched. Considering today's growing wealth divide both between countries and within them, it is entirely possible that at some stage some will say 'enough' and seek forcible change".

We must all contemplate the ultimate nightmare, an Armageddon in the making, so that we all join in resolving to fight the culture that has brought the world to this precipice.

The Responsibility on All of Us

People who enjoy the luxury of time to think, to write and to speak in public have a special responsibility to shift their mind-sets. Their past negligence (even if by default alone) has placed all of us at risk to the looming life-threatening dangers. Introspection has begun in the academies and corridors of power, but fundamental pre-conceptions are not being radically challenged. Rather, the resort is to metaphors that represent what I call trauma thinking.

Representative of the economics profession is Andrew Haldane, the Executive Director responsible for Financial Stability at the Bank of England. He admits that analytical failure contributed to the financial crisis of 2008. He and his colleagues were apparently assailed by a virus. "This virus had contaminated almost everyone by 2007, causing them to view the pre-crisis world through spectacles far rosier than subsequent events have shown was justified."[24] Under the influence of that "virus", economists at the Bank of England compounded their failures by making the rich richer, and the poor poorer. The Bank achieved this by printing money (Quantitative Easing: QE), which was distributed to favour the asset-rich section of society. The Bank revealed that households in

---

24 Haldane (2012: 133).

the richest 10% of the population enjoyed an average rise in the value of (largely land-based) assets of £129,000. Households at the lowest end of the income scales endured a drop in incomes and bore the brunt of unemployment.[25] In Britain, the top 5% of households hold 40% of the assets that mopped up the money (hundreds of billions of pounds) supplied by the Bank.

Historians and political scientists are similarly failing to acknowledge the driving force behind global events. An example is the analysis by Graham Allison. He shares my fear of a possible China-US military conflict. Allison is director of the Belfer Center for Science and International Affairs at Harvard's John F. Kennedy School of Government. He employs historical precedent to warn that when a ruling power is challenged by a rising power (as with the rise of China today), war tends to follow.

> In 11 of 15 cases since 1500 where a rising power emerged to challenge a ruling power, war occurred. Think about Germany after unification as it overtook Britain as Europe's largest economy. In 1914 and in 1939, its aggression and the UK's response produced world wars.[26]

Historical precedents, analogies and metaphors have their value; I use them. But they should not serve as substitutes to camouflage the root causes of conflicts for which there are rational remedies.

My final point relates to the burden of responsibility on all of us. As moral beings, we cannot out-source our obligations to the "experts". If we want solutions to be formulated and implemented on a democratic basis, the *minimum* that can be expected from every one of us is a contribution towards the creation of the thinking-and-acting space needed by a new generation of political leaders. That means we need to show tolerance to those who offer to grapple with our problems. The present short electoral cycle (4-5 years) is biased to favour shallow short-term strategies. These offer instant gratification, but that is all. To abolish the cheating syndrome, time is needed (i) to discuss the issues, leading to a democratic consensus and mandate for change, (ii) to implement reforms, and put in place the safeguards to protect vulnerable people from disruptions during the transition, and (iii) to monitor the results.

---

25 Bank of England (2012: 11). The disingenuous presentation of the facts is illustrated by the Bank's preferred presentation of the impact of its policy. It admits to "an estimate of the total increase in household wealth stemming from the Bank's £325 billion of asset purchases up to May 2012 of just over £600 billion, *equivalent to around £10,000 per person if assets were evenly distributed across the population*" (p.10: emphasis added). Assets, and the distributional effects of the Bank's policy, are not distributed evenly, either between individuals or between assets. The pro-land value bias in policy is obliquely acknowledged in the statement that "the fall in house prices during the crisis is likely to have been smaller than would otherwise have been the case" (p.9). The Bank does not mention by name the one asset that reaped the largest benefit from its policy: *land*.
26 Allison (2012).

We should not insist on instant relief from pathologies which have been incubated over the course of 500 years. Those pathologies embedded themselves in our lives through the enactment of the laws which nourished them. Those laws made it possible for the pathologies to mutate by corroding the culture and collective consciousness of the peoples of the commons. Nonetheless, the therapeutic work needs to begin immediately. Democracy, which is the single most important starting point, needs to be adapted. The first step is the *reinterpretation* of the functions of democracy. Parliamentary democracy, as evolved by feudal cheats, was confined to (a) its information gathering technique (votes measure the views of the electorate), and (b) its decision-making attributes (representatives are authorised to enact laws). Not surprisingly, the cheating culture's version of democracy has alienated the majority of people, who boycott elections.

The therapeutic powers of an open and honest democratic politics need to be articulated. One starting point is the model of *self-actualising* person-centred therapy developed by humanist psychologists like Carl Rogers (1902-1987). This model leads to the reframing of political institutions as trauma-solving agencies that meet the simultaneous needs of *everyone*. We need to reconceptualise democracy as a therapeutic model that can achieve renewal on a population-wide scale. This new approach to democracy is aided by insights from psychotherapists like Kenneth Evans and Maria Gilbert, who acknowledge the need to expand the terms of reference of their discipline. In their introduction to integrative psychotherapy they recognise the need to locate psychotherapy in the wider cultural and ecological environments.

> *Psychologists are in the front line in hearing the voices of people victimized by the pressures towards personal and technical development. We see them as anxious, pressurized by work, depressed by their disrupted relationships, failing to find meaning in a society that depicts consumption as fulfilment, struggling to cope with illness that might have been prevented, loss of control over decisions to impersonal corporate and governmental actions, and unable to gain sustenance from the beauty of nature.*[27]

By linking personal trauma to the cultural and environmental ramifications, it becomes apparent that, *if we wish to restore health to the individual we need a multi-disciplinary collaboration that also rehabilitates culture and people's relationship to nature.* The cathartic renewal of personality entails the recovery of the commons for the benefit of us all.

---

27 Evans and Gilbert (2005: 60).

Bibliography

Acemoglu, Daron, and James A. Robinson, (2012), *Why Nations Fail*, London: Profile Books.

Ahmed, Nafeez Mosaddeq, (2010), *A User's Guide to the Crisis of Civilisation*, London: Pluto Press.

Aldrick, Philip, (2012a), "Illiterate and innumerate risk Britain's economic success", *Daily Telegraph*, May 31.

Aldrick, Philip, (2012b), "Treasury reveals millionaires paying less than basic tax rate", *The Daily Telegraph*, April 17.

Alexander, Michelle, (2012), *The New Jim Crowe: Mass Incarceration in the Age of Colorblindness*, New York: The New Press.

Allison, Graham, (2012), "Thucydides's trap has been sprung in the Pacific", *Financial Times*, August 22.

Andelson, R.V., (1979), *Critics of Henry George*, Rutherford: Fairleigh Dickenson University Press.

Andelson, R.V., (1991), *Commons Without Tragedy*, London: Shepheard-Walwyn.

Andelson, R.V. (ed.), (2000), *Land-Value Taxation Around the World*, 3rd edn., Oxford: Blackwell.

Anderlini, Jamil, (2011), "We just need a bit of land, say siege villagers", *Financial Times*, December 21.

Anderlini, Jamil, (2012), "China fears resurgence of property bubble", *Financial Times*, July 6.

Appiah, Kwame Anthony, (2010), *The Honor Code: How Moral Revolutions Happen*, New York: W.W. Norton

Armistead, Louise, (2012), "Sands: no grounds for revoking NY licence", *Daily Telegraph*, August 9.

Atkinson, Anthony B., and Joseph E. Stiglitz , (1980) *Lectures on Public Finance*, London: McGraw-Hill.

Attack, R.S., (2010), *John Clare: Voice of Freedom*, London: Shepheard-Walwyn.

Avila, Charles, (1983), *Ownership: Early Christian Teaching*, Maryknoll, NY: Orbis Books.

Barrell, John, (1972), *The Idea of Landscape and the Sense of Place 1730-1840: An Approach to the Poetry of John Clare*, Cambridge: Cambridge University Press.

Bate, Jonathan, (2005), *John Clare*, London: Piccador.

Becker, Gary S., (1992), "How is affirmative action like crop subsidies", *Business Week*, April 27.

Bell, Daniel, (2012), "The real meaning of the rot at the top of China", *Financial Times*, April 24.

Bingham, Tom, (2010), *The Rule of Law*, London: Penguin.

Binmore, K., (2005), *Natural Justice*, New York: Oxford University Press.

Bland, Ben, (2011), "Hanoi's $3m pad fuels property battle", *Financial Times*, April 19.

Blundell, V.H., (1994), "Flawed Land Acts 1947-1976", in Nicolaus Tideman (ed.) *Land and Taxation*, London: Shepheard-Walwyn.

Bowater, Donna, (2012), "Blasphemy is everyday talk, BBC tells vicar", *The Daily Telegraph*, March 17.

Boyle, Nicholas, (2010), *2014 – How to Survive the New World Crisis*, London: Continuum.

Braithwaite, Tom and Sharlene Goff, (2012), "US accuses StanChart on Iran", *Financial Times*, August 7.

Braithwaite, Tom, *et al*, (2012), "Wells settles loan discrimination claims", *Financial Times*, July 13.

Branigan, Tania, (2012), "Beijing cuts growth target", *Guardian Weekly*, March 9.

Breadun, Deaglan de , (2012), "Graft about more than 'brown envelops' of cash", *Irish Times*, July 24.

Brittan, Sam, (2012), "It is time to tax England's green and pleasant land", *Financial Times*, February 24.

Brody, H., *et al*, (2000) "Map-making and myth-making in Broad Street: the London cholera epidemic, 1854", *Lancet*, vol. 356.

Brueggemann, Walter, (2002), *The Land: Place as Gift, Promise, and Challenge in biblical Faith*, 2nd edn., Minneapolis: Fortress Press.

Busey, James, (1995), *Latin American Political Guide*, New York: Robert Schalkenbach Foundation

Case, Karl, and Ray Fair , (1994), *Economics*, 3rd edn., London: Prentice Hall.

Cave, Stephen, (2012), *Immortality: The Quest to Live Forever and How it Drives Civilisation*, London: Biteback.

Cha, Ariana Eunjung , (2012), "'Economic suicides' shake Europe as financial crisis takes toll on mental health", *Washington Post*, August 14.

Chamberlain, Gethin, (2012), "In Brazil, the world's most endangered tribe cries for help as loggers invade", *The Guardian Weekly*, April 27.

Childe, V. Gordon, (2003), *Man Makes Himself*, 4th edn., Nottingham: Spokesman Books.

Cicarelli, James, (2012), "Economic thought among American Aboriginals prior to 1492", *The Am. J. of Economics and Sociology*, (71:1), January.

Clayton, Peter, (2012), *Octavia Hill*, Andover: Pitkin Publishing.

Coates, John, (2012), *The Hour Between Dog and Wolf: Risk Taking, Gut Feeling and the Biology of Boom and Bust*, London: Fourth Estate.

Cobden, Richard, (1842), "Corn Bill – Burdens on Land", HC Deb 14 March, Vol.61, col.560.

Corning, Peter, (2003), *Nature's Magic: Synergy in Evolution and the Fate of Humankind*, Cambridge: Cambridge University Press.

Coronella, Steve, (2012), "Emigration can be door to opportunity and adventure", *Irish Times*, June 21.

Cosmides, Leda, and John Tooby, (1992), "Cognitive adaptations for social exchange", in J. H. Barkow, L. Cosmides, & J. Tooby (eds.) *The Adapted Mind: Evolutionary Psychology and the Generation of Culture*, Oxford: Oxford University Press.

Daragahi, Borzou, (2012), "Revolution leads Tunisians to reduce dependence on French", *Financial Times*, January 27.

Davis, Carl, *et al*, (2009), *Who Pays? A Distributional Analysis of the Tax Systems in 50 States*, 3rd edn., Washington, DC: Institute on Taxation and Economic Policy.

Davis, Evan , (2012), "Reasons to be cheerful, part five", *Financial Times*, August 4.

Demsetz, H., (1967), "Toward a Theory of Property Rights", *American Economic Review* (57:2).

Diamond. Jared, (2005), *Collapse: How Societies Choose to Fail or Survive*, London: Allen Lane.

Dinmore, Guy, and Giulia Segreti, (2012), "Monty draws up spending cuts to avoid tax rise", *Financial Times*, May 1.

Docker, J., (2004), "Raphael Lemkin's History of Genocide and Colonialism", Contribution for United States Holocaust memorial Museum, Center for Advanced Holocaust Studies, Washington DC, February 26.

Dorling, Daniel, (2010), *Injustice*, Bristol: Policy Press

Dorling, Daniel & Bethan Thomas, (2011), *Bankrupt Britain: An atlas of social change*, Bristol: Policy Press.

Dorling, Danny, (2011), *So You Think You Know About Britain?* London: Constable & Robinson.

Douglas, Roy , (1976), *Land, People and Politics*, London: Allison & Busby.

Driver, H.E., (1969), *Indians of North America*, 2nd edn., Chicago: University of Chicago Press.

Dunbar, Robin, (1992), "Neocortex size as a constraint on group size in primates", *J. of Human Evolution*, Vol. 22(6).

Dunbar, Robin, (1997), *Grooming, Gossip and the Evolution of Language*, Cambridge, Masss: Harvard University Press.

Dunbar, Robin, (2011), "Friends to count on", *The Guardian*, March 25.

Dutton, Denis, (2009), *The Art Instinct*, New York: Bloomsbury Press.

Dyer, Geoff, (2011), "Two Chinese cities face property tax", *Financial Times*, January 28.

Eisenstein, Charles, (2011), *Sacred Economics*, Berkeley: Evolver Editions.

Eleftheriadis, Pavlos, (2012), "Only a new political order can rescue Greece", *Financial Times*, May 28.

Evans, Kenneth R., and Maria C. Gilbert , (2005), *An Introduction to Integrative Psychotherapy*, Basingstoke: Palgrave Macmillan.

Falk, Richard A., (1973), "Environmental Warfare and Ecocide – Facts, Appraisal, and Proposals", in Marek Thee (ed), *Bulletin of Peace Proposals*, 1973, Vol. 1.

Ferguson, Niall, (1997), *Virtual History: Alternatives and Counterfactuals*, London: Picador.

Ferguson, Niall, (2011), *Civilisation: Is the West History?* London: Penguin

Ferguson, Thomas, (1948), *The Dawn of Scottish Social Welfare*, London: Thomas Nelson and Sons.

Figley, Charles R., (1988), "Post-traumatic family therapy", in Frank M. Ochberg (1988), *Post-Traumatic Therapy and Victims of Violence*, New York: Brunner/Mazel.

Financial Crisis Inquiry Commission, (2011), *The Financial Crisis*, New York: Public Affairs.

Fitzgerald, Rory, (2011), "Exodus begins", *The Tablet*, March 12.

Flint, Hannah, (2012), "Buenos Aires Governor decrees land re-valuation", *The Argentina Independent*, May 31.

Frankfort, H. & H.A., (1949), "The emancipation of thought from myth", in Frankfort *et al*, 1949.

Frankfort, Henri, H.A. Frankfort, John A. Wilson & Thorkil Jacobsen, (1949), *Before Philosophy: The Intellectual Adventure of Ancient Man*, Harmondsworth: Penguin.

Funk, T. Marcus, (2010), *Victims' Rights and Advocacy at the International Criminal Court*. Oxford: Oxford University Press

Gaffney, Mason, (2009), *After the Crash*, Oxford: Wiley/Blackwell.

Gaffney, Mason, (1998), in Harrison (1998).

Gaffney, Mason and Fred Harrison, (1994), *The Corruption of Economics*, London: Shepheard-Walwyn.

Gainsbury, Sally, (2012), "Gu's sister fronted property purchases", *Financial Times*, August 9.

Galbraith, James K., (2012), *Inequality and Instability*, Oxforsd: Oxford University Press.

Gauger, Anja, Mai Pouye Rabatel-Fernel, Louise Kulbicki, Damien Short and Polly Higgins, (2012), "Ecocide is the missing 5th Crime Against

Peace", Human Rights Consortium, School of Advanced Study, University of London.

George, Henry, (1879), *Progress and Poverty*; New York: Robert Schalkenbach Foundation (1979 Centenary Edn.)

Giles, Chris, George Parker and Vanessa Houlder, (2022), "Threats to the edifice", *Financial Times*, April 2.

Goldstone, Jack A., (1991), *Revolution and Rebellion in the Early Modern World*, Berkley: University of California Press.

Guha, Ramachandra, (2012), "Fantasies of power in my land of muddle along", *Financial Time*, August 2.

Guy Donna J., (1991), *Sex & Danger in Buenos Aires: Prostitution, Family, and Nation in Argentine*, Lincoln: University of Nebraska Press.

Haldane, Andrew, (2012), in Diane Coyle, *What's the Use of Economics*, London: London Publishing Partnership.

Halperin, Mark, (2012), "Between the Lines", *Time*, August 12-20.

Hancock, Matthew and Nadhim Zahawi, (2011), *Masters of Nothing: How The Crash Will Happen Again Unless We Understand Human Nature*, London: Biteback.

Hannington, Wal, (1937), *The Problem of the Distressed Areas*, London: Victor Gollancz.

Harrison, Fred, (1979), "Gronlund and Other Marxists", in R.V. Andelson (1979).

Harrison, Fred, (1983), *The Power in the Land*, London: Shepheard-Walwyn.

Harrison, Fred, (1997), "The Coming 'Housing' Crash", in Frederic J. Jones and Fred Harrison, *The Chaos Makers*, London: Othila Press.

Harrison, Fred, (1998), *The Losses of Nations: Deadweight Politics versus Public Rent Dividends*, London: Othila.

Harrison, Fred, (2005), *Boom Bust: House Prices, Banking and the Depression of 2010*, London: Shepheard-Walwyn.

Harrison, Fred, (2006a), *Ricardo's Law: House Prices and the Great Tax Clawback Scam*, London: Shepheard-Walwyn.

Harrison, Fred, (2006b), *Wheels of Fortune: Self-funding Infrastructure and the Free Market Case for a Land Tax*, London: Institute of Economic affairs.

Harrison, Fred, (2008), *The Silver Bullet*, London: theIU; Madrid: Ediciones Gondo (2010).

Harrison, Fred, (2010a), *The Predator Culture*, London: Shepheard-Walwyn; Madrid: Ediciones Gondo.

Harrison, Fred, (2010b), *2010: The Inquest*, London: D.A. Horizons

Hassell, Michael P., and Robert M. May, (1985), "From Individual Behaviour to Population Dynamics", in R.S. Sibly and R.H. Smith (eds), *Behavioural Ecology*, Oxford: Blackwell.

Hawking, Stephen and Leonard Mlodinow, (2010), *The Grand Design*, London: Bantam.

Hennigan, Tom, (2012), "Former Argentinean dictator says he told Catholic church of disappeared", *Irish Times*, July 24.

Herman, Judith Lewis, (2001), *Trauma and Recovery: From Domestic Abuse to Political Power*, London: Pandora.

Herring, Hubert, (1968), *A History of Latin America from the Beginnings to the Present*, 3rd. edn., New York: Knopf.

Heseltine, Michael, (2011), "We'll only mend society from the bottom up", *The Times*, August 23.

Hesse, Erik, Mary Main, Kelly Yost Abrams and Anne Rifkin, (2003), "Unresolved States Regarding Loss or Abuse can Have 'Second Generation' Effects", in Solomon and Siegel (2003).

Higgins, Polly, (2012), *Earth is our Business: changing the rules of the game*, London: Shepheard-Walwyn

Higgins, Polly, (2010), *Eradicating Eco-cide: Laws and Governance to Prevent the Destruction of our Planet*, London, Shepheard-Walwyn.

Hobson, J.A., (1920), "Ruskin as Political Economist" in *Ruskin the Prophet*, ed: J. Howard Whitehouse. London: George Allen & Unwin.

Holmes, Bob, (2011), "Total re-boot", *New Scientist*, March 26.

Hope, Christopher, (2012), "Pin photos of benefit cheats to lampposts, says official", *Daily Telegraph*, Jul 4.

Hurst, Greg, (2012), "A levels have got easier, says exam chief", *The Times*, May 2.

Institute for Security Studies, (2012), *Citizens in an Inter-connected and Polycentric World*, Paris: ISS/EU

International Energy Agency, (2011), *World Energy Outlook, 2011*, Paris.

Jack, Andrew , (2012), "Pfizer fined $60m for bribery", *Financial Times*, August 8.

Jacob, Rahul, and Zhou Ping, (2012), "Wukan authorities rattled as polls keep legacy of dead activist alive", *Financial Times*, March 6.

Jacobsen, Thorkil, (1949), "Mesopotamia", in Frankfort *et al*, (1949).

Johnson, Paul, (2011), "The poverty claptrap", *The Guardian*, October 11.

Jones, Cheryl, (2010), "Frank Fenner sees no hope for humans", *The Australian*, June 16.

Jupp, Kenneth, (1999), *The Formation and Distribution of Wealth: Reflections on Capitalism*, London: Othila Press

Jupp, Kenneth, (2005), *The Rule of Law*, London: Shepheard-Walwyn.

Kay, John, (2012), *The Kay Review of the UK Equity Markets and Long-term Decision Making. Final Report*. London: BIS.

Kay, John, and Mervyn King, (1990), *The British Tax System*, 5th edn., Oxford: Oxford University Press.

Keenan, Douglas , (2012), "My thwarted attempt to tell of Libor shenanigans", *Financial Times*, July 27.

Keynes, John Maynard, (1936), *The General Theory of Employment Interest and Money*, London, MacMillan.

King, Mervyn, (2010), "Banking: from Bagehot to Basel, and back again", The Second Bagehot Lecture, New York, October 25.

Kington, Tom, (2011), "Italy calls on neighbours to help with north African migrant influx", *The Guardian*, April 1.

Kohler, Heinz, (1992), *Economics*, Lexington: D.C. Heath & Co.

Kolk, Bessel A. van der, Alexander C. McFarlane, and Lars Weisaeth (eds.), (2007), *Traumatic Stress*, New York: The Guilford Press.

Krugman, Paul and Robin Wells, (2006), *Economics*, New York: Worth Publishers.

Labaye, Eric, *et al.*, (2012), *French Employment 2020: Five Priorities for Action*, Paris: McKinsey Global Institute.

Lansley, Stewart, (2012), *The Cost of Inequality: Why Equality is Essential for Recovery*, London: Gibson Square.

Laqueur, Walter, (2012), *After the Fall*, London: St. Martin's Press.

Layard, Richard (2012), "Why a new mindset on mental health can allay our economic ills", *Financial Times*, September 12.

Lefmann, Ole, and Karsten K. Larsen, (2000), Ch. 10, in R.V. Andelson (2000).

Lemkin, Raphael, (1944), *Axis Rule in Occupied Europe*, Washington, DC: Carnegie Endowment for International Peace.

Lévi-Strauss, Claude, (1955), *Tristes Tropique*; translated by John and Doreen Weightman, London: Penguin, 1992.

Lewis-William, David and David Pearce, (2009), *Inside the Neolithic Mind: Consciousness, Cosmos and the Realm of the Gods*, London: Thames and Hudson.

Lipsey, Richard G., (1979), *Positive Economics*, 5th edn., London: Weidenfeld & Nicolson.

Löhr, Dirk, (2011), "The Cambodian Land Market: Development, Aberrations, and Perspectives", *ASIEN* (July).

Löhr, Dirk, (2010), "External Costs as Driving Forces of Land Use Changes", *Sustainability* (April).

Löhr, Dirk, (2012), "Capitalisation by Formalisation? – Challenging the Current Paradigm of Land Reforms, *Land Use Policy*.

MacAskill, Ewen, (2012), "UN inquiry into Native Americans", *The Guardian Weekly*, April 27.

MacMurray, John, (1957), *The Self as Agent*. London: Faber & Faber.

MacMurray, John, (1935), *Reason and Emotion*, London: Faber & Faber.

Mallet, Victor, and James Crabtree , (2012), "Coal deal lost $33bn, says New Delhi auditor", *Financial Times*, August 18.

Masalha, ====, (2012), ==========

Mason, Ian, and Begonia Filgueira, (2009), "Wild Law: Is Earth Jurisprudence a practical philosophy of law?", *Environmental Law & Management* (21).

Mathieson, Nick, and Melanie Newman, (2012), "Finance industry's multi-million pound lobbying budget revealed", *The Guardian*, July 20.

McIntosh, Alastair, (2012), "The challenge of Radical Human Ecology to the Academy", in Lewis Williams, Rose Roberts and Alastair McIntosh (eds.), *Radical Human Ecology: Inter-Cultural and Indigenous Approaches*, Farnham: Ashgate.

Mill, John Stuart, (1891), *Principles of Political Economy* London: Routledge.

Miller, G.J, (2000), *On Fairness and Efficiency: The privatisation of the public income during the past millennium*, Bristol: Policy Press.

Miller, G.J., (2003), *Dying for Justice*, London: Centre for Land Policy Studies.

Mirrlees, James et al (eds), (2011), *Tax by Design: the Mirrlees Review*, Oxford: Oxford University Press.

Mohanty, Madhu S., and Aman Ullah , (2012), "Why Does Growing up in an Intact Family during Childhood Lead to Higher Earnings during Adulthood in the United States?" *Am. J. of Econ. And Sociology*, Vol.71(3).

Monbiot, George, (2012), "John Clare, the poet of England's rural crisis", *The Guardian Weekly*, July 20.

Moses, Dirk, (2008), "Empire, Colony, Genocide: Keywords and the Philosophy of History", in Moses, D. (ed), *Empire, Colony, Genocide: Conquest, Occupation, and Subaltern Resistance in World History*, Oxford: Berghahn Books.

Mount, Ian, and Phillip Sherwell, (2012), "The Argentine president and her empire in the South", *Daily Telegraph*, February 12.

Muller, Anders, and Gregers Morch-Lassen, (1989), Ch. 11 in Ronald Banks (ed.), *Costing the Earth*, London: Shepheard-Walwyn.

Mumford, Lewis, (1967), *The Myth of the Machine*, Vol. 1, San Diego: Harcourt Brace Jovanovich.

National Intelligence Council, (2000), *Global Trends 2015*, Washington, DC.: NIC.

National Intelligence Council, (2004), *Mapping the Global Future*, Washington, DC: NIC.

National Intelligence Council, (2004), *Global Trends 2025: A Transformed World*, Washington, D.C: NIC

Novaes, Sylvia Caiuby As casas na organização social do espaço Bororo., (1983),"The houses in the social organization of Bororo space", iIn: -------- (Org.).n *Indigenous Dwellings*,São Paulo: Nobel; Edusp, 1983. São Paulo: Nobel.

Noyes, Ricahrd, (1991), *Now the Synthesis*, London: Shepheard-Walwyn.

O'Hara, Mary, (2011), "'Troubled lives", *Society Guardian*, March 16.

Palmer, Stephen, and Ray Woolfe (eds.), (2000), *Integrative and Eclectic Counselling and Psychotherapy*, London: Sage.

Parker, Matthew, (2012), *The Sugar Barons*, London: Windmill Books.

Partnoy, Frank , (2012), "Who are the true villains of the StanChart tragedy?", *Financial Times*, August 9.

Patten, Chris, (1998), *East and West: The Last Governor of Hong Kong on Power Freedom and the Future*, London: Pan Macmillan.

Peacock, Louisa, (2012), "Graduate pay is squeezed as salaries dwindle", *Daily Telegraph*, April 16.

Pickard, Jim, (2012), "Tax officials reveal 4,000 companies under investigation", *Financial Times*, June 28.

Piffano, Horatio L.P., and Adolfo C. Sturzenegger, (2011), "El Impuesto Inmobiliario Rural", La Plata: National University of La Plata (mimeo).

Pistoletto, Michelangelo, (2010), *The Third Paradise*, Venice: Marsilio.

Posner, R.A., (1980), "A Theory of Primitive Society, with special reference to Law", *J. of Law and Economics* (23:1).

Quinn, James, (2012), "HMRC chairman quits after tax-deal controversy", *Sunday Telegraph*, April 29.

Rabinovitch, Simon , (2012), "The road to nowhere", *Financial Times*, July 17.

Rajan, Raghuram G., and Luigi Zingales, (2003), *Saving Capitalism from the Capitalists*, London: Random House.

Redfearn, David , (1992), *Tolstoy: Principles for a New World Order*, London: Shepheard-Walwyn.

Redgrave, Steve, (2012), "This verdict is a dispiriting victory for the drug cheats – it is time to fight back", *The Daily Telegraph*, May 1.

Rock, David, (1975), *Argentina in the 20ᵗʰ Century*, Pittsburgh: University of Pittsburgh Press.

Rommen, Heinrich A., (1998), *The Natural Law: A Study in Legal and Social History and Philosophy* (translator: Thomas R. Hanley), Indianapolis: Liberty Fund

Roth, Kenneth M., (2002), *Annihilating Difference: The Anthropology of Genocide*, University of California Press.

Ruskin, John, (1867), *Time and Tide*, London: Smith, Elder.

Russell, Alec, (2007), "Anan to lead revolution for African farmers", *Financial Times*, June 15.

Russell, Bertrand, (1949), *The Scientific Outlook*; London: Routledge, 2009.

Sachs, Jeffrey, (2008), *Common Wealth: Economics for a Crowded Planet*, London: Penguin.

Sack, Robert David, (1986), *Human Territoriality: Its theory and history*, Cambridge: Cambridge University Press.

Sahlins, Marshall, (1965), "On the Sociology of Primitive Exchange", in M. Banton (ed.), *The Relevance of Models for Social Anthropology*, London: Tavistock Publications.

Sahlins, Marshall, (1974), *Stone Age Economics*, London: Tavistock Publications.

Samuelson, Paul A. and William D. Nordhaus, (1985), *Economics*, 3rd Edn., New York: McGraw Hill.

Sandler, Héctor, (2008), *In Search of Lost Treasure: Roots of Permanent Crisis and Proposals for their Solution*, Buenos Aires: Instituto de Capacitación Ecónomica.

Schiermeier, Quirin, (2011), "Climate cycles drive civil war", *Nature*, August 24.

Schneider, H.K., (1974), *Economic Man: The Anthropology of Economics*, New York: Free Press.

Schore, Allan N., (2003), "Early Relational Trauma, Disorganised Attachment, and the Development of a Predisposition to Violence", in Solomon and Siegel (2003).

Scott, Matt, (2012), "What City Sheikh really spent to rule English game", *The Daily Telegraph* May 10.

Sharot, Tali, (2012), *The Optimism Bias*, London: Robinson.

Sherwell, Philip, (2012), "The Whole World in its Hands", *The Sunday Telegraph*, March 11.

Shiller, Robert J., (2000), *Irrational Exuberance*, Princeton: Princeton University Press.

Shiller, Robert J., (2012), *Finance and the Good Society*, Princeton: Princeton University Press.

Smith, Adam, (1776), *The Wealth of Nations*; Edwin Canaan (ed.), Chicago: University of Chicago Press, 1976.

Smith, Henry Nash, (1970), *Virgin Land: The American West as Symbol and Myth*, Cambridge, Mass.: Harvard University Press.

Smyth, Jamie, (2012), "A peace to protect", *Financial Times*, August 15.

Solomon, Marion F., and Daniel J. Siegel, (2003), *Healing Trauma*, New York: W.W. Norton.

Spengler, Oswald, (1932), *The Decline of the West*, London: George Allen & Unwin.

Stacey, Kiran, (2012), "Thousands of civil servants face tax avoidance probe", *Financial Times*, May 3.

Stevenson, Harold W., (1991), "The development of prosocial behavior in large-scale collective societies: China and Japan", in Robert A. Hinde and Jo Groebel (eds.), *Cooperation and Prosocial Behaviour*, Cambridge: Cambridge University Press.

Stiglitz, Joseph, (2010), *Principles and Guidelines for Deficit Reduction*, Washington, DC: The Roosevelt Institute.

Stiglitz, Joseph`, (2012), *The Price of Inequality*, New York: W.W. Norton.

Sugar, Alan, (2010), *What You See is What You Get*, London: Pan Books.

Summers, Lawrence, (2012), "Growth not austerity is the best remedy for Europe", *Financial Times, April 30.*

Thomas, Daniel, and Cynthia O'Murchu, (2011), "Ukraine's richest man revealed as buyer of £136m Hyde Park flat", *Financial Times*, April 19.

Thompson E.P., (1993), *Customs in Common*, London: Penguin.

Toynbee, Arnold, (1890), *Lectures on the Industrial Revolution of the 18th Century in England*, 3rd edn., London: Longmans Green.

Tsui, Enid and Rahul Jacob, (2012), "China slowdown test limit of property market", *Financial Times*, June 22.

Tuchman, Barbara W., (1994), *The Guns of August*, New York: Ballantine Books

Tutu, Desmond, and Bettina Gronblom, (2012), "Camels can pass through the eye of a needle", *Financial Times*, April 5.

Tweedie, Neil, (2012), "We must draw on our historians", *Daily Telegraph*, August 1.

Vernant, Jean-Pierre, (1982), *The Origins of Greek Thought*, London: Methuen.

Vickrey, William, (1999), four chapters in K.C. Wenzer (ed)., *Land-value Taxation*, Armonk, NY: M.E. Sharp: London: Shepheard-Walwyn.

Wainwright, Martin, (2011), *The English Village*, London: Michael O'Mara Books.

Wallace, Alfred Russel, (1901), *The wonderful Century*, London: Swan Sonnenschein.

Wang, Zheng, (2012), *Never Forget National Humiliation: Historical Memory in Chinese Politics and Foreign Relations*, New York: Columbia University Press.

Weisberg, Barry , (1970), *Ecocide in Indochina*, San Francisco: Canfield Press.

Welshpool, (2011), "Charity Shops Issue", Welshpool Town Council, RAR/5.12.2011

White, Eugene N., (2009), "Lessons from the Great American Real Estate Boom and Bust of the 1920s", Washington, DC: NBER Working Paper No. 15573.

Wilcken, Patrick, (2010), *Claude Lévi-Strauss: The Poet in the Laboratory*, London: Bloomsbury.

Wilson Edward O., (2012), *The Social Conquest of Earth*, New York: Liveright Publishing.

Wilson, Edward O., (1975), *Sociobiology*, Cambridge, Mass.: Belknap Press.

Wilson, Harry, (2012), "Barclays hit with £290m fine over Libor fixing", *Daily Telegraph*, June 26.

Wilson, John A., (1949), "Egypt", in Frankfort *et al*, (1949).

Wilson, William Julius, (1978), *The Declining Significance of Race: Blacks and Changing American Institutions* Chicago: University of Chicago Press.

Wink, Walter, (2002), *The Human Being: Jesus and the Enigma of the Son of Man*, Minneapolis: Fortress

Wolf, Martin, (2012), "Seven ways to clean up our banking 'cesspit'", *Financial Times*, July 13.

Wolf, Martin, (2011), "Britain's experiment in austerity", *Financial Times*, February 9.

Wolf, Martin, (2010), "Why we must half the land cycle", *Financial Times*, July 9.

Acknowledgements

W RITING this volume was not a joyous experience. It was a task that I began nearly 40 years ago (with research for a PhD thesis). I set the doctorate aside to write *The Power in the Land*, and I did not return to it. In the interval since then, my constant companion was my wife, Rita. She willingly afforded me the space to explore the world's unfolding dramas. Finally, I could no longer postpone the return to my starting point: the investigation into how the fate of modern societies was sealed by an obsolete social class. Feudal barons and knights, sensing that they were due to be paid off to make way for the professionals of the emerging modern state, were not satisfied with redundancy money. They wanted pensions in perpetuity. *The Traumatised Society* is the opening broadside on behalf of the heroes of this narrative, the people of the commons. Rita once again undertook the copy-editing. My daughter, Nina, drew on her insights as a teacher and on her post-graduate studies in psychology to provide valuable comments on my application of the concept of trauma. My gratitude to them is unbounded.

About the Author

FRED Harrison studied economics at Oxford, first at Ruskin College and then at University College, where he read Philosophy, Politics and Economics. His MSc is from the University of London. He cut short his career in Fleet Street and embarked on a 10-year sojourn in Russia, following the collapse of communism. That turned out to be a fruitless bid to help the people to avoid the economics favoured by rent-seekers. Boris Yeltsin swallowed the advice from consultants paid by Western governments, and Russia was delivered to the oligarchs.

Index

ETHICAL ECONOMICS

'Today we live in a world that is divided. A world in which we have made great progress and advances in science and technology. But it is also a world where millions of children die because they have no access to medicines. We live in a world where knowledge and information have made enormous strides, yet millions of children are not in school…It is a world of great promise and hope. It is also a world of despair, disease and hunger.'

Nelson Mandela

Dear Reader,

Mandela's words reflect the stark reality in the world today. They stand in sharp contrast to the metaphor of 'a rising tide lifting all boats', quoted by John F Kennedy to imply that economic growth would naturally benefit everybody, or to the rather less optimistic 'trickle down theory' promoted by the IMF and World Bank.

These imbalances and the recent financial crises stem from a failure of economics, of which there is a growing recognition: for example, the lead article in *The Economist* (23/08/1997) entitled 'The puzzling failure of economics', or more recently Anatole Kaletsky in *The Times* (28/10/2009): 'one of the few benign consequences of last year's financial crisis was the exposure of modern economics as an emperor with no clothes'.

In March 2012 Victoria Chick, Emeritus Professor of Economics at University College London, in a public lecture went so far as to draw a comparison between Gresham's Law (Bad money drives out good) and what has happened to economics: 'far from there being progress in economics, bad economic theory has driven out good theory'.

These admissions are the exception, however, for, as Professor Ormerod pointed out in *The Death of Economics*, 'tenure and professional advancement still depend to a large extent on a willingness to comply with and work within the tenets of orthodox theory'.

As Professor Chick went on to point out: 'We are all paying the price of the success of bad economics', for governments still rely on economists steeped in orthodox thinking for advice. If things are to change, a clearer understanding of how the economy works is needed, not just by economists and policy-makers, but also by the wider general public – a voter who votes in ignorance forges the chains that bind him.

Economists have erected round their subject an intimidating barrier of jargon and maths, but Shepheard-Walwyn have built up a range of books which re-examine the work of the classical economists in a search for a more accurate understanding of how the economy works. While thoroughly researched and referenced, the books are also intended to give the layman, the voter, a grasp of the basic principles. For those who prefer a lighter read, we have three novels by John Stewart which explore some of the issues and the likely outcomes. For details, visit *www.ethicaleconomics.org.uk*

Anthony Werner
Publisher

'*The world cannot get out of the current state of crisis with the same thinking that got it there in the first place*'

Albert Einstein